# A PILGRIM IN YOUR BODY

## ENERGY HEALING AND SPIRITUAL PROCESS

**ALSO BY JIM GILKESON**
*Energy Healing: A Pathway to Inner Growth*

# A PILGRIM IN YOUR BODY

## ENERGY HEALING AND SPIRITUAL PROCESS

*Using Energywork for the Health and Well-Being
of the Spiritual Traveler Within You*

BY JIM GILKESON

iUniverse, Inc.
New York   Bloomington

**A Pilgrim In Your Body**
**Energy Healing and Spiritual Process**

*iUniverse books may be ordered through booksellers or by contacting:*

*iUniverse*
*1663 Liberty Drive*
*Bloomington, IN 47403*
*www.iuniverse.com*
*1-800-Authors (1-800-288-4677)*

*ISBN: 978-0-595-46645-0 (pbk)*
*ISBN: 978-0-595-90940-7 (ebk)*

*Printed in the United States of America*

*iUniverse rev. date: 3/6/2009*

Illustrations copyright by Aimee Eldridge, 2008. All rights reserved.
Author photo copyright 2008 by Andrew Yavelow. All rights reserved.
Leaf photo copyright 2008 by Diane Tegtmeier. All rights reserved.
Internal photographs by Andrew Yavelow and Diane Tegtmeier.
Cover design by Aimee Eldridge. All rights reserved.
Madronna was the Pilgrim photo model.

NOTE:
PLEASE UNDERSTAND THAT THE PRACTICES IN THIS BOOK ARE NOT INTENDED TO BE A SUBSTITUTE FOR CARE BY A QUALIFIED HEALTH PROFESSIONAL. IF YOU HAVE QUESTIONS ABOUT HOW THESE PRACTICES WILL AFFECT YOUR PHYSICAL, EMOTIONAL, OR MENTAL CONDITION, PLEASE CONSULT YOUR DOCTOR BEFORE DOING THEM. IN THE SAME LIGHT, YOU MAY ALSO WANT TO WORK WITH A MENTOR WHO IS SKILLED IN ENERGY HEALING.

Author Web site: http://www.jimgilkeson.com

In loving memory of

Bob Moore
1928-2008

*To journey without being changed*
*is to be a nomad.*
*To change without journeying*
*is to be a chameleon.*
*To journey and to be transformed*
*by the journey*
*is to be a pilgrim.*

Mark Nepo

# PATRONS AND ANGELS OF THE PILGRIM PROJECT

*A Pilgrim in Your Body: Energy Healing and Spiritual Process* was made possible in part due to the generous financial support of a group of special people. I would like to express my sincere gratitude and appreciation to the following donors to this book's publication:

Peg Anderson
Dawn Beye
Liza Braude
Marna A. Burgess
John and Eileen Caldwell
François Candela
Cecilia Cavalier
Kent Comfort
Mimi and Tom Cudzilo
Brian Dean
Venus Elyse
Ruth and Leif Erickson
Lorindra Moonstar Frances
Cindy Free
Bonnie Fitz-Gibbon
Bruce Gilkeson
Mary Sue Gilkeson
Amy Gilligan

Ethan Grunstein
Leon and Maggi Jones
Diane Kobrynowicz
Annette Kuhlmann
KeiLin Kramer-Yin
Kathy Loo
Caroline Macarah
Susanne Meyer
Lorenzo and Vicki Mitchell
Luca Moen
Patty Muhl
Steve Robinson
Callia Erica Shapiro
Rainer Simmelbauer
Keesha and Kent Standley
Betty Swarthout
Coleen Trimble

# CONTENTS

## SECTION 1
## A BROADER PICTURE OF ENERGY HEALING
## THE LANDSCAPE OF THE INNER PILGRIM

### CHAPTER 1: SPIRITUAL PROCESS: SPIRITUAL INITIATION ON THE MASSAGE TABLE. . . . . . . . . . . . . . . . . . . . . . . . . . . . . . . . . . . . . . . . . . . . 3

Energywork is anything you do on purpose to influence the human energy field, including energy-oriented practices used in therapeutic bodywork. It invites spiritual process, which is ultimately about the renewal of the age-old human experience of awakening to our most essential nature. This chapter explores the connection between energywork and spiritual process.

### CHAPTER 2: THE THREE-FOLD SPIRITUAL PATH. . . . . . . . . . . . . . . . . . . . . . 8

There is a universal pattern to spiritual process: it carries us out of the world in some sense, into sacred space, and then back into the world again. This pattern could rightly be referred to as the three-fold spiritual path. A healer's work, no matter what the discipline, is enhanced by his or her ability to recognize phases of this perennial three-fold pattern, which provides the healer with an elegant and simple lens with which to view spiritual process.

### CHAPTER 3: MAKING THE CASE FOR DOING INNER WORK. . . . . . . . . . . . . . 19

Stepping into the arena of energy healing necessitates the personal work of self-healing and self-exploration on the part of the healer. This chapter presents the perspective that any energetic work techniques you might use are at their best and most responsible when they are informed by your own direct, personal experience.

### CHAPTER 4: ANCIENT SPIRITUAL TECHNOLOGY . . . . . . . . . . . . . . . . . . . . . 25

In the process of doing energy-oriented exercises, you will master the skills of conscious movement (inner pilgrimages) within the sacred space of your body and energy system. Here, the stage is set for the kinds of energetic practices found in the rest of the book.

INNER PILGRIMAGE #1: *The Pilgrimage of the Orange*

INNER PILGRIMAGE #2: *The Pilgrimage of the Six-Pointed Star*

INNER PILGRIMAGE #3: *Energetically Balanced Breathing: A Ritual of the Meeting of Heaven and Earth*

INNER PILGRIMAGE #4: *The Bear and the Tulip Bulb: An Inner Pilgrimage for Winter*

INNER PILGRIMAGE #5: *A Summer Spiral for the Light of Summer*

FROM THE STORYBOOK: "A Visit with Two Scottish Healers"

# SECTION 2
## PERENNIAL THEMES IN ENERGYWORK

Your calling plays an important role in your development. This chapter explores the nature of callings and examine some of the recognizable phases of learning energy healing.

> INNER PILGRIMAGE #6: *The Pilgrim's Secret Training: Getting Guidance About Your Path*
>
> INNER PILGRIMAGE #7: *Your Inner Advisory Board*

Beliefs play a critical role in the life of an emerging energy healer. Not only do your beliefs tend to expand or limit the range of your perceptions, they also become focal points around which the skills and techniques you acquire will tend to organize themselves. This chapter is a self-administered mini-workshop designed to help you find deeply held, often unconscious beliefs operating in the background of your healing work.

> MAPPING PROJECT #1: *Spiritual Autobiography*
>
> MAPPING PROJECT #2: *Synoptic Personal History*
>
> FROM THE STORYBOOK:   "Signs and Miracles"
>                       "Angelic Voices"

Holism is the perspective that a whole system is accessible in each of its parts. In this chapter, a series of holistic appreciation exercises is provided to help you extend your senses and expand your conceptual world. This is a necessary skill in energy healing, since energetic work entails a shift to the holistic or holographic level of organization of yourself and the person you treat.

> INNER PILGRIMAGE #8: *Expanding Awareness of Two Heavenly Bodies*
>
> INNER PILGRIMAGE #9: *Touch Water*
>
> INNER PILGRIMAGE #10: *Touch Air, Breathe Sky*
>
> INNER PILGRIMAGE #11: *Touch Earth*
>
> INNER PILGRIMAGE #12: *Touch Fire*
>
> INNER PILGRIMAGE #13: *Of Roses, Dogs, and Gold*

Mindfulness, an essential ingredient of meditation practice, goes hand in hand with the art of energetic healing. Exercises are provided for honing your ability to connect energetically with yourself or another in a mindful, present, non-agendized way. One of the fruits of practicing these skills is the trust and subconscious cooperation that make healing processes easier when there is mindful connection between you and your healing partner.

> INNER PILGRIMAGE #14: *The Starfish Exercise*
>
> PARTNER TREATMENT #1: *"May I Come Closer?"*
>
> PARTNER TREATMENT #2: *Differentiated Listening*
>
> PARTNER TREATMENT #3: *Following Tissue Movement: "Alien Communication" with Your Partner*

# ACKNOWLEDGMENTS

I owe a great debt of gratitude to many people who contributed, sometimes inadvertently, to *Pilgrim*. To all of you, my heartfelt thanks.

Stephanie Brock for the babushka doll. Stephanie sent these unpainted wooden nesting dolls after I had talked about babushka dolls in a workshop. I sent them to Aimee Eldridge, the artist for *A Pilgrim in Your Body*, who transformed them into colorful Pilgrim Path Babushkas for all seasons. Come to my Web site[1*] to see them!

Hal Zina Bennett for encouragement and guidance and for the suggestion to invite others into the project by becoming patrons and angels, an old idea whose time may be coming back.

Diane Tegtmeier, Andrew Yavelow, Jan Allegretti, Liza Braude, Sanna Durk, Niel Murphy, Rebecca Ferguson, Elaine Watt, Ann Prehn, Gloria Cox, and Inika Spense for reading early versions of this manuscript and for editorial assistance.

Jessica Jackson, for keeping me from grievous error in homeopathic matters.

Anodea Judith, for tuning me in to the needs of today's readers. Our talks fomented my *Note on Terminology* and a correspondingly de-jargonized text.

Ursula Gilkeson and Bob Moore, my original teachers in energywork.

Lois Wilkins, PhD, a dear friend who erroneously went unacknowledged for her wise contributions to *Energy Healing: A Pathway to Inner Growth*.

Vajra Matusow, for providing me with the alchemical elements assigned to the four modes of breathing in Chapter Four.

The land, waters, and residents of Harbin Hot Springs, as well as my colleagues at Harbin Health Services.

Aimee Eldridge, this project's artist, for her constant pluck and good humor.

Mr. Virgil Klotz, for teaching me to type long, long ago—may we all be forgiven for things we said, and wrote, in high school.

All my clients and workshop participants. You have been my teachers.

Special thanks to Diane Tegtmeier for her love and wisdom and support.

I am grateful for the following permissions to reprint from the works of other authors:
Pilgrim poem (no title) from *The Book of Awakening* ©2000 by Mark Nepo. Used with the kind

---

1    Instructions on how to find the Babooshkas and other Pilgrim Extras on my Web site are on the final page.

# PREFACE

Limentour Beach in Northern California. I'm watching the waves as they rise and fall. Pelicans fly an undulating line, scanning the waters for fish. The lead pelican stops flapping its wings; an impulse, almost visible to my eyes, passes through the line. One by one, they all stop flapping and glide, cutting a silent streamlined arc through the air. Then, beginning with the leader, one by one, they resume flapping.

I'm watching instinctual behavior, millions of years old, against a backdrop of rising and falling tides, rhythms as old as the planet. I'm watching something that has always been taking place in more or less the same way. Pelicans have been flying these undulating lines, and the tides have been ebbing and flowing for time out of mind.

In the pelicans and tides of Limentour Beach I glimpse a level of life that is old beyond calculation, wise beyond human definitions, perfectly balanced, and diversified. The answers to my questions about what is relevant in this life have more to do with these ancient rhythms than with the superficial concerns occupying my heart and mind at this moment.

These rhythms seep in and remind me that I, too, am part of *that*. Behind the scenes in my own body and conscious mind is a primordial intelligence that partakes of the eternal rhythms of life. That deep natural wisdom is represented, in part, by the subtle energy system that enlivens my body and mind; the instant I open my awareness to this level of life, there it is.

For thousands of years, healers and mystics have known that we are surrounded and penetrated by intense subtle activity, dotted with points of pulsating energy, and sketched with radiant pathways of energy movement. What is more, they have understood the importance of attending to this energy and tracking its movement throughout the body, along what classic Chinese medicine calls *energy meridians*. By following these songlines of the body, we can be drawn into an inner journey toward the hidden, but accessible, wholeness that makes up each of us. This book is dedicated to that journey, and to that subset of humans who take it upon themselves—each in their own way—to answer a call to embody the spirit of healing.

Jim Gilkeson,
Limentour Beach and Harbin Hot Springs, California,
August, 2007

# STARTING POINTS

The shockwave caused by the events of September 11, 2001, reached me in Northern California in many forms. First there was the strange, brooding, slightly agitated atmosphere—similar to what happens among animals just before an earthquake—that descended on the retreat center where I live and work the day or so before the attacks. Then there were the events themselves that rippled across the country, leaving a tremendous energetic and emotional shake-up in their wake. Finally, as everyday life started to reassert itself, waves of guests arrived at the retreat center, people who were clearly taking temporary refuge from the turbulence. Even here, five thousand miles from the site of events that changed our world, many of us bodywork and energywork therapists felt that we were on a psycho-spiritual frontline in our work with clients who had witnessed the events of 9/11. It was a time of heightened awareness that, in our work, we were privileged to touch the wounds of the greater body of humanity.

When I touch the body and psyche of the individual on my treatment table or in the water, I am more aware than ever that I am holding in my hands a mystery much larger than any of us. In different ways, I handle the same mystery as a teacher and writer, as well. The mystery is this life we all share. We share it with our loved ones, we share it with people we don't even know, and we share it with people who fly big airplanes into buildings. How we choose to hold and handle that mystery affects all of us.

The way I see it, *energywork*—the intentional use of the energy field that enlivens our life processes—would be a small and inconsequential sector of human endeavor indeed if it did not join actively with the human longing for peace, unity, and self-realization, and with the concerns of the pilgrim, or spiritual traveler, within each of us. I believe that those who would follow the calling of the healer and the schools that train them ought to be prepared to rise to the challenge presented in a new confluence of factors: first there are the new consumers of bodywork who come not just as people with a collection of symptoms to be fixed but also as secret spiritual travelers with a heightened need to find support for their pilgrimage; then there are the new students of what I will call energy-active bodywork, who are driven in their choice of careers by the journey of their own inner pilgrimage; and finally there is the accelerated pace of change on all levels of life.

My hope is that this book will contribute to a growing understanding of how we can attend to the sacred mystery of life when we hold it in our hands. The events of 9/11 highlighted anew the challenge of meeting with compassion a world that is exploding all around us, emerging within us, and pleading for attention in those we serve. Maybe these things have occurred to you, too.

### My Story with Energy Healing

*A Pilgrim in Your Body* is a product of my personal journey with energy healing, which started in about 1983. In that time, my understanding and appreciation for what energywork is about has, of course, gone through many phases. When I first began, I focused on the work within myself, almost completely unconnected to work with other people. This was not by design, but because I simply didn't know that energywork was good for anything else. Indeed, my first exposure to energywork practice was mostly in the form of personal meditative exercises like those scattered throughout this book. I had been a member of a spiritual order for nine years prior to being introduced to Bob Moore, an Irishman living in Ringkøbing, Denmark, who became my main teacher of energywork. Bob led our group through a comprehensive experiential exploration of the human energy field, and most of this work was focused on individual inner growth. It fit wonderfully with my understanding of spiritual practice up to that time, which was based on the classic disciplines of the inner life: prayer, meditation, and contemplation. For years, that is what energywork was about for me.

By and by, the desire grew in me to work with others in ways I vaguely imagined to be at once spiritual and psychotherapeutic while also somehow involving the physical body. But I didn't know how to present what I was interested in, much less how to make a living doing it. By then, I had developed a loose framework for giving energetic treatments, but they were presented as an esoteric specialty and not very connected to the concerns that most people had in their everyday lives. Becoming some kind of psychotherapist occurred to me, and for a couple of years I pressed my nose against the windows of various schools of transpersonal psychology. But something always stood in the way of actually going in the door.

Conceptually, I was all over the map. Spirituality, though a real force in my life, was still in a compartment that never quite touched the earth. Psychology was fascinating to me, especially transpersonal and Jungian psychology, except that I was utterly unmotivated when it came to actually becoming a Jungian analyst. Massage and bodywork were in their own compartment, too, either somewhere in the realm of physical therapy or rehabilitation in a hospital, which held no interest for me, or, more interesting at least, something slightly lascivious—God knows what—that people out in California did in their hot tubs. This all reflected the way I was holding the various dimensions of life apart in myself. Deep within me, though, I sensed that my body and mind, my spirituality and my mundane life, were trying hard to come together, but hadn't yet.

If there was a turning point for me—and there must have been one, because I now see things from a completely different perspective than the one I had when I first started—it came around the time when, as a bodywork therapist in the 1990s, I witnessed the effect that my personal energywork practice was having on my clients. My personal energetic and meditative practice made it impossible to ignore the energy system of my client. With the addition of techniques like Craniosacral Therapy and Zero Balancing that allowed me to work on the cusp between the structure of the physical body and the energy that moves around and through it, I realized I was bringing energywork out of the ethereal realms and into people's bodies. It was no longer something that only my most sensitive clients could appreciate. Clients began having physical and emotional releases that were part of their process of squeezing through knotholes in their inner world and connecting consciously with a source of renewal within them. I was able to recognize this process from my own meditative and energetic work.

With my physical body and my inner life finally able to be on board the same boat, I gradually understood that I had a means of facilitating what I have come to see as an inner pilgrimage in those who come to me, and of helping these modern-day spiritual travelers to bring what they gained through their inner experiences into their everyday lives and offer their much-needed gifts and insights to the world. For me, this amounted to a new vision of what bodywork and healing could become.

### This Book

I used to tell people that *A Pilgrim in Your Body* was the outgrowth of what fell on the cutting-room floor from my first book, but I've stopped saying that because it isn't so. While this new book does carry on with some of the themes of its predecessor, it has a life and a world of its own.

Both books were born in protest about failures in the necessary communication task I see in the world of energywork. I started writing *Energy Healing: A Pathway to Inner Growth* out of my dislike for the unnecessarily occult way energywork was being presented in many books and public forums. The germ of *A Pilgrim in Your Body: Energy Healing and Spiritual Process* was my argument with the narrow, symptom-focused way energy healing was taught in some schools of bodywork and massage. These protests may have served to get the books started, but in both cases the protest phase soon gave way to something more adventurous than merely carping about what's wrong.

In the case of *Pilgrim*, I set out with the goal of presenting energywork in its spiritual context. As the writing progressed, however, my thoughts began organizing themselves around a number of recurring psycho-spiritual themes and principles in energy healing. So, a second impulse started coursing through the writing. Friends who read earlier versions wanted this to be two books, one on the spirituality of energywork, the other on its perennial themes. But, try as I might, I couldn't find a way to separate them. Perhaps these early readers, in their wisdom, were being like King Solomon, urging me to use my sword in order to force me into the realization that this is one baby, not two.

*A Pilgrim in Your Body* is laid out with the intention of serving three different, but interlocking purposes. The first of these is to paint a big enough picture of energy healing to set it in the context of a psycho-spiritual undertaking and spiritual process, where it belongs. The second is to present fifteen major recurring themes that show up in all energywork, regardless of the modality or flavor. The third of these intertwined purposes is to present personal energy-oriented practices for the internal work of anyone interested in opening new pathways to inner growth and cultivating their spiritual qualities and potentials. These personal practices turn outward in the form of practical, hands-on partner treatments for addressing the same perennial psycho-spiritual themes in healing work with other persons.

I assume that a good number of you who pick up this book are interested in what the disciplines of energy healing have to offer in your personal development and inner growth, or you work with others in some kind of healing capacity, or you would like to learn to do so. I also assume that, if you are a practitioner, perhaps a massage or bodywork therapist, aquatic bodyworker, psychologist, or spiritual mentor, you see people who go through intense internal experiences under your hands, in your counseling office, or even over the telephone. In my work, it is evident to me that sensitive individuals, the kind who seek out energetic healing practitioners and who might well be coming to you, are, more than ever, in need of help in grounding and centering themselves, as well as facing and moving through their fears.

If you are involved with energy-oriented healing work, you might find yourself in a unique position with regard to how the dramatic events taking shape in our world affect people. For it is in the energy field that surrounds and penetrates our physical bodies that we process, mostly unconsciously, the dramas and traumas of our lives. Never before have so many individuals been in need of therapies that address the level of deep transformation that is erupting in their worlds, not to mention in the world we all share. The tools of energy healing give us access to this dimension.

It is my experience that energy healing can be presented as a holistic and psycho-spiritual tool without in any way excluding its use for what ails us physically. I have found that techniques that make use of our energy field not only help in alleviating pain and stress but can quite often help us to make significant inroads into understanding the background of what is going on when we have a physical condition. Indeed, modern inquiry into the effectiveness of prayer, an active spiritual life, and a sense of being part of something greater than one's individual self has provided convincing evidence of the relationship between our psycho-spiritual life and our physical health, our longevity, and our enjoyment of life.

This book is an invitation to you to enter into the journey of energywork practice. The tools, techniques, and perspectives presented in this book all partake of the understanding that our inner and outer lives—from our health and well-being to our aspirations and callings, from our identities as unique individuals to our very essence as universal beings—are joined and interdependent and in need of being engaged.

*The New Client, Student, and School*

With increasing frequency, I am finding that my clients are using energywork and bodywork sessions, whether fully consciously or not, as an entry point into transforming transpersonal experiences that go way beyond whatever specific complaint might have gotten them into my practice in the first place. Obviously, this is not going to be attractive to everyone. And yet, in the years I have pursued energy healing as a teacher and practitioner, I have come to realize that many people appreciate subtler approaches to healing that afford them opportunities for self-exploration and transpersonal experience, as well as attention to what ails them.

I'm not suggesting here that each and every symptom has to be understood as a deep and meaningful spiritual process. My practice has shown me, however, that when energywork practices are used, there is a fairly predictable progression in which the focus of activities moves along a continuum from problems and symptoms to internal exploration to transcendent experience, often followed by the task of integrating one's experiences into everyday life. That is to say that the discomfort or symptom can, under certain circumstances, become an entry point into a much deeper process. It may begin with a special kind of deep relaxation many people encounter in receiving an energywork session. Sooner or later, the same person might experience a shift into nonordinary states of consciousness in which the entire gamut of internal experiences unfold within her. Sometimes during a session or in its immediate aftermath, experiences emerge from hidden, forgotten corners of her being and make themselves felt. Energy healing has a way of inviting us into zones where our bodies, minds, and spirits come together in experiences that leave us changed, broadened, and deepened.

The frequency of encounters I have with this new kind of client is for me a sure indicator of the general accelerated pace of people's inner worlds. Meanwhile, the bodyworker or psychotherapist who incorporates energywork into his or her practice, in order to be prepared for the kinds of responses energywork can evoke, needs to have ridden the rapids of their own inner world and be on some kind of stable footing with spiritual process.

Energy healing presents a parallel challenge for educators of bodyworkers. Although the addition of energywork into the curricula of massage schools may be seen by some as a passing fad, existing because of a current demand for "new-age energy stuff," the fact is that energywork is increasingly becoming linked with massage and bodywork. In the process, two phenomena are occurring side by side. For one, with the inclusion of energywork practices, the nature of massage and bodywork is evolving in the direction of a spiritual discipline. This necessitates a new kind of teaching, one that is of the body and of the spirit. The other result is that a new kind of student is arriving at the doors of massage schools, students with different kinds of callings and needs from those of many of their counterparts of twenty years ago. This difference needs to be met with a deeper, more truly holistic offering for students who are ready to take on the task of cultivating their spiritual gifts as healers. As a result, a silent transition is taking place in massage schools as well as in the hands-on bodywork scene in general.

In his book, *The Courage to Teach*, Parker J. Palmer makes some telling distinctions among books and studies on the art of teaching. Most books on the subject, he points out, are dedicated to *what* to teach and *how* to teach. Some are devoted to the question of *why* we teach. But few, if any, take up the question of *who* it is that teaches. I find that the same questions, the same paradigm, exist in healing work. It is a consideration that badly needs to be deepened in settings where healing work is taught. Too often, courses on energy healing, especially those taught in massage schools, are entirely focused on technique, in other words, on the *what* and the *how* of energy healing, with a few general assumptions about *why* we do it, but with little or no attention to *who* it is that is doing the healing work.

This book will attempt to address this oversight. I would like to offer something not only for the what, how, and why of energy healing practice, but also for the *who* as well. This question of who it is that is involved with healing brings with it a number of sub-questions. What kind of interior development and spiritual path is the energy healer involved with? What is the calling of *healer* about? What does a healer need in order to truly scratch the deep itch of such a calling?

If you have this itch, then this book is dedicated to you.

*About the Anecdotes from the Storybook*

The anecdotes at the end of some chapters are based on real encounters with real people. I have provided the persons in these little stories with other names, when it seemed appropriate to do so, in order to protect their identities. Here and there, I take some artistic license and get a trifle whimsical in the telling of these little tales—mostly in order to further cloak their identities, but also because it's fun to tell stories—and no offense is intended to either the living or the departed.

# A Note on Terminology

*If you want to talk to people, you'd better find a language that you
share, and if there's some obstacle,… unless you're indifferent to the
problem, well, then you change it.*

Paul Simon

In this book, I will use rather generic language to refer to things like chakras, energy points, and energy streams, which are among the stable features of the human energy field. For example, in the exercises and treatments you will find throughout the text, I will use terms like *energy centers* and *energy-active positions* to identify key energetic locations on your body, along with instructions on how to develop your awareness of them. By doing so, my hope is to find a language that works for an experience-based approach to learning energy healing, one that honors the venerable traditions that have fed world spirituality, and at the same time allows me to point to ways of using these energy systems of ours to generate authentic experiences that are not unduly burdened by lots of ideas about what's supposed to happen.

Why is the choice of terminology so important? A teacher of bodywork once told me, "One of the nice things about teaching physiology is that no matter if a person is an atheist or a Christian or an Islamic fundamentalist, an elbow is still an elbow, a knee is still a knee, flexion is still flexion, and extension is still extension." Unfortunately, the study of energywork does not have the luxury of a universally agreed upon language and description of its subject matter. Many people, especially those who are likely to pick up this book, already know what a *chakra* is, and for the most part, that is a good thing. Paradoxically, though, it is also part of the problem.

We are heir to a number of traditions when it comes to teachings about the chakra system. When you dip into the readily available lore about the chakras, you will most likely be confronted with updates of classic teachings from yogic, Taoist, or Tibetan sources. Or you might run into representations of the chakra system passed through Western Hermetic traditions. Each of these strands of teaching has its own inflection and serves a different facet of spiritual growth and understanding. While some come wrapped in astrological or alchemical interpretations, others have a strong bias toward stimulating the rise of the kundalini and the movement of consciousness beyond duality.

Therein lies the dilemma. Those of us who would teach about such things as chakras are speaking to a much more informed audience than was the case even ten years ago. With the greater volume of information available, the interested student of energywork inevitably comes with more associations and preconceived notions. As a result, I have found that I need to do something unconventional if I don't want to automatically trigger a whole array of assumptions drawn from one or another of the various traditions you may already have studied. Hence, my use of the more generic terminology.

As you read this book, do the exercises, and go on the inner pilgrimages described here, try to enter each of these inner connections and experiences like a naturalist entering a field or pond. The naturalist knows something about fields and ponds, of course, but doesn't know what he or she is going to find in *this* particular field, on this particular day. Similarly, an instruction like this:

> "Move your attention to the highest point on the top of your head, and then find a position slightly forward of that and slightly up in your hair. Now simply relax your awareness and allow this energy-active position to draw your attention into itself …"

is not intended to give a lot of information about Crown Chakras, but rather to point you in as simple a way as possible to a trailhead of experiences that are your own—without the limitation or distraction of a prior assumption.

It is my hope that you will enjoy the energy practices in this book with a fresh and open mind. They are an invitation to discovery, and to a pilgrimage to the Source of Life to which we all have access.

# SECTION 1

## A BROADER PICTURE OF ENERGY HEALING
### The Landscape of the Inner Pilgrim

# CHAPTER ONE

## SPIRITUAL PROCESS
### SPIRITUAL INITIATION ON THE MASSAGE TABLE

*Next time you give or get a massage, ask yourself the question, "In what other historical contexts have people been carefully rubbed with oil?"*

Whether you use energywork as part of your personal practice or as a healing modality in your work with others, it can evoke changes in consciousness and perspective that are best understood in the context of the human spiritual journey. At its core, energywork—basically, anything you do in a knowledgeable and purposeful way to influence the human energy field, your own or someone else's, for healing and growth of consciousness—invites spiritual process, and spiritual process is ultimately about the renewal of an age-old human experience. That experience is often not communicable except in the language of human transformation associated with spiritual traditions, so it is given names like enlightenment, illumination, transcendental experience, self-realization, and others. These are life-changing events when they occur in one's inner life, and the processes surrounding these experiences—let's refer to them collectively as spiritual process—are among the perennial themes of energywork.

Though it has applications in every sphere of life and healing, energywork is a decidedly psycho-spiritual undertaking. Whether it takes the form of personal meditative practices or treatments with another person, it can bring long forgotten and repressed material from our personal subconscious to the surface of our awareness, but it goes further than that. The practices of energywork contain within them the seeds of spiritual practice. They are the not-so-distant cousins of the classic disciplines of the inner life: prayer, meditation, and contemplation. These are all practices that invite experiences into our consciousness from what is beyond our individual spheres of awareness and personal biographies, from what Swiss psychologist Carl Jung called the *collective unconscious*, and beyond, into ecstatic dimensions of pure consciousness and revelation. This is not to say that each energywork session results in enlightenment any more than every prayer is met immediately by an intelligible answer from God. Still, it behooves anyone who makes use of energetic practices to develop an appreciation for the patterns of spiritual process.

All of this might sound a trifle strange if you have been involved with energy healing mainly in the context of therapeutic bodywork and are accustomed to thinking in terms of therapeutic outcomes, symptom management, and basic health care. To grasp the connection between energywork and spiritual process, it is important to gain an understanding of what energywork is at its most essential level. Begin by taking an inventory of the subtle energetic practices you yourself are involved with already—maybe without even thinking of them as energywork—either as part of your healing work or in your efforts to become a more conscious individual. In your subtle energy practice inventory:

- Include all hands-on and hands-off energywork modalities like Therapeutic Touch, Reiki, Polarity Therapy;

- List subtle energy therapies like acupuncture and homeopathy;

- Include all spiritually oriented practices like meditation, prayer, chakra exercises, toning, breathing exercises, chanting and singing spiritual hymns, overtone singing;

- Don't leave out practices that slow down and intensify your perception of the energy movement in your body and around it, such as yoga, t'ai chi, and qi gong;

- Add to these all forms of spiritual ritual you might be involved with, such as sweat lodges, vision quests, ritual movement, sacred dance and walk;

- And don't forget massage, which often helps you shift into deep relaxation, essentially an altered state of consciousness.

What all of these practices have in common—and the reason they stimulate spiritual process—is that each of them steps up the interaction between your energy field and your body and enlivens the interplay between your conscious and non-conscious processes[2]. If there are differences among energywork practices in their usefulness as holistic healing tools, those differences lie mainly in the conscious awareness, beliefs, orientation, and intention of the one using them. There is a difference, for example, between a bodywork session in which the practitioner is consciously aware of and intentionally working with the energy field of his partner while doing the session, on the one hand, and a session in which he might be doing the same set of physical maneuvers but without that awareness, presence, and set of intentions, on the other hand. It could be said that some practices are more explicitly geared toward facilitating psycho-spiritual processes than others. In reality, though, each healing modality and each meditative style is potentially a holistic, *energy-active* form of healing work with the potential to activate what psychologist Robert Johnson calls the "source of our evolving character," and "the process whereby we bring the total self together."

*Glimpses of the Inner Pilgrim*

Many people come to an energy healer because of an emerging spiritual process, though they probably don't call it that. They run into something discontinuous with their usual consciousness. Spiritual process can emerge spontaneously. It can be small, quiet, simple. I remember my brother telling me that once, while riding on the train, he looked out the window and realized that everything was perfect, and a profound peace arose within him. Other times, spiritual process is jarred into action. Sudden loss of a job, illness, the break-up of a relationship, and the birth of a

---

2    I have decided to go, here and elsewhere, with osteopath John Upledger's word "non-conscious" because, as he points out, it does not seem to have the limitations that cling to words like "unconscious" and "subconscious" from various psychological schools of thought. By "non-conscious," I mean everything that is not (currently) accessible or available to one's conscious awareness, be it of a repressed or suppressed nature, collective unconscious or archetypal in nature, or a part of one's higher consciousness which one hasn't owned yet.

baby are examples of this. A long-time student of mine dates her spiritual awakening back to a head-on collision in which she could easily have lost her life. When the timing is right, our deep psyche will use just about anything as tinder to ignite change. These experiences can be both exhilarating and upsetting.

If you are a practitioner, bear in mind that under the influence of an energy treatment, your partner's body and symptoms often serve as a doorway into his or her deep inner world. Next time you give a healing treatment, keep in mind that the person you are working on might be experiencing, to one degree or another, elements of dream, memory, emotion, or insight. They might be nursing an inner wound or piecing together a broken sense of humanity. A healing session with you can help them slip a bit more gracefully into a new world of experience.

Spiritual process may or may not be obvious at first, but as you awaken to your own spiritual process, you will, with increasing frequency, find yourself encountering a pilgrim, or spiritual traveler, in others. When it comes to pilgrims, it typically takes one to know one. Becoming intimately and courageously aware of the spiritual process active in you is what prepares you to discern spiritual process in others and work purposefully with it. Your personal growth and development is therefore crucially important if you want to use the tools of energy healing responsibly with others.

Once you get an eye for spiritual process and a feel for its shapes and patterns, it is not uncommon to witness the drama and beauty of spiritual initiation[3] right there on your massage table or in your therapy room. Your challenge is to catch on to where your partner is in the arc of her inner pilgrimage. She might be moving along quite well on her spiritual quest and coming to you as something of a "pit stop." Or she might be in one or the other of the predicaments that spiritual travelers get into. She may arrive in a state of disarray as she comes to realize she is being led out onto a dimly-lit path, away from the world she has known and the company she has heretofore kept. She might be lost, sick, injured, in a trance or a state of suspended animation, buried deep in stone or ice, or incubating in a deep wintry slumber, awaiting what poet Denise Low called "the searing call of one hot star."

The pilgrim on your massage table, in your counseling office, or the one in your own body might come in need of refuge; she could be making the first rustlings of awakening from a long sleep, needing nourishment, or demanding breathing room, a space to unfold, expression, and recognition. She might be ready to take wing into realms of discovery in the worlds of the spirit. Or she might find herself on a path of return to the everyday world after a time of absorption in the spiritual realms, charged with the need to share herself and her spiritual gifts with others. Other pilgrims might be facing some life-altering task or ordeal, or even death, in the form of life's inevitable losses, the death of a former worldview, or even literal death. The upshot is that, in the early stages of this inner pilgrimage, she might not be conscious of any of this. All she might know at the time she comes to you is that something hurts.

If you are a practitioner, this does not mean you are abandoning your treatment of your partner's aches and pains in favor of going for spiritual process. On the contrary, the aches and pains are probably the very things that brought her to you in the first place, and you are using your skills to alleviate unnecessary suffering while at the same time recognizing that symptoms are part of something larger. On most days you are a companion, hopefully, a wise and compassionate

---

3     For more discussion of spiritual initiation and its parallels in energywork practice, see the Appendix: "Two Reflections on Spiritual Process and Initiation" at the end of the book.

one, having swum the waters and hiked the inner terrains of your own soul. On occasion, you play the role of spiritual midwife.

*Hallmarks of Emerging Spiritual Process*

Marilyn Ferguson, the founder of the *Brain/Mind Bulletin*, articulated a principle from quantum theory that gets to the heart of emerging spiritual process. She said, "Things fall apart, so they can fall together at a higher level of order." What this says about the constant organization, break down, and reorganization of the stuff of the universe also applies to our work with energy and consciousness and the way our inner and outer lives change and grow. Let's recast this statement in such a way as to shed light on spiritual process so we can recognize it as it unfolds within us and in those we serve. Here are some hallmarks:

*I had been my whole life a bell, and never knew it until at that moment I was lifted and struck.*

Annie Dillard

- *Disruption*: In big and small ways, something interrupts the continuity of a person's life. In some people, it can be the breaking in of external events, such as a sudden loss, or input from other dimensions of consciousness, perhaps in the form of a profound insight or a dream or an inner awakening in a meditation. In other people, it's not a case of something breaking in, but rather it is the person who breaks out of the status quo, like a baby chick pecking its way out of its shell, an egg no longer. Either way, the mold is broken.

- *Reshuffling*: This is a fluid phase, marked in many people by uncertainty, disorientation, and vulnerability. A person might feel lost and directionless without their old orientation, but these are also times of new opportunities to shape the world in which they live. Circumstances are plastic and malleable in this phase, and new choices can be made because the former pattern is gone and the new one hasn't yet emerged.

- *Reorganization*: Sooner or later, new patterns crystallize out of the chaos. Remember Marilyn Ferguson's statement that things fall apart, so they can fall together at a higher level of order. That new, higher level of order will, in its turn, fall apart and give rise to what comes next. That's the way things progress in nature and in us. Our spiritual process is no different.

What you can do if you work with other people and detect this pattern:

- *Work on yourself.* Your inner work is what you do to tend your own fire and your own inner garden. It's what you do to become more conscious, and it can take any number of forms, from your daily meditations, retreats, and spiritual practices to therapy of one kind or another. It could include energetic practices like those in this book. Whatever the form, your inner work is an indispensable ingredient in anything you would undertake to cultivate and express your spiritual qualities.

  I have found that people who get involved with energy healing strictly in order to "fix" others, without working in a parallel way on their own inner growth and development, tend to hit a wall early on. Without active participation in your own pathways of spiritual growth and personal healing and development, it is easy to restrict your notions of what energywork is about. In addition, whatever your path or discipline, your inner work is how you unlock your potentials, become comfortable with processes of inner change, and gain a wider perspective on life, based on your own experience. Your inner work is the basis for compassionate work with others.

- *Learn to create a safe environment* for those who come to you for help. So much happens all by itself in inner work if the setting is right. An adept energy healer who has learned to be comfortable, centered, and grounded in herself becomes a safe environment for those who come to her.

- *Learn to support the process at hand* and nurse it along. This begins with recognizing the underlying spiritual process and then finding ways to support it and make it easier. From there, you are in a position to trust that process and help it to go where it needs to go.

I think of spiritual process as the big umbrella over all perennial themes of energywork that we will go into in this book. Each of the following chapters will elaborate on an aspect of spiritual process in the context of energy healing. Together, they form a vision of the path of the pilgrim in your body and of what you can do to empower this spiritual traveler in your life and in others.

# CHAPTER TWO

## THE THREE-FOLD SPIRITUAL PATH

*The legend of the Traveler appears in every civilization, perpetually assuming new forms, afflictions, powers and symbols. Through every age he walks in utter solitude …*

Evan S. Connell Jr.

Spiritual process is about the renewal of the age-old human experience of waking up to our essential spiritual nature. The events that make up spiritual process in a person's life all contain within them a universal pattern: they carry us out of the world in some sense, into sacred space, and then back into the world again. This pattern of leaving our familiar world, moving into what is extraordinary, and then returning, changed, to our known world could rightly be referred to as the *three-fold spiritual path*. A healer's work, no matter what the discipline, is enhanced by the ability to recognize phases of spiritual process and, to that end, this perennial three-fold pattern provides an elegant and simple lens to look through. It will add immeasurably to your appreciation of the various magnitudes of initiation—from the most mundane to the most sublime— contained in life's events.

We will mainly explore the three-fold spiritual path in terms of what comes up in energywork practice, but in truth this is a universal pattern, present in all your inner growth, in everything you have ever learned and made your own. In what follows, we'll look at some of the ways the three-fold path shows itself in classic lore about the spiritual path, its manifestation in our personal paths and those of the people who come to us in the context of energetic healing.

*Leaving the World: The Pilgrim's Journey Begins*
Classical stories and myths are full of accounts of individuals faced with the need to go off on some kind of quest. They leave for different reasons, of course. They are often forced onto their path, compelled somehow by outrageous fortune. Frequently something—often relating to personal power—has been lost and needs to be retrieved, and that retrieval involves some kind of journey.

One of the best-known ways of describing this universal cycle of initiatory activity is to speak of the *Hero's Journey*. Part of the work of Joseph Campbell and Paul Rebillot was to articulate the abiding image of the hero embedded deep in our psyche. The hero is the one who responds to what Joseph Campbell liked to call the "call to adventure," forced by necessity, or carried along by his own adventurous spirit into something bigger than himself, to leave his familiar ground in order to go into the unknown on a quest of some kind. Along the way, the hero meets any number of challenges, often in the form of adversity: the misunderstanding of those he leaves behind, the "demons of resistance" in his body, emotions and thoughts. Mentors and allies are at hand as well to teach him new skills and disciplines, and how to consort with forces he has never dreamed of before. The hero's journey takes him out of time and place, away from his former identity—he might adopt a new name while on his journey into the core of his being. Somewhere along the line, he is challenged unto death. He resurrects and is reborn and returns to the world, bearing gifts of wisdom and healing. The Hero's Journey presents a complete picture of the three-fold spiritual path.

Spiritual literature is full of tales whose basic story line is that of the three-fold spiritual path, and their basic form is alive and well in such bestsellers as Paulo Coelho's *The Alchemist* and James Redfield's *The Celestine Prophesy*, which, quite aside from whether they are based on factual events, follow this classic form. It is the perennial initiation story: leaving, discovering something extraordinary, and then returning. The original title of *The Hobbit*, the prelude to Tolkien's *The Lord of the Rings*—a classic hero's journey if there ever was one—was *There and Back Again*.

One strand of the basic story goes something like this: the hero finds himself on a quest, which puts him on a search for a temple where he has heard that the mysteries of life are revealed. Or he is looking for a secret order of initiates, or a spiritual master who can open the mysteries for him. Typically, the hero is put upon to pass through tests before he can enter. He is confounded. He is asked to do things that he doesn't want to do. He might be tricked into believing that he is looking for a far-off temple when, as it turns out, he has already entered the temple. Or he thinks he is waiting for an audience with the spiritual master. He is told to wait outside, to go take a seat on that bench over there underneath the banyan tree. Time passes, he gets bored, then impatient. Meanwhile, he strikes up a conversation with the gardener, who tells him dirty jokes. Typically, in stories of this kind, our hero subscribes to middle-class moral notions more than he thought, and so he is scandalized. The gardener is a bit naughty, maybe even a bit crazy, our hero decides, but better than nothing for keeping him company while he waits. Their conversation turns strange. Maybe they engage in a game or a bet. Or the gardener says he'll show him his prize roses, but only in exchange for the hero's Kansas City Royals baseball cap and his Reeboks. He'll gladly show him his medicinal plants, and maybe even let him try them out, but only if the hero gives him his T-shirt with "Visualize Whirled Peas" stenciled on it. And on and on, until the pilgrim is standing there naked, metaphorically or literally. Of course, it turns out that the gardener is the master of the temple. This symbolic stripping has to take place before our hero's eyes are eventually opened and the master guides him through initiation into the mysteries. Then he is sent back out into the world, charged with a mission of service.

The three-fold spiritual path is strewn with obstacles, both within ourselves and outside us. Let's have a look one of the most pervasive and most camouflaged obstacles to conscious spiritual growth.

*Mass Mind*

What is it that we are "leaving" when we "leave the world," as we take the first step on the ever-cycling three-fold spiritual path? What is it that we leave in order to move into sacred space, after which we return to the world with something to offer? Obviously, it does not mean killing yourself, or getting in a space ship and blasting off (although there are people who have interpreted the idea in this way). As any monk or nun will tell you, simply renouncing the world, donning robes, and climbing up on a mountain or disappearing behind the walls of a cloister do not make you holy. Could spiritual teachers have something else in mind when they say, "leave the world"?

One of the (many) jarring moments in spiritual life is the disconcerting realization that, try as we may, we are deeply conditioned by our upbringing and our culture. It is a jolt to

*If you don't know the kind of person I am and I don't know the kind of person you are a pattern that others made may prevail in the world and following the wrong god home, we may miss our star.*

William Stafford
(used with permission)

realize that your reality, your connection to your very self and your worldview, are thoroughly influenced by the particular mass culture in which you live. It is as though your culture hands you a prism through which you experience life, and this prism is then reinforced at every turn by the culture.

One of the wonderful insights available in subtle energy practice is that your physical body and the earth are part of spiritual life. Scriptures speak of a "new heaven and a new earth." Mystics speak of a merging of heaven and earth, of spirit and body, and if there is something specific about "the world" that we need to break free of, it is the particular mindsets and belief systems that keep this process of merging from happening.

Let's call it the *mass mind*, that inevitable amalgamation of all the unexamined assumptions that make up consensus reality in any group of people. You only need to turn on the television to see an effective conduit for the mass mind at work. Sit in any pubic place and listen to what people talk about. Most conversation and most of what comes to us via the mass media deals in products of the mass mind and, suffice it to say, genuine spiritual growth is typically not one of those products. That is why in classical texts the spiritual seeker is told to "leave the world," which can be translated as *disconnect from the mass mind*.

Italian Journalist Luigi Barzini attested to the power of the mass mind in his witty and wise book, *The Europeans*. He noted that in World War II the commanding officers in the British army were able, if the need arose, to entrust critical missions to even the lowest-ranking foot soldiers. According to Barzini, the secret to the success of the British in times of adversity was the fact that all of them could be counted on to be thinking exactly the same seven things. Unfortunately, Barzini didn't enumerate the seven things—I'd be interested in knowing just what those seven things were—so I take this to be the author's metaphoric comment on the fact that the British mass mind was formidably consistent and pervasive.

It is perhaps useful in wartime to have everyone, from the generals down to the infantry, thinking the same thing, and apparently the British excelled at that. But what seems useful at one level can be an obstacle when it come time to grow beyond it. Cultures whose members all think the same "seven thoughts" can create mountainous obstacles for those who begin to have eight thoughts, or nine, or God forbid … ten.

The mass mind is the box of conventional thinking and the unexamined acceptance of what a group of people assumes to be true and real. Your process of personal development, and definitely your involvement with energywork, have probably already challenged you to think outside the box of consensus thinking and may have even gotten you into trouble with those who are dedicated to maintaining the status quo. If you would like to examine your relationship with mass mind, reflect a bit on these questions:

- Do you live in a culture, or family, or group, in which everyone seems to share the same "seven thoughts" or set of assumptions?

- What are the pervasive, unquestioned assumptions in the mass mind of your family, culture, or group?

- What experiences and points of view do you have that are outside of the mainstream of your culture or family?

- What have you encountered when you have tried to communicate about your experiences or act on them?

See if you can identify some mass mind assumptions and write them down. Examples might include things like "everyone should be self-supporting by the age of twenty-one"; "everyone ought to be married"; "the material world is the only reality." Look at widely held unquestioned beliefs that prevail among your people about physical appearance and about persons who are different from your particular group, political, or religious persuasion. Look at stereotypes about other races, sexual orientations, nationalities, and cultures. Look at advertising, which makes broad assumptions about what you value. This can be a way of gaining insights about the particular mass mind you live in. And by all means, look into the particular unquestioned assumptions of the mass mind that you have collided with as you make new discoveries in the world of energy and consciousness, and note especially what happens as you have acted on decisions resulting from thinking outside of the box.

The mass mind affects how you see things, literally. I'll tell you about a striking instance of this which I experienced. Few films have become part of our cultural vocabulary more than *Star Wars*. When it opened in 1977 in Salt Lake City, I went to the opening day matinee with a friend. We were the only two in the theater and we got quite a kick out of it. We talked later with friends who saw it, and we all agreed, along with the majority of the millions of viewers who would see it after us, that *Star Wars* was a delightful, sci-fi comic strip with campy humor and spiritual overtones.

The next year I moved to Germany at about the time the dubbed version of *Star Wars*, *Krieg der Sterne*, opened in theaters. Seeing it in German, sitting in a German audience in Cologne, I had many moments when I couldn't have sworn that it was even the same film. I saw no humor and detected no hint of spirituality. People left the theater buzzing about the fantastic *machinery*. Machinery stood out from everything else. It is what stood out to *me*. I was baffled; it definitely was the exact same film, so how could my perception be so different?

Shortly thereafter, an American friend who lived in Spain mentioned that he had seen

*Star Wars* in Madrid, in Spanish, with the name *Guerra de las Estrellas*. He, and everybody else in the theater, saw it as a love story.

What a shock! The fact of the mass mind is fairly hidden. It is like being a fish, swimming around in the same waters all its life, an element so familiar, so taken for granted that it is practically invisible. One way that many people discover the particular mass mind in which they have lived all their lives is to live outside it. Living for a significant time in another culture with its own language and history—and, of course, its own mass mind—can bring with it many insights into the phenomenon of mass mind, because you have a contrast. You encounter and, to some degree, enter another mass mind.

The mass mind will even color how you approach energy healing. Think about it: if a person walked in off the street and witnessed an energy healing session in progress—let's say one in which the practitioner was using her hands off her partner's body to influence the aura structure—what would that person think? Chances are, it would look pretty weird. What if he or she went away and tried to describe to another person what this healer was doing, waving her hands over the body of the other person? What categories could he count on in the person to whom he is trying to describe the scene? What common language and concepts could the two draw upon in order to discuss it in any way at all? The problem is that we do not share much, if any, consensus reality about energy healing, which lies mostly outside the field of what is considered real in our culture's mass mind.

The three-fold spiritual path begins with "leaving the world" by breaking your identification—if only for a moment at a time in a meditation—with the mass mind. "Leaving," in this sense, has a great deal to do with releasing what has been holding us, physically, mentally, emotionally. Much of formal spiritual training, especially at the outset, is about breaking this identification, often ruthlessly, as novitiates in spiritual orders can tell you.

But you don't have to be a monk or nun, or even consider yourself to be a spiritual seeker, for processes of internal change, processes that bring you out of the mass mind, to be active. Sometimes that active process presents itself in the urge to differentiate yourself from your family, from your background. A common example of this is the plight of a young person who returns home after living elsewhere for a period of time only to find that old friends and family can't acknowledge any change in him because they still see him as the same person as he was before he left home. He feels they have put him in a box, and are blind to the changed, more mature person he has become.

The Swiss psychologist Carl Jung referred to this process of differentiation as "individuation," and even predicted that it would become the most challenging task of our time as more and more individuals found themselves growing beyond the confines of the mass mind of their tribe or nation. Interestingly, when asked once in a letter from a patient to explain, in a single written paragraph, how to individuate, Jung rose to the challenge and told his reader that if she would do whatever she did wholeheartedly, not holding back, and then do the next thing she did completely wholeheartedly, and the next thing, and so on, she would come into what was truly hers. By following her heart in this way, she would individuate, no longer dependant on the mass mind to tell her who she is.

The process of individuation described by Jung is one way of describing how life leads us, sometimes by tricking us, to leave our familiar world and set off on our journey of awakening. The mass mind is hypnotic, and exiting from it is literally about waking up from a trance. Most people's investment in the mass mind is so entrenched that this rarely happens without resistance. A first awakening to a sense of yourself beyond the one your group has laid out for you means breaking open core assumptions that have been in operation all your life. It can be a moment of great revelation that cuts like a bolt of lightning, or it might enter stealthily in the gradual realization that you "aren't in Kansas anymore." Sometimes it happens in periods of disillusionment, illness, hardship, depression, even in events that look to others like a psychotic break. St. Paul, whose extreme awakening and spiritual transformation included getting blasted out of his saddle by the presence of Christ, was speaking about a very intense version of spiritual process when he said, "It is a terrible thing to fall into the hands of the living God" (Heb. 10:31).

Whether you are knocked off your horse on the road to Damascus, jolted by some life-changing realization that causes you to see everything differently, or ease slowly into a new point of view all your own, you are constantly being induced to leave the mass mind. The classic disciplines of spiritual life, such as prayer, meditation, contemplation, solitude, fasting, and silence, to which I will add energywork practices like those in this book, are all aimed at opening a door through which to exit from the mass mind and enter what is beyond it, and then return to the world. Whether or not you are aware of it at the time, each time you exit from the mass mind and enter sacred space, you return slightly changed and more immune to the mass mind.

*Stillness: Being in the Holy Place*

What happens when you are not in the web of thoughts, assumptions, and feelings that keep you tied to the mass mind? Spiritual practices offer us many ways of taking the second step of the three-fold spiritual path, which has to do with being in sacred space. One of the surest signs that you are *not* in the mass mind is when you are in deep silence. If there are nameable goals in meditation and subtle energy practice, stillness is certainly one of them. Subtle energy practices help you, or the person you are working on, come into stillness, a hallmark of contact with universal consciousness.

Subtle energy practice, by its nature, draws you into

*… and it seemed to him in that moment he had actually struggled up and out of a whole customary system of living and emerged a small basic essence of the basic man.*
Margery Allingham

*The myth is the public domain and the dream is the private myth. If your private myth, your dream, happens to coincide with that of the society, you are in good accord with your group. If it isn't, you've got a long adventure in the dark forest ahead of you.*

Joseph Campbell

finer and finer levels of appreciation for the quality of stillness. Paradoxically, stillness is not the absence of sound; instead, it may be the very heart of sound. One of the most profound meditative experiences I ever had was in the rush hour chaos of a Chicago train station. Many people who become absorbed in great works of music report that they are drawn into a timeless state filled with a *resounding stillness*, or the *music of the spheres*.

It is not uncommon nowadays for someone who you just met for the first time in a weekend personal growth workshop to go into confessional mode—pour their insides out, revealing their traumas and dramas and innermost secrets to anybody who will listen. Indeed, sometimes listening isn't even required for them to spill forth. The practice of sharing one's experiences, common in personal development workshops, plays an important role in the process of releasing the excess energy and emotion of long-held fears and pain, learning communication and intimacy, and facing the challenge of self-honesty.

But a balance must be struck between the need to release excess energy and articulate experiences on the one hand, while at the same time preserving their potency on the other. At some point, the catharsis that might clear the way for a deeper experience to emerge gives way to containment, your capacity for holding something as sacred. This may well mean that you *aren't* talking about it much at all. Traditionally, initiates in spiritual schools were sworn to silence about their inner experiences, perhaps sharing only with a mentor or spiritual guide skilled in helping students make the most of inner events. In this sense, people who truly value their inner experiences tend to be not secretive so much as *selective*. If they choose to share their experiences at all, they select people who can help them contain their experience.

The reason for this is a very practical one. There are special initiatory moments in spiritual process in which something is revealed. The moment of the actual revelation may be but a split second, but it is powerful and initiates a process of change in you. It could come in a flash of intuition, a symbol or an image that is worth more than a thousand words. Or, it may come as … stillness. The more you talk about these experiences and the more people you talk about them with, however, the more the energy of that original experience becomes *diffused*—and as a result, less potent—and, consequently, less useful in the service of transformation.

The breakthrough of consciousness from another dimension plants seeds that often need to slumber for a season. An intuitive flash, in its embryonic state, is like a cake you have just put into the oven. It needs heat and the passage of time before it becomes a cake as opposed to a pan of gooey batter. If you open the oven so you can show off your beautiful cake to all your friends before it is ready, it will fall.

The second phase of the three-fold spiritual path is this encounter with the Divine. The energy healer maintains a protective space in which her partner can go deeply into this encounter and then return to normal consciousness without wasting its power with needless chatter. It can be a moment of personal transformation for the individual who enters this sacred space, and also have profound meaning for how she will be able to express her spiritual qualities. With each encounter with divine stillness, the pilgrim in your body and in those you might be treating is gaining a more complete means of engaging with the world and expressing his or her calling. The wise healer teaches respect for this ripening process.

*Return*

The Zen Buddhists have a way of communicating the paradox of the return phase of the three-fold spiritual path: "Before enlightenment, chop wood, carry water. After enlightenment, chop wood, carry water." You leave the ordinary, encounter what is extraordinary, and return again to the ordinary. Nothing changes, and yet, everything changes because you return a bit more, or a lot more, awake to the nature of your being. Many people on a spiritual path envision an ultimate goal of ascension into heaven, or absorption into the Light, but as a *next* step in the development of most of us, there is the inevitable question of how we will engage with the world in the light of our big and little extraordinary encounters.

*The modern pilgrim seeks a passionate connection to his or her individual gifts, and the grace to use them to better humankind.*
Lauren Artress

*Ten Bulls*

Possibly the first representation I ever saw of the initiatory journey—and a slightly nuanced telling of the three-fold spiritual path of leaving the world, finding the sacred place, and then returning, enriched, to the world—was *Ten Bulls* by the twelfth century Chinese Zen master Kakuan. I first saw it accompanied by woodcut drawings in Paul Reps' compilation of Zen writings, *Zen Flesh, Zen Bones*. The text and drawings of the ten bulls represent in very simple form the progressive steps of enlightenment. According to Paul Reps, in Zen tradition, the bull represents "the eternal principle of life, truth in action." What follows is a brief walk through these steps in which I have tried my hand, helped by an understanding of the three-fold path, at catching the flavor of this teaching. It presents a pattern, or cycle, that shows up repeatedly in spiritual process.

## Leaving the World

- *The Search for the Bull:* I call myself a seeker, even while admitting I don't quite know what it is I am seeking. But I sense that there is a far greater reality than the one I am living. Something propels me to take some kind of *action* in the name of my search.

- *Discovering the Footprints:* Teachings abound; many disagree with each other. Yet I have an intuitive sense that all these teachings are pointing to *something*. I haven't yet decided what to do about it, but I do notice that *something* has left a trail.

- *Perceiving the Bull:* Seeking and learning about "it" are one thing, but this attitude allows me to pretend that my goal is "out there," far away. Now, because of direct experience, I see "it" everywhere, and in myself.

- *Catching the Bull:* What made me think this would be tame, fair-weather undertaking? I have invoked heaven! I'm dealing with primal forces! Tiger by the tail or bull by the horns, this is going to take discipline.

## Going into the Sacred Place

- *Taming the Bull:* My discipline is now part of me. It may look severe to others, but I am relaxed. It's what I do. It's who I am.

- *Riding the Bull Home:* I am mindfulness itself, content to let this process unfold as it will. I neither make anything happen, nor do I prevent anything from happening. My art and my work are all a front. My real job is listening.

- *The Bull Transcended:* I don't practice any more. I have no discipline. It is of no more use to me. I am home.

- *Both Bull and Self Transcended:* There is nobody home. I am gone, like a bullet fired into the sun. Not even the vapor remains.

- *Reaching the Source:* Stillness is the only sound, and now even that ceases. I have no other identity but this.

## Returning

- *In the World:* You can see me in town most days. I drive an old car, I wear a shirt I got ten years ago. Most people don't even see me, but I don't care. My treasure is in my heart, and my heart is open.

Each step on the three-fold path has its own kind of character. "Leaving the world" involves seeking and discovery. It necessitates developing a sharp eye for the clues laid down in front of us. It requires a daring spirit and risk-taking, especially when the process becomes real, moving from theory to practice. Like the one who finds the bull, you have to learn the disciplines of taming this primal force of life and grow the trust it takes to ride it. Ultimately, the move into stillness is as natural as night turning to day. Like a river that sooner or later finds its way to the sea, the life force carries you on your journey into the place of intimacy with the Divine Source. The same applies to the return to the world, where what you now bear with you by virtue of this experience finds expression through you, turning outward into the world in which you live.

Energy healing connects us, and those we treat, with more of the totality of who we are. What might start as an attempt to rein in the effects of an injury or disease can become an opening to new perspectives on what this life is all about. When we engage the world of energy and consciousness available within us by means of energetic practices and treatments, we are setting the table for experiences which partake of the deep wisdom within us, and the potential for expanded awareness.

If we think at all about enlightenment, we tend to highlight the big moments of awakening—the impact of the big "AHA!" moments of deep insight is indisputable—and yet, this is a process that is also going on continuously in the background of our consciousness, bit by bit. As you learn the ropes of going in and out of the mass mind and cultivating contact with the Divine Source within you, a curious thing starts to happen. Early on, the experience of finally "connecting" in meditation indeed feels like you are completely leaving the world and trekking to some mystic mountaintop. At first, spiritual teachings seem vague and metaphorical. Heaven is far away and getting there is a journey of a thousand days and much hardship. By and by, however, as you cultivate your relationship with the Source, it is as if heaven and earth start to approach each other and grow together, and more of your spiritual life seeps through, so to speak, into your body and your everyday life. As you grow spiritually, your gifts also grow. At some point, they turn outward and begin to have an effect on other people. This is the process by which your deep insight turns into action and your spiritual gifts connect, through you, with the world.

## RETREAT

*Decision made*
*in earnest*
*arrangements made*
*appropriate place, open space*
*in the appointment book,*
*gather provisions,*
*finally alone,*
*it starts.*

*Outer resistance behind me, I turn*
*within. But now the dwellers*
*on my inner thresholds*
*make their presence known, there*
*all the time, but now*

*we do battle.*
*My body hurts,*
*craves stimulation,*
*I'm frustrated. I'm bored. I want light,*
*but my heart is closed.*
*I'm depressed.*
*My practice is empty.*
*I decide to pray*
*forever*
*for something ... what?*
*A hammer!*
*Something to crack the hard nut*
*of my symptoms, my misery, my stupidity.*
*I sleep,*
*dream,*
*wake,*
*rise,*
*move*
*through days of silence.*
*Inner turmoil becomes thin, a veil*
*between me and ... stillness.*
*I listen,*
*Stillness listens to me.*
*Nature's sound does not clash*
*with that deepening sense. I enter.*
*Senses elongate,*
*they braid together.*
*I move now with wind.*
*I touch air*
*that touches all surfaces*
*of all creatures.*
*My prayer echoes from the hills;*
*my invocation opens all gates,*
*heals all wounds.*
*Time starts again.*
*I am ready.*

—JG

# Chapter Three

## MAKING THE CASE FOR DOING INNER WORK

*How can you expect to do energywork if you can't even meditate?*

Vajra Matusow

In the laboratory of your personal energywork practice, you find out, first hand, what energetic practices actually do. In time, this transfers to your external work with others. That is part of the uniqueness and excitement of this work. No one in the world can tell you ahead of time exactly what is going to happen, *this* time, within *you*, if you sit down and connect your awareness, for example, with the energy center in your sacrum or your throat. It is exactly the same fresh and mysterious unpredictability that a naturalist thrives on, who returns, day after day, season after season, to the same field, the same stream, the same grove of trees. The more you look, the more you see. It is not the same field or stream as it was yesterday. In your personal energywork practice, *you* are that field, that grove, that stream, and you are that naturalist who is learning the secrets held there.

Inner work is anything you do in order to interact with your non-conscious world, and practices like the energy exercises in this book are examples of ways of implementing this interaction. With practice, over time, they give you a means of actually leaving the world of the mass mind, going within, and then returning to your ordinary consciousness with intact, potent experiences. They create a means of forging a communicative link with your inner world, and this, in turn, helps you grow a trusting relationship with your intuition and the other processes of your inner life. When you do inner work, you are finding out, first hand, how you tick.

Inner work involves more than merely mastering a set of techniques; you are attending to *qualities* in yourself. By this I mean you are cultivating the potentials and spiritual gifts that you carry in you, for example those of an artist, healer, teacher, or

*Everything in the world, every baby, city, tetanus shot, tennis ball, and pebble, was an outcrop of some vast and hitherto concealed vein of knowledge, apparently, that had compelled people's emotions and engaged their minds in the minutest detail without anyone's having done with it. There must be bands of enthusiasts for everything on earth—fanatics who shared a vocabulary, a batch of technical skills and equipment, and, perhaps, a vision of some single slice of the beauty and mystery of things, of the complexity, fascination, and unexpectedness.*

Annie Dillard

*If you don't have room in your house for an elephant, don't make friends with the zookeeper.*

Sufi saying

leader, not to mention the unnameable blend of qualities that are uniquely yours. They will grow, following their own natural cycles, and at some point turn outward and touch others.

Whatever you feed and water with the energies of your attention and caring will grow. Imagine tearing a hole in the floorboards of your house, digging right down through the cement foundation until you strike earth, and then planting a cottonwood sapling. You will probably find you have to do any number of things to your house in order for the young tree to mature, beginning with cutting skylights and new windows and constructing mirror-lined sun tunnels to let light in. Sooner or later, you will have to cut a hole in the ceiling and then the roof to accommodate the tree's crowning branches and leaves and learn ways to appreciate how the pervasive cottony seed fluffs look on your furniture. By and by, you become conscious of having given a home to a creature of great strength and beauty, a habitat to numerous plant and animal species that arrive to nest in its branches and bark, a landmark to the eye of all who know your neighborhood, and an inspiration to the poet next door who closes his eyes and imagines the rustling of the wind in the cottonwood leaves to be the surf of a vast upside-down ocean of air breaking above our heads. In the same way, attending to your spiritual qualities will mean accommodating the changes that take place.

Although most of what follows is addressed to readers who feel drawn to energetic healing work, the essential kernel of these ideas can apply to you, whatever the specific spiritual qualities you feel are yours to cultivate. In other words, even if you feel that your calling lies somewhere other than in healing work, you are invited to try the energetic practices in this book to nourish your inner world and shed light on the calling that is yours.

*Six Reasons for Doing Inner Work*

1. *Your work with yourself is your way of activating your healing potentials.* Your effectiveness as a healer, if it is to go beyond technical mastery, depends on the interaction between the healing potentials active in you and that same area of potential which is latent in the person you are working with.

2. *The work with yourself is your laboratory for learning directly about the human energy system.* Information can never replace experience, and your inner work is an opportunity to gain experience.

3. *Your work with yourself is your side of the bargain when it comes to gaining the subconscious cooperation needed when working with others.* Your connection and comfort, or your lack

thereof, with your own inner world will communicate itself wordlessly to those you work with and signal to them how trustworthy you are for them and their healing process.

4. *Your inner work will help you to clear long-standing, highly-charged issues from your body and your subconscious* that would otherwise create an attraction point for unwanted transfers of energies from other people.

5. *Your inner work is a way of connecting with your ongoing spiritual process.* In the words of psychologist Robert Johnson in his book *Inner Work*, "The purpose of learning to work with the unconscious is not just to resolve our conflicts or deal with our neuroses. We find there a deep source of renewal, growth, strength, and wisdom. We connect with the source of our evolving character; we cooperate with the process whereby we bring the total self together; we learn to tap that rich lode of energy and intelligence that waits within."

6. Among the by-products of your inner work are *confidence in the nature of life and a belief in the deep wisdom of the body.*

### *The Noble Tradition of Self-Experimentation*

In the general field of complimentary and alternative healing, perhaps especially energy healing, there is a discernable tradition of self-experimentation. Some people seem to really like the sound of this, while others definitely do not. Maybe it will console you to know that when it comes to any self-experimentation you undertake—the meditations and exercises in this book all have that character—you will be in interesting company. William Sutherland's *cranial bowl* experiments on himself in the 1930s come to mind. He had the (then) totally unconventional belief that the bones of the cranium are mobile. As any craniosacral therapist can now attest, cranial bones do indeed have tiny but significant movements that occur with the contraction and expansion of the head in what is called craniosacral rhythm, instead of being fused together at the sutures. To test out his theory that cranial bones not only move, but that immobile cranial bones also lead to pathology, Sutherland crafted a helmet fitted at strategic positions with thumbscrews. He would strap on his cranial helmet, tighten the thumbscrews down on an individual cranial bone in order to immobilize it, and then take note of the symptoms that arose in him. While he noted his physical symptoms, his wife, unbeknownst to him at the time, was busy noting his emotional symptoms and mood swings. Once he succeeded in taking a cranial bone out of its normal movement pattern, he then had to devise ways to restore its proper movement. Sutherland's self-experimentation led to the founding tenants of cranial osteopathy, which further evolved into modern-day craniosacral therapy.

Another notable self-experimenter was Samuel Hahnemann, the father of homeopathy, one of the truly remarkable forms of energy medicine, which makes use of highly diluted forms of plant, animal, and mineral substances. Hahnemann was a doctor in Germany in the eighteenth century in an era when bloodletting and the pervasive use of mercury were part of standard medical practice. If you examine the derivation of the word "quack," when not being used to refer to the language spoken by ducks, a tiny window will open on the history of Western medicine. Our word "quack," in this context referring to a disreputable medical practitioner who makes claims that he or she cannot fulfill, comes to us from German, in which the word is *Quacksalber,* which is related to the word *Quecksilber,* German for "quicksilver," also known as mercury.

The connection is this: mercury was widely used by physicians in eighteenth century Europe, along with bloodletting and opiates, and while mercury actually cured some ailments, it also left immense toxic side effects in its wake. Seen from this perspective, the essence of the quack mentality is the unquestioned practice of following one undifferentiated regimen or approach for everyone. As the saying goes, "If you're a hammer, every problem looks like a nail."

The development of homeopathy was driven, in part, by Samuel Hahnemann's outrage at these practices and this mentality. According to homeopath Jessica Jackson, "Hahnemann was a vitriolic opponent of the practice of medicine in his time, would never use mercury or venesection in his practice. His 'radical' ideas included recommendations for exercise, fresh air and the application of water in the form of bathing," and extended to his methods of research.

The proven cure for malaria at that time was Peruvian bark (the plant source of quinine). Hahnemann made an extract of the bark, diluted it using a formula he could replicate, took it at regular intervals, and awaited the onset of symptoms, which he then carefully noted. As he continued to take his diluted extract of Peruvian bark, he developed malaria-like symptoms of alternating fevers, chills, and shaking. When he stopped taking the extract, his symptoms subsided. This and other similar experiments led him to base an entire science of medicine on the *Law of Similars*, an ancient idea in medicine, written of by Hippocrates and Paracelceus. It states that "Like cures like," along with its corollary that says, "That which causes certain symptoms in a well person will have a curative influence on similar symptoms in an ill person." These became the guiding principles of homeopathy.

Hahnemann went on to subject a wild array of animal, mineral, and vegetable substances to the same type of testing. And not only on himself; he gave new meaning to self-experimentation by including his students and his children in the experiments. His children all lived well into their nineties, by the way, and when he himself was in his eighties, Hahnemann moved to Paris, married a second time, and started a new career.

The tradition of self-experimentation continues in modern homeopathic research in the form of *provings*, systematic trials in which the researcher takes a dose of a remedy and notes what happens. In many schools, these provings form one of the cornerstones of how homeopathy is taught. I once attended a seminar at the *Homöopathiewoche* in Bad Boll, Germany. Firsthand reports about provings were a feature of the week's studies. In this course, there were two small groups of participants who took part in controlled provings. At the beginning of the week, one group of a half dozen participants took a known remedy, the properties of which were already established in the homeopathic literature. The other group took a dose of a remedy *without* knowing its identity. The idea in both cases was that the participants would monitor the symptoms that arose over the days of the seminar. In the case of the group with the unknown remedy, their task was to deduce the remedy from the symptoms it caused to arise. One of the seminar participants made a crack about how conventional physicians also ought to take the drugs *they* prescribe before giving them to their patients in order to learn firsthand about their effects.

Homeopathic provings can sound utterly hair-raising to the uninitiated, but provings of this kind are done all the time with a number of safeguards. No one is allowed to take part in provings if they are ill, for instance, and symptoms evoked in provings clear up quickly when the remedy is no longer being taken. And as it turns out, not every "symptom" is even unpleasant.

Predictably, the group that took the known remedy came up with a mild but discernable constellation of symptoms, both physical and intrapsychic. Some of the participants reported dreams and even serendipitous events over the course of the week-long seminar that struck them as significant. Under the guidance of the instructor, they constructed a composite of their reportings, which, in essence, confirmed the widely known *portrait* of the remedy they had taken.

More interesting, of course, was the group who did not know what remedy they had taken. These were doctors, for the most part, and they knew how to catalog symptoms in an orderly way. But now they had to turn into detectives as well and deduce, from the composite of their experiences, the substance that had evoked their particular constellation of symptoms. Each in turn reported from the notes they had taken on themselves, and little by little, like a Polaroid photo developing before our eyes, a picture evolved. The kicker was the mysterious happenstance that four out of five of the participants in the proving developed a marked, untypical craving for beer during the time they took the remedy. This unusual symptom was part of the established *portrait* of a particular homeopathic remedy and it ended up tipping the scales in favor of *Bryonia*, the remedy they had taken. They got it right!

I once met an old osteopath in Kansas City who had an unmistakable touch of the self-experimenter about him. Everybody loved Dr. Whim, a quiet saint on Linwood Boulevard in midtown Kansas City. He kept his fees very low, $20 per visit, regardless of the services he performed, so everyone could afford his services in that transitional neighborhood. His waiting room was World War II vintage. So were the *National Geographics* on the magazine racks, as well as the dust balls that lined the baseboards. Inside his practice room, an ancient treatment table set at knee level, yellowed, curling acupuncture charts in Chinese, medicine cabinets, and several unnamable contraptions on wheels. Every available surface was covered with snapshots taped to the walls and medicine cabinets, photos of children he had treated.

Old school, Dr. Whim wore a white shirt with the sleeves rolled up and his necktie stuck into the front of his shirt between the buttons like an old Scotsman out on the golf links. Dr. Whim had "veterinarian hands"; they had an instant calming effect on whatever creature he touched; in this case, me. He would adjust my spine, finding exactly the right spot and the precise vector so that he could accomplish what he intended with minimal force. He would sometimes prepare my body for the adjustment using what he called "physiotherapy," electrostimulus guided into tight muscles from one of his ancient contraptions on wheels.

One day, I was lying face down on Dr. Whim's therapy table while he applied the electrodes of what was surely the original physiotherapy machine to my upper back. I wondered if frayed wires were going to be the death of both of us. After a while of feeling my rhomboids convulse and release, convulse and release with the alternating doses of current, my mind wandered away from imminent death by therapeutic electrocution. I began to examine the dust bunnies under the medicine cabinet in front of me when my eyes lit upon a couple of tiny white globular objects.

"Dr. Whim, are those homeopathic pellets under your medicine cabinet?"

Dr. Whim left the electrodes stuck in position on my back and got down on his hands and knees to look. After a moment of close scrutiny, he lightly licked a fingertip and brought up one of the white pellets stuck to it.

"Well, I believe they are," he said, apparently as surprised as I was.

He asked if I was interested in homeopathy and other forms of energetic healing. I told him I was. For the next thirty minutes, Dr. Whim reminisced about "strange phenomena" he had studied. He confided that it was great to find someone else who was interested in energywork. As he talked, I had a fantasy of him in the 1930s, an odd, lonely young man, thrilled with his new discoveries but feeling unable to talk about them outside of a small circle and getting to feel what it's like to be seen as a crackpot. And now, here he was, an old man with great, compassionate hands, surrounded by baby pictures and the ancient tools of his craft, hidden away in a musty office in midtown Kansas City. From what he told me, he had been busy with some of the same things that had kept *me* busy since my early twenties.

At one point, Dr. Whim got a mischievous look in his eyes.

"You know something," he said, "if you take little copper disks and put them on your body at certain positions …"—and here, he commenced to point out, on his shoulders, hips, knees, and the sides of his head, some of the *exact* same energy-active positions that I use in energy treatments and inner work—"and string them together with copper wires, and then go to sleep with them on …" Dr. Whim's eyes grew more mischievous. "you'll really have strange dreams."

When I told him I had been doing more or less the same thing, minus the copper wires, we had a good laugh. Nothing new under the sun.

When I finally got up off the table (he got around to adjusting my spine after I reminded him), I felt better. I went out to the reception desk to pay for my visit. I had been in there for fifty minutes, and the waiting room was full of mothers and children. The receptionist was a woman in her seventies.

"Twenty dollars," she said.

"But I was in there so long," I protested. "Shouldn't it be more?"

She just smiled and shook her head. "No. He does the same thing with everybody. Just seems you needed more time today."

As I made my way through the crowded waiting room, I looked back to see Dr. Whim welcoming his next patient, a young mother with a baby in her arms. He must have felt me watching him because he turned and called to me across the room.

"Don't forget to try the copper wires!"

It is not required that you strap helmets with thumbscrews onto your head and wire yourself up with copper discs or perform experiments on your children in order to learn energywork. Still, the pathway to learning energywork, by its nature, will always have a strong nontraditional— that is to say personal and experiential—quality to it, because so much of what happens in energy and consciousness is impossible to get next to unless you encounter it in yourself. William Sutherland, Samuel Hahnemann, and Dr. Whim are inspiring examples of how knowledge and the wisdom to put it to use have to be dug out of the ground of personal experience. Indeed, the energy healer often truly has nothing but his or her own experience to turn to for insight. We humans have a rich legacy of teachings and practices designed for the pilgrim within, practices that generate the kind of experiences from which our inner pilgrim can learn and grow. In the chapters to come, we will explore some modern updates of ancient spiritual technologies that will serve your inner spiritual traveler.

# CHAPTER FOUR

## ANCIENT SPIRITUAL TECHNOLOGY
### An Introduction to the Inner Pilgrimage

*The seat of the soul is there, where the inner and the outer worlds meet.*
Joseph Campbell

When Alex Grey, the visionary artist famous for *The Sacred Mirrors*, traveled to the North Pole in search of insight about the principle of polarity, he found himself performing an impromptu ritual in the middle of a vast desert of snow. He had made his way to the magnetic North Pole, the place all compass needles point to, where all the lines of the earth's magnetic force converge. Grey found out that instead of being in one constant position on the map, the magnetic North Pole "wanders" in a circle about one hundred miles in diameter, so he reasoned that he, too, must wander in a circle in order to capture the essence of this mysterious phenomenon. In a work entitled *Polar Wandering*, he photographed himself walking, naked, a circular pattern in the dazzling snowscape. He would later describe the experience as an ecstatic ritual act.

The patterns that run deep in nature are among the most ancient starting points for conscious ritual. When we trace the contours of a natural cycle with our mind, senses, and imagination, or even emulate them through ritual, our awareness is invited into what the ancients thought of as a basic idea in the mind of God. The patterns that run deep in nature also run deep in us, and our energy healing practices partake of this as well.

Though we might not think of it as ritual, each time we use our awareness to "walk" the labyrinthine energetic pathways in and around our bodies, we create the possibility of entering sacred space. More so when we do it purposefully, mindfully, reverently. This is ritual space.

As you continue in this book, you will find it full of practices in which you consciously use your awareness to trace the contours of your energy body, the subtle energetic architecture of the temple in which you live. The conscious movement of your deep awareness within this temple is an internal pilgrimage. The pilgrim in your body is you.

### *"Through World Contemplate World"*[4]
Our spiritual ancestors had great reverence for the natural world. They understood nature to be the mirror of the cosmos and their spiritual technology was what they had at hand. Contemplation of the life patterns of the natural world is a way to get a handle on the holographic universe in which the whole is accessible through any of its parts. In ritual, when we consciously mirror the cosmos with love, mindfulness, and heart in our small worlds, we are learning about the place "where the inner and the outer worlds meet," and we invite connection with the great cosmos. This, again, is

---

4    Lao Tsu

the basis for all effective ritual. Each natural cycle, down to the tiniest submicroscopic event in a drop of pond water, is a mirror of the cosmos as electrons and protons gyrate like planets around an atom's nucleus. The dervish whirls, turning a spinning orbit around his teacher, replicating the motion of the planets around the sun. Soon, the dervish's consciousness is drawn into the cycling of the heavenly bodies.

What follows is a meditative exercise that demonstrates this idea. Exercises like this one have been used for eons to help humans to, as the poet Blake put it, "see the world in a grain of sand."

INNER PILGRIMAGE #1: *The Pilgrimage of the Orange*

Preparation: Read through all the instructions before starting. This is a good idea with all the exercises and inner pilgrimages.

1.  Find a fresh orange.

2.  With your eyes open, settle into a restful and alert frame of mind, sitting comfortably with the orange in your hand. Slowly, carefully inspect each detail of its surface, its color, texture, and shape.

3.  Send your sight (your "x-ray vision," if you like) down into one of the countless, breathing pores in the orange's skin and bring your awareness below the skin surface into the white pulpy protective layer beneath its surface.

4.  Examine the arrangement of these fibers as they completely upholster the fruit's sections. Note how this same layer differentiates and forms the stringy cord that makes up the center line of the orange, extending from the "north pole" of the orange, where the stem links it to the branch and to the tree, down to its "south pole."

5.  Now move your awareness from one section of the orange to the next. Count them in your mind's eye as you go. How many are there?

6.  In your mind's eye, choose one of the sections and separate it from the rest of the orange. Look at how that same layer of tissue that protects the orange from bumps and bruises and wraps up each section in a neat bundle also forms the thin, translucent membrane covering each of the juice-filled cells inside the section. This is how nature ensures that if the orange gets pierced—if you stuck a pencil through it, for example—only the cells that are pierced will lose their juice, while all the others remain intact.

7.  Now move your awareness to the seeds in the center of the orange. Count them. Select one of the seeds and examine it. It is covered with the same pulpy tissue. Strip that tissue away and in your mind's eye open that seed so you can examine what's inside. Take a good look at the colors, textures and shapes in the core of the seed.

8.  Now close the seed back up and see it being planted in the ground. See it being covered over with soil and tamped down a bit.

9.  See the orange plant gradually sprout and grow through all its cycles: See the sun's warming energy and the rain soaking into this buried seed as it passes through many cycles of dark and light, hidden in the ground.

10. At some point, there is an imperceptible stirring in the seed, a shudder of life force as something changes. A tiny feathered root forms and begins to descend into the earth. Almost simultaneously, a miniscule tendril sprouts and ventures upward toward the earth's surface. At one point, the tender sprout breaks through the surface of the ground. Below the surface, the root reaches downward into the earth.

11. Together, they grow; the young orange tree reaches a height above the ground, mirrored almost exactly by the network of roots that extend into the earth. Day and night pass, rain and sunshine, cycle upon cycle, until one day it is a tree with leaves and blossoms.

Orange blossoms in which tiny buds form. A tiny, hard bud grows, drinking in the waters of the tree's sap. Time passes, and the bud swells toward ripeness. It weighs heavily on its stem. It is only a matter of time …

12. See a hand, your hand, reaching up toward the orange. Just before you touch the orange, it drops into your hand. It is the orange you are holding.

13. Eat the orange. Slowly.

See a hand, your hand, reaching up toward the orange. Just before you touch the orange, it drops into your hand. It is the orange you are holding.

*Now You Are the Orange*

Now let's move our contemplation of an orange into a new dimension by applying Alex Grey's ancient style of reasoning: *if the earth and natural world around me behave in a certain way, then I come into harmony with her and learn her secrets by emulating what she does.* The contemplation of the architecture of the orange that we just completed revealed that it has a "north pole," and a "south pole." It also has a core of fiber that connects these two poles through its center. Close examination reveals that the same fiber that makes up this core also forms the orange's skin. Like the orange, you—or to be more precise, your personal energy field—also have a "north pole" and a "south pole" and an energetic core connects the two, and this core is of one piece with the rest of the energetic sheath that makes up your individual aura.

The pilgrim moves in sacred space as he walks the pathways between heaven and earth. Every stop along the way is a potential site of divine insight and renewal. In the practice that follows, the pilgrim in you will travel pathways learned by the study of the form of his ally, the orange.

*Preparation for the Journey*

Your inner pilgrim first needs to know the landmarks, the holy shrines, on the path of this pilgrimage. Let's introduce the locations of the energy-active positions we will be using, one by one, to help you find them.

- *Crown Center:* The easiest way to connect your awareness with your Crown Center is to move your attention to the highest point on the top of your head, then find a position slightly forward of that and slightly up in your hair.

- *Heart Center:* This will be the beginning and the end of this pilgrimage. Locate it in the middle of your chest.

- *Perineum Center:* This is an energy-active position located at your perineum[5], between your anus and your genitals.

- *South Pole:* If you were to drop a slow, conscious line straight down from your perineum to a position that feels like it is about three feet (one meter) in the floor or ground below the level of your feet[6], and then relax your awareness, you can be drawn into the energy of the "south pole" of your individual energy field. If you are sitting on the floor or the ground, you will get a *feeling contact* with your energetic South Pole by moving your awareness to what feels to you like three feet below your perineum.

- *North Pole:* To locate this position, move your awareness slowly, consciously straight upward from your Crown to a position that feels like it is about three feet (one meter) above your head. This might be regarded as the "north pole" of your personal energy field[7].

If any of these energy-active positions are unfamiliar to you, try locating them individually, using the above descriptions as guidelines, and spending some time with them. This way, they will have the time and attention they need in order to "bloom" in your awareness. The advantage is that you will then know how to find them when it comes time to use them in an inner pilgrimage.

*Five Tips for Connecting Your Awareness with Energy-Active Positions on Your Body*

1. *Know the location:* Each energy-active position we use in these inner pilgrimages can be accessed by bringing your attention to the appropriate physical landmarks on your body. These physical landmarks are not one and the same with the energy-active position, but

---

5    In *A Pilgrim in Your Body*, I capitalize the names of energy-active positions like Heart Center and Perineum Center, but use lower case for physical anatomical references like "heart" and "perineum."

6    This is a subjective guideline for finding your energetic South Pole, since you move into a different relation with space and distance when you move your awareness off your body. The same idea will apply to finding your energetic North Pole, which will feel like it is about three feet above the crown of your head.

7    Interestingly, this position is also referred to as the "Individuality Point" in some circles, and the "Transpersonal Point" in others. It is typical of terms like this to reflect the point of view of those who coin them. As the name "Individuality Point" suggests, this position relates to the unique set of spiritual qualities you have brought with you into this life. One clairvoyant I know describes it as the first energy-active position to incarnate when a soul is being born, and the last to go when the person dies. On the other side of the coin, the same position is also called the "Transpersonal Point," no less correctly, but the perspective is different. Here, it is seen as a gateway from the world of individual consciousness into that of universal consciousness.

they serve as easy positions from which your awareness can be drawn into the energy movement at that position. Since most of us can feel our physical body more easily than our energy field, it makes sense to first bring attention to specific positions on our bodies that act as gateways to the energetic.

2. Get a *feeling contact* with the position, as opposed to thinking about the position, or even visualizing it.

3. Relax. *Don't try to force your way into a connection.* It just doesn't work. Energy contact is best made if you create a feeling contact with the place on your body that you are working with, and then let go and relax your awareness. Let your attention be "loose" and let the energy-active position do the work of drawing you in.

4. *Cultivate mindfulness*: This means that when you make an energetic connection you are present and paying attention, but you are not trying to make anything happen, nor are you trying to prevent anything from happening.

5. *Move slowly and consciously between positions*: Whether you are moving your attention within your body, on your skin-surface, or in the energetic space around your physical body, there is much to be experienced *between* the landmarks of your inner journey. Moving slowly between positions, not leaping spasmodically between positions, especially when you are moving your awareness outside your physical body, also helps you to develop a necessary sense of control over the movement.

## *The Pilgrimage*

1. When you have settled into a comfortable sitting position, drop your awareness into your *Heart Center* and allow this contact to deepen. Relax your awareness and give this initial contact a couple of minutes to deepen before you move on from there.

2. Release your Heart contact and slowly move your awareness down in your body until you reach your *Perineum*, located between your anus and your genitals. When you have a feeling contact with this position, make sure your focus is loose and relaxed. Give this contact a minute to respond.

3. After allowing this contact at your Perineum Center to deepen, release it and slowly drop your awareness further, *straight down to your energetic South Pole.* This will feel like it is about three feet (one meter) in the ground or floor beneath your Perineum Center. Let this position draw you in, and *stay with it for one minute.*

4. From your South Pole, move your awareness out and around your body in a slow, conscious arc extending to *about three feet from your body*[8]. Travel up to your *energetic North Pole.* This will feel like it is approximately three feet (one meter) above the crown of your head. As with all energy-active positions, your energetic North Pole has its own feel and it will draw you into itself in its own way. Give this contact with your North Pole a minute to deepen.

5. Now, after you have gently released your contact with your North Pole, move your awareness *slowly downward to your Crown* and allow that contact to develop for a minute or so.

6. Releasing your Crown Center contact, slowly drop your awareness *back into your Heart and re-establish your contact there, letting it deepen a minute.*

7. *Move along this pathway a second time*: downward to your South Pole, out and around your body to your North Pole. Once you have mastered this movement with a single

___

8     Here, too, you are moving to what feels like it is about three feet away from your body. Bear in mind that your aura structure is a fluctuating field of energy. As such, it expands and contacts. Sometimes it will feel like it is expanding well beyond the three feet, other times like it is hugged in closer to your physical body.

arc, try moving your awareness out from your South Pole all around your body up to your North Pole—imagine you are spreading your awareness out over the whole skin of the orange as you travel up to your energetic North Pole—and then back down through the crown of your head and finally coming to rest in your Heart. On the way, pause momentarily at each of these stations (Perineum, South Pole, North Pole, Crown and Heart Centers) and let the connection deepen before moving on.

8. *Finish in your Heart* and allow a ten-minute period for a meditation. Allow what wants to come up in you to do so.

9. End the exercise.

The orange is a perfect outward image of the energy field that surrounds and infuses our physical bodies. In this inner pilgrimage you follow the shape of your energy field's structures.

Reversing the Direction

The Pilgrimage of the Orange can be done in the opposite direction. Where you have a downward, grounding movement in the above exercise, you will find that reversing the direction will bring you into a different set of experiences. In both cases, begin and end the pilgrimage in your Heart Center, a good place to begin and end any journey. Here are the stations in the reversed direction:

1. *Heart Center*
2. *Up to your Crown Center*
3. *Up to your energetic North Pole*
4. *Out, around, and down to your energetic South Pole*
5. *Up to your Perineum*
6. *Up to your Heart*
7. *Repeat a second time*
8. *Finish in your Heart and allow a ten minute period for a meditation and release phase*
9. *End the exercise*

TIP: Try this circulation in one direction one day, then in the other direction the next. Alternate these directions for two weeks and keep track of what comes up within you. Pay special attention to what happens from one sitting to the next. All energy-oriented exercises need to be done over a period of time in order for their broader effects to become known to you.

### *Consulting Nature—As Above, So Below*

One of the best-known of ancient cosmological maxims is "As above, so below." Other ways of expressing this are:

- "As within, so without."

- "As in the manifest world, so in the unmanifest world."

- "On earth as it is in heaven."

- "As in the macrocosm, so in the microcosm."

The pilgrim within you is a modern descendant of seekers who throughout history have looked to nature for guidance about life. They looked down at what was below their feet, out at the world around them, and, of course, they also looked up and searched the skies for guidance.

> *From my journal notes:* Today is November 8, 2003, the day of a full moon eclipse and the day of what many are calling the Harmonic Concordance, a long-awaited configuration of six major planets. In astrological terms, this is a powerful moment in the progression of starry influences as it is the convergence of two Grand Trines.
>
> What gets my attention in this is the fact that these major planets form a six-pointed star, the ancient symbol of the balanced interpenetration of heaven and earth.

The event referred to in my journal entry was an occasion for creating the following inner pilgrimage, an energetic example of a basic kind of ritual in which we enact "here below" what is happening "up above."

### INNER PILGRIMAGE #2: *The Pilgrimage of the Six-Pointed Star*

In Vedantic teachings, the six-pointed star is a symbol for the Heart Center, but it can be used elsewhere in your energy system to enhance balance. Wherever it is used, it symbolizes the balanced interpenetration of heaven and earth and the harmonious blend of masculine and feminine, yin and yang. We'll start this inner pilgrimage by inviting the influence of this geometric figure into a part of our energy system that often needs help with its energetic balance, namely, the Solar Plexus Center.

### Preparation

- On a piece of paper, *draw a six-pointed star* made with two intermingled equilateral triangles, one pointing upward, the other one pointing downward.

- *Consciously disconnect this symbol from any specific religion, and from all national or political associations.* The idea here is to make use of it as an energetic symbol and tool of consciousness.

- If you feel the need to do so, review the five tips for making conscious contact with an energy-active position.

- Sit or stand comfortably in an upright position and breathe gently as you settle into a meditative state.

## Part 1: Contact and Color

1. Drop your awareness into your Solar Plexus Center, three finger-breadths above your navel. Relax your attention and allow some time for your contact to deepen. Give this first contact two minutes.

2. *Add color:* Disconnect from your Solar Plexus Center and visualize a field of *bright yellow color* (like the sun) in front of you.

3. Place this color on your Solar Plexus Center.

> *Note On Working With Color:* When you work with color in your energy field in this way, the color you start with will probably change to another color, or move around, once you place it in a position. Just allow that to happen after you place it there.

4. Stay with this bright yellow color (or whatever it changes into) for two minutes. The point is to *allow the energy center and the color to interact in their own way.*

5. Release this color connection and settle into a short meditation: sit with whatever comes up into your awareness. Give this a couple of minutes.

## Part 2: Add the Six-Pointed Star *(see illustration)*

6. Now open your eyes and look at the six-pointed star you have drawn on the piece of paper in front of you.

7. When you have spent a bit of time looking at this figure, close your eyes and in your visualization place it on your Solar Plexus Center. The idea here is to *allow the symbol and the energy center to interact.* Again, don't try to force the symbol to stay fixed in one place. After some time at your Solar Plexus Center, it might change in appearance, size, or position. Just allow that to happen. Stay with this connection for two minutes.

8. Short meditation: disconnect your attention from the symbol and allow whatever wants to come up in you to do so. Give this little meditation a couple of minutes.

## Part 3: Enlarge the Symbol *(see illustration)*

Start by building the upward-pointing triangle:

9. Bring your awareness down to your *left big toe.* Get a feeling contact with it, and allow about a minute for the contact to deepen.

10. Now slowly, consciously move your awareness on your skin surface up your left leg, up the left side of your body, neck, and face until you arrive at *the middle of your forehead.* This is the Pineal Extension Point, a good position for contacting your Pineal Center.

Allow your attention to rest there a moment. Give this connection a minute to deepen.

11. Now disconnect from your Pineal Center and move your awareness slowly *down the right side of your body*, following the contours of your skin surface. Move down your body and your right leg until you reach your *right big toe*. Make a good conscious connection with your right big toe and allow this contact to deepen. One minute.

12. Now move your awareness in a slow, conscious line *from your right big toe back to your left big toe*, completing a triangle.

13. Repeat steps 1–4 and sit in your awareness of the entire triangle for a minute and then disconnect.

Now it's time to create the downward-point triangle:

14. Bring your awareness now to the zone *above your left shoulder and directly out from the side of your head above your left ear*. Relax and allow your contact to build there. *One minute.*

15. Release your awareness from this position above your left shoulder *and slowly move your awareness in a line through the center of your head*, in through the left side, above your left ear, passing through the middle of your head and out the right side, above your right ear. You will be coming to a position above your right shoulder that corresponds to the position you found to the left of your head. Give this contact a minute to deepen.

16. Disconnect from this position above your right shoulder and move your awareness slowly down to a point on the floor *midway between your feet*. Let your awareness rest there for a minute before disconnecting.

17. Move your awareness in a slow line up to the position to the *left of your head*.

18. Repeat this triangle and place your attention on this entire downward-pointing triangle. One minute.

19. You have now formed a downward-pointing triangle and an upward-pointing triangle. See if you can feel both of these triangles *at the same time*. Sit with your awareness inside these two triangles, which form a six-pointed star. One minute.

20. Release this contact and take a few minutes and allow what comes up within you to do so.

Final Phase: Sit or Stand Within the Six-Pointed Star *(see illustration)*

21. Expand the two triangles so that you can place them *around your entire body*. See yourself standing or sitting in the center of these interpenetrating triangles, which form the six-pointed star. Give this a minute.

22. Now release your awareness of the triangles and take ten minutes for a meditation. Allow whatever wants to come into your consciousness to do so.

23. End the exercise and take note of your experiences.

The *Journey of the Six-Pointed Star* at a Glance:

Part 1: Contact and Color
1.  Solar Plexus Center. Two minutes.
2.  Place bright yellow color on your Solar Plexus. Two minutes.
3.  Release color and settle into a short meditation: sit with whatever comes up into your awareness. Give this a couple of minutes.

Part 2: Add the Six-Pointed Star *(see illustration)*
4.  Now open your eyes and look at the six-pointed star.
5.  In your visualization place it on your Solar Plexus Center. Two minutes.
6.  Short meditation.

Part 3: Enlarge the Symbol *(see illustration)*
Start by building the upward-pointing triangle:
7.  Left big toe. One minute.
8.  Move your awareness on your skin surface up to your pineal extension point, allowing one minute to deepen.
9.  Move your awareness slowly down the right side of your body to your right big toe. One minute.
10. Move your awareness to your left big toe.
11. Repeat steps 1–4 and sit in your awareness of the entire triangle for a minute and then disconnect.

Now it's time to create the downward-point triangle:
12. Bring your awareness to the zone above left shoulder and directly out from the side of your head above your left ear. One minute.
13. Slowly move your awareness in a line through the center of your head to a position above your right shoulder that corresponds to the position at the left of your head. One minute.
14. Move your awareness slowly down to a point on the floor midway between your feet. One minute.
15. Move your awareness back up to position to the left of your head. One minute.
16. Repeat this triangle and feel entire downward-pointing triangle. One minute.
17. Feel both of these triangles at the same time. One minute.
18. Release this contact and take a few minutes and allow what comes up within you to do so.

Final Phase: Sit or Stand Within the Six-Pointed Star *(see illustration)*
19. Expand the two triangles so that you can place them around your entire body. See yourself sitting in the center of these interpenetrating triangles, which form the six-pointed star. Give this a minute.
20. Now release your awareness of the triangles and take ten minutes for a meditation.
21. End the exercise and take note of your experiences.

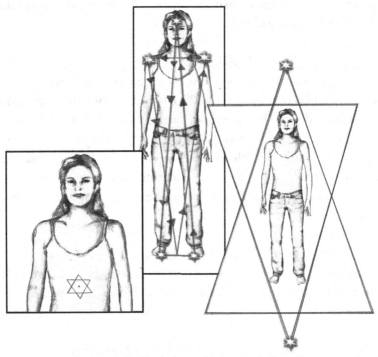

The six-pointed star is a symbol of the balanced interpenetration of heaven and earth. Here, it is applied in three different positions: your navel, your torso and around your entire body.

INNER PILGRIMAGE #3: *Energetically Balanced Breathing: A Ritual of the Meeting of Heaven and Earth*
Probably the most universal spiritual exercises have to do with breathing. All religious and spiritual traditions have some kind of teaching about the breath and spirit. Yoga and qigong practices are full of specific breathing practices for enlivening your body and raising your spiritual tone. The nexus of breath and spirit is embedded in Hebrew, Latin, and Greek, and dates back to the Indo-European roots of all our modern European languages. It's not just a coincidence that the German word *atmen* (to breathe) strongly resembles *Atman*, the Sanskrit word for the Universal Spirit. Look at the way the Latin word *spiritus* creates the linguistic bridge between "breath" and "spirit" in English. Here are some examples that shed interesting light on this connection; in each case, many of the words tell what is happening to breath and spirit:

> Respiration: Breath/spirit goes in and out again.
> Inspiration (also a synonym for inhalation): Breath/spirit goes into you.
> Expire: to "breathe out"; "to die" [i.e. when you breathe your last breath, you "give up the ghost (spirit)."]
> Aspire (to): Your spirit goes toward something when you aspire to it.
> Conspiracy: literally "breathing together," joining spirits.
> Spire: vertical structure of a church or temple, places you go for in-spir-ation.

Breath and spirit are inseparable, and the first way we can make use of this fact is to become aware of our breath. Among the most ancient spiritual and energetic practices is the act of consciously following your breath as it passes into and out of your body. Of course, we are drawing in oxygen and other gasses from the atmosphere around us and breathing out gasses like carbon dioxide, which we need to release from our bodies. But we are also involved with an exchange of energy as well. Consciously or unconsciously, we are constantly regulating our energetic metabolism with our breathing.

### Four Modes of Breathing for Energetic Balance

Each of the following breathing patterns is associated energetically with one of the alchemical elements: fire, air, earth, and water. Here is a simple breathing practice that combines four modes of breathing. This is intended to introduce an energetically balanced blend of forces to your energetic system and, in so doing, positively influence your energy metabolism.

Do this exercise consciously and slowly, paying attention to every part of the breath and the pauses between your inhalation and your exhalation. You might want to breathe a bit more intensely when you do this, but remember, the purpose here is not to rev up your energy system, but rather to balance it.

### The Basic Exercise: Twelve Breaths—The Pilgrim Honors the Elements

This is our basic exercise for energetically balanced breathing, using a twelve-breath cycle: *Take three long, slow, conscious breaths in each mode.* The four modes of breathing and their respective alchemical elements are:

- In through your NOSE and OUT through your NOSE (Earth)
- In through your NOSE and OUT through your MOUTH (Water)
- In through your MOUTH and OUT through your NOSE (Fire)
- In through your MOUTH and OUT through your MOUTH (Air)

### Applications and Variations

As you practice this little exercise, you will find that as you breathe in the above pattern, you will be able to follow the way energy moves into and out of your system. You will also probably find that each of these modes of breathing adds something different to the energetic mix. Since energetic balance is one of the first prerequisites for healing and expansion of consciousness, this twelve-breath cycle has all kinds of uses. Here are some applications for your work, both with yourself and with others.

### Step 1: Start at Your Heart

This is a simple exercise for breathing energies from the earth and the cosmos into your Heart Center and then out into the world around you.  Try this:

1. Bring your awareness into your Heart Center and allow a minute for the contact to deepen.
2. With your awareness in your Heart Center, introduce the Twelve-Breath Cycle (three breaths in each of the four modes described earlier in this chapter). As you do this, visualize that you are breathing *into and out of your Heart Center.*

### A Variation

1. Starting with your awareness in *both your Perineum and Crown at once*, try this breathing pattern: as you breathe in, move your awareness into your Heart from above and below at the same time.
2. On your out-breath, move your awareness out from your Heart *in all directions at once.*

3. Introduce a round of energetically-balanced breathing: apply the Twelve-Breath Cycle while moving your awareness in this pattern.
4. Come to rest in your Heart, breathing normally.
5. Give yourself several minutes to allow what wants to come up in your awareness to do so.
6. End the exercise.

Typically, this exercise starts with the feeling that you are drawing energy into your Heart Center along a couple of straight lines, one up from your Perineum and the other down from your Crown, and then out from your Heart in a straight line, like a cross. As you relax into the movement (this may take a bit of practice), you can develop the sense that you are drawing energy into your Heart Center from all directions and sending energy out from it in all directions.

Draw energy into your Heart Center from above and below on your in-breath, then send it out in all directions on your out-breath.

<u>More Variations</u>
*Combining Energetically Balanced Breathing and Physical Gesture*[9]
An excellent way to enhance the effect of this practice is to introduce some physical movement or gesture that follows the energy movement as you progress through the four modes of breathing.

---

9    There is a photo series of this exercise on my Web site. Turn to the last page of the book for instructions on how to find the Pilgrim Extras.

This is a moving gesture of gathering energy from both heaven and earth into your Heart and then sending it out into the world. Try this:

1. Use your hands to trace the movement of energy into your Heart Center as you breathe in.
2. Bring your hands together at your Heart.
3. Pause there briefly before following the outward-moving energetic ripple of your exhalation back out into the space around you as you exhale.
4. Pause there briefly before following the next breath in.
5. Continue in this mode through a Twelve-Breath Cycle.

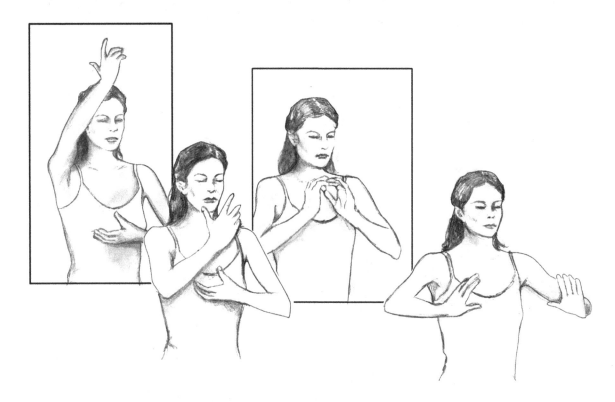

Use your hands to trace the movement of energy into and out of your body as you do this balanced breathing practice. This dynamic gesture enhances your awareness of that energy movement. For a detailed look at this exercise, come to the Pilgrim Extras on my Web site. (See the instructions for finding the Pilgrim Extras on the last page of this book.)

Add a Silent Invocation

An additional option is to accompany this dance of inward and outward movement of breath, energy, consciousness, and hand gesture with a silent invocation that matches the cycle—silent mainly because it is hard to stick with the four modes of breathing if you do this out loud. This could be any two-part invocation, prayer, or chant; one part for the in-breath and another for the out-breath. An example might be, "Spirit of the Living God" on the in-breath, "Fall afresh on me" on the out-breath. Get creative with this. It is wonderful in groups, by the way, to join this kind of silent prayer or invocation with physical gestures and energetically coordinated breathing.

Other Centers and Circumferences

I have called this series "A Ritual of the Meeting of Heaven and Earth" because here, too, you are following, in microcosmic form, a universal pattern observable throughout nature. The movement of breath, spirit, and energy into and out of your body reflects an aspect of how energy moves: in toward a center, and back outward in an expansion. With practice, you can use your breathing to direct energy and awareness into and out of any place, anywhere that you can bring your consciousness. Remember that in the world of energy and consciousness you are not restricted by considerations of time and place. On that basis, it is not at all farfetched to extend your energetic outreach to people and events in other places, even other times. Your Heart Center, combined with these four modes of breathing, is a great starting place for learning to cultivate this capability.

Try combining each of these variations with the Twelve-Breath Cycle:

- Breathe IN to your Heart Center and OUT, down your arms and into your Hand Centers (good preparation for hands-on healing work);

- Breathe IN to your Hand Centers and OUT to the tiny energy centers in your fingertips;

- Breathe IN to your Perineum and OUT, down your legs and into your Foot Centers;

- Breathe IN to your Foot Centers and OUT to the tiny energy centers in the tips of your toes;

- Breathe IN to the center of the Earth and OUT to the atmosphere around her;

- Breathe IN to the nucleus of all the cells in your body and OUT to the cells' membranes;

- Breathe IN to your Heart and OUT to your world: the circle of your family and friends, your surroundings, community, nature, and the Earth;

- Breathe IN to your Heart and OUT to people you know are in trouble or ill;

- Breathe IN to your Heart and OUT to war-torn places, natural disaster sites;

- Breathe IN to the nuclei of all the atoms in the universe and OUT to the sub-atomic particles that orbit around their nuclei;

- Breathe IN to the sun and OUT to the planets of the solar system;

- Breathe IN to your Heart and OUT to all sentient beings.

If you move your awareness slowly and consciously in these breathing practices, you will find your attention being drawn into finer and finer states of energy and perception. What this means is that you are becoming aware of other dimensions of life within and around you. What may start as a slightly hyperventilated feeling will give rise, as you come into greater energetic balance, to a feeling of how the life-force moves into and out of your body.

With a Partner

Explore what this twelve-breath cycle can do. This type of simple breathing practice has a lot of uses in your exploration of the world of energy and consciousness. It can also be a way to relax and then enliven a part of your body that may be in need.

In treatments with another person, realize that this also extends to the energetic unit you create with a partner when you give a treatment. Try this:

- Simply hold a restricted area of your partner's body between your hands, turn your attention to the natural exchange of energy between your hands.

- Now silently apply a twelve-breath cycle of energetically balanced breathing. Your partner will automatically become part of that energetic cycle, and benefit from this silent behind-the-scenes addition to the treatment you give.


INNER PILGRIMAGE #4: *The Bear and the Tulip Bulb: An Inner Pilgrimage for Winter*
In its most basic terms, ritual is what we do to create a link between our small individual worlds and the great cosmos. We do ritual in order to leave the riverbank where we spend most of our time, and enter the river of life. All seasons have their rituals, but winter is a time of year when rituals abound. Not surprisingly, rituals of this time are about light that shines in the darkness. Scandinavian cultures mark this time of year by feasts of light, bright stars, blazing trees, and Solstice processions of white-clad girls entering pitch-dark rooms wearing evergreen wreaths with candles, lit ones, on their blonde heads. All this as if to dramatize to ourselves over and over again that during this time when the physical sun is least evident, we have greatest access to spiritual light.

Here is one such inner pilgrimage, a spiral of light for wintertime, although you can do it year-round.

*Preparation*:
- *Contact with energy centers*: You have probably by now established some contact with your energy centers. If not, you might want to brush up on your understanding of how to do this by turning back to the five tips, listed earlier in this chapter, for making a good, basic contact with energy-active positions on your body.

- *Prayers for contact with energy centers*: Each of the stations in this energetic inner pilgrimage is a major energy center, and at each of these stops a prayer or invocation is offered as a means of entering more deeply into its mystery. I have included a prayer for each of your energy centers, but I invite you to substitute prayers and invocations of your own.[10]

- *Pay attention to the directions of movement* after you leave your contact with each of these energy centers. You will be moving your awareness in a spiral, out to the side of the energy center, and then up or down to the next center contact. This movement conforms to the dominant flow of energy in the etheric,[11] up the left side of the front of your body and down the right side.


This pilgrimage spirals inward, appropriate for winter, a time when much of nature goes within and hibernates. The images for this exercise are the bear hibernating in his cave, and the tulip bulb lying buried beneath frozen earth, waiting for spring, gathering Light from the Source

---

10    For more prayers for your energy centers, see "Prayers for an Energyworker Pilgrim" in *Energy Healing: A Pathway to Inner Growth*.

11    For more about etheric movement, see the "Fourth Etheric Laboratory" in *Energy Healing: A Pathway to Inner Growth*.

of Life to feed the seed of secret new life germinating there. This pilgrimage is dedicated to the bears and tulips hibernating within you.

Exercise Steps:
1. After you have settled into a comfortable sitting position, drop your awareness slowly straight down to your energetic South Pole. This will feel like it is about three feet (one meter) down in the ground or floor beneath you. Spend a minute to allow your contact to deepen in this position.
2. Release this South Pole connection and move your awareness up slowly and consciously, through your Perineum, up into your Heart Center.
3. *Heart Center:* Bring your awareness into your Heart Center in the center of your chest.

> *Heart Center Prayer:*
> I silently bless the sleeper in my heart, the one whose time has not yet come to rise and shine. Let Heaven and Earth join in me and keep each other warm.

Spend a minute here at the Heart Center and allow the contact to build up.
4. Now slowly move away from your Heart Center in an arc to the left and up to your Energetic North Pole.
5. *Energetic North Pole:* To connect with your Energetic North Pole, move your awareness slowly upward from the crown of your head to a position that feels like it is an arm's length or about three feet (one meter) above your head. Once your awareness is in position, however, the strategy is the same as with any other energy-active position: make your awareness loose and allow it to be drawn into the energy activity that is there.

> *North Pole Prayer:*
> I turn toward my star, the piece of Heaven that has guided me since I was conceived in the Mind of God. Let Heaven infuse me with Light.

Allow about a minute for this contact to build up.
6. After this contact with your energetic North Pole, move your awareness out to your right and down to your Sacral Center. The Sacral Center contact for this exercise is in the center of your sacrum.

> *Sacral Center Prayer:*
> I invite the stillness of the winter Earth up into me. Let

*Tulip Elegy IX*
*Not simply a wizened husk*
*and pulp, but some future*
*wound into a vegetable*
*locket, some clock*
*waiting to be unsprung*
*by cold hours, water,*
*a star's close pass.*

Denise Low,
(used with permission)

41

Heaven and Earth join even in the densest bones of the world,
through me. We will awaken into the Light together.

Allow about a minute for the contact to build up.

7.  Now, leaving your Sacral Center, move your awareness out around your body in a slow, wide sweeping arc to your left and up to your Crown Center.

8.  *Crown Center:* To contact your Crown Center, move your awareness to the crown of your head, that is, the highest point on your head. From there, move your awareness slightly forward and up a bit into your hair.

> *Crown Center Prayer:*
> Heaven's jewels shine down into my heart. Let all the colors of
> Heaven and Earth mingle and cascade into this world, through
> me.

Spend a couple of minutes with this contact, allowing it to intensify.

9.  After you have allowed your contact to deepen in your Crown Center, move out to your right, away from your body and down to your Hara Center.

10. *Hara Center:* The contact position for your Hara Center is located three finger-breadths below your navel.

> *Hara Center Prayer:*
> Time to rest and regenerate the creativity and juiciness of living.
> Let Heaven and Earth join and create the world, through me.

Spend about a minute with this contact.

11. Now it's time to move out of this center contact in a sweeping arc to the left and up to your Pineal Center. Remember to move your awareness slowly and consciously.

12. *Pineal Center:* A simple way to contact your Pineal Center is at the center of your forehead. Energetically, this position is sometimes called the *Pineal Extension Position* because it is a good place to be drawn into the movement of the Pineal Center.

> *Pineal Center Prayer:*
> I turn toward the luminous darkness and wait for new vision. Let
> Heaven and Earth join and shine in the darkness, through me.

Stay with this contact for about a minute.

13. After you have allowed your contact to deepen in your Pineal Center, move your awareness out to your right, away from the center, and down to your Solar Plexus Center.

14. *Solar Plexus Center:* Move your awareness to a point three finger-breadths above your navel.

> *Solar Plexus Center Prayer:*
> My fears are quiet. My love is still. Let Heaven and Earth join
> without fear in me.

Spend a minute in your Solar Plexus Center before moving on.

15. Now move away from your Solar Plexus Center by bringing your awareness in a slow, conscious arc out to your left and up, this time to your Throat Center.

The winter spiral moves inward, toward your heart. Think of gathering your energies into yourself.

16. *Throat Center:* Bring your awareness to the area at the front of your throat, just under your Adam's apple. This is the area where it is easiest for your awareness to be drawn into the activity of the Throat Center.

> *Throat Center Prayer:*
> In sound, stillness; in stillness, all sound.  Let Heaven and Earth join and speak, through me.

    Go with a feeling contact in this position for about a minute.

17. Move from your Throat Center down to your Heart Center.
18. *Heart Center:* Here you are, back where you started, having spiraled through your energy centers and contacted the very top and bottom of your personal energy field at your energetic North and South Poles. Now you are bringing what you have gathered on your inner journey into your Heart Center.

> *Heart Center Prayer:*
> Let Heaven and Earth meet and spread Light, Life and Love to all creation, through me.

> *Meditation:* Now that you have come full circle in your inner pilgrimage, Spend some time in this position, allowing whatever wants to come up in you to do so.

19. End the exercise.

*The Winter Spiral at a Glance:*

Note: The movement upward is around the left side of your body and the movement downward is on your right side.

1. Energetic South Pole—one minute.
2. Move your awareness up through Perineum into Heart Center—one minute.
3. Move your awareness away from Heart Center in an arc to the left up to your energetic North Pole—one minute.
4. Move your awareness out to the right and down to Sacral Center—one minute.
5. Spiral up to Crown Center—one minute.
6. Hara Center—one minute.
7. Pineal Center—one minute.
8. Solar Plexus Center—one minute.
9. Throat Center—one minute.
10. Heart Center—one minute.
11. Settle into a meditation, allowing whatever wants to come up in you to do so—ten minutes.
12. End the exercise.

INNER PILGRIMAGE #5: *A Summer Spiral for the Light of Summer*

Here, we reverse the direction of our Winter Spiral. Instead of spiraling inward, this time we'll travel a widening gyre into the Light of Summer. Here, too, you can use the above prayers for each of your energy centers, or bring in your own. Either way, an invocation is a good way to mark and sanctify the steps you take on your inner pilgrimage.

Once you reach your Heart Center the first time, the Summer Spiral reverses the path you traveled in the Winter Spiral.

Exercise Steps:

1. After you have settled into a comfortable sitting position, drop your awareness slowly straight down to your energetic South Pole. Spend a minute to allow your contact to deepen in this position.

2. Release this South Pole connection and move your awareness up slowly and consciously, through your Perineum, up into your Heart Center.

3. Heart Center: Bring your awareness to your Heart Center in the upper center of your chest. Spend a minute here at the Heart Center and allow the contact to build up.

4. Now slowly move away from your Heart Center in an arc to the left and up to your Throat Center. One Minute.

5. Now move away from your Throat Center in a slow conscious arc out to your right and down to your Solar Plexus Center. Let your contact deepen there for a minute before you move on.

6. Now move away from your Solar Plexus Center and bring your awareness in a slow conscious arc out to your left and up, this time to your Pineal Center for one minute.

7. After you have allowed your contact to deepen in your Pineal Center, move out to your right, away from the center, and down to your Hara Center. Spend about a minute with this contact.

8. Now it's time to move out of your Hara contact in a sweeping arc to the left and up to your Crown Center. Spend a minute with this contact, allowing it to intensify.

While the winter exercise spiraled inward, as befits hibernation, the summer version spirals outward.

9. After this contact with your Crown Center, move your awareness out to your right and down to your Sacral Center. Allow about a minute for the contact to build up.
10. Now, leaving your Sacral Center, move your awareness out around your body in a wide sweeping arc to your left and up to your Energetic North Pole. Allow about a minute for the contact to build up.
11. Now, slowly, consciously bring your awareness straight down from your Energetic North Pole, through the top of your head and down into your Heart Center.
12. Meditation: Spend some time in your heart, allowing whatever wants to come up in you to do so, now that you have come full circle in your inner pilgrimage.
13. End the exercise.

*The Summer Spiral at a Glance:*

While the winter exercise spiraled inward, as befits hibernation, this journey spirals outward. The movement upward is around the left side of your body and the movement downward is on your right side.

1. Energetic South Pole—one minute.
2. Move awareness up through Perineum into Heart Center—one minute.
3. Throat Center—one minute.
4. Solar Plexus Center—one minute.
5. Pineal Center—one minute.
6. Hara Center—one minute.
7. Spiral up to Crown Center—one minute.
8. Sacral Center—one minute.
9. Energetic North Pole—one minute.
10. Down to Heart Center—one minute.
11. Meditation: allowing whatever wants to come up in you to do so—ten minutes.
12. End the exercise.

*Guidelines for Inner Pilgrimages*

With practice, energetic exercises like the ones you will find in this book will teach you how to move within your body and psyche and give the pilgrim within you an opportunity to walk the three-fold spiritual path. The inner world that these pilgrimages open is potent both in its capacity to heal and to confront, so these practices ought not to be done lightly. In most cases, an incorrectly done exercise will simply not do much at all. In other cases, where instructions about sequence of steps, length (in time), frequency of the practice, and direction of movement are not followed, some people will get momentarily "spaced out." Others will find unconscious material surfacing in ways that can be confusing or uncomfortable, especially for persons unused to working on themselves. As you venture into this exploration, be advised of the following, which I borrow from Robert Johnson's book *Inner Work*:

> You must understand that when you approach the unconscious you are dealing with one of the most powerful and autonomous forces in human experience. The techniques of inner work are intended to set in motion the great forces of the unconscious, but in a sense this is like taking the cap off a geyser: Things can get out of hand if you are not careful. If you fail to take this process seriously, or try to turn it into mere entertainment, you can hurt yourself.
>
> None of this should dissuade you from doing inner work. We are only observing a universal law: Anything that has great power for good can also be destructive if the power is mishandled. If we want to live intimately with the powerful forces of the inner world, we must also respect them.

And so I urge judicious use of this material, which comes out of many years of my own practice and the experiences of my teachers, clients, and workshop participants. Much of the inspiration for this material has been drawn from ancient world traditions as well. To do these traditions justice, I wish to promote a sense of the sacred in the responsible use of this knowledge.

There is an intentional design to each exercise. They are put together with a beginning, middle and end. They are constructed specifically to:

- Allow you to enter some area of experience;

- In some cases, create the opportunity for emotional, physical, and mental release;

- Draw in energy from higher dimensions of consciousness (this is what makes them *healing* exercises); then come back to normal body awareness and integrate what has been contacted during the exercise.

Energy Exercise Guidelines

1. *Find an appropriate time.* There might be certain times of day that are better than others for doing energy exercise. Experiment around until you find good times for you and your personal rhythms. Find times when you will not be disturbed. Tell others with whom you live that you need this time to yourself. Unplug the phone. Know also that doing certain exercises just before going to bed can keep you awake.

2. *Allow time between exercises.* Unless otherwise recommended, allow a day or two between days when you do a specific exercise. If you are doing two different exercises concurrently, simply do them on alternate days. Note that it takes about thirty-six hours for the altered

movement caused in your energy field by the exercise to register at the level of bodily consciousness. This time period allows for the grounding and integration of the energy you draw into your body by doing the exercise.

3. *Be precise.* Check the subtle anatomy guidelines where new positions are introduced if you are uncertain as to how to find a specific point or energy center. It is important to know where they are in order to get a good contact with them.

4. *Observe good body posture.* Unless otherwise indicated, do these exercises sitting upright or even standing, but not lying down. An erect, relaxed posture with your feet on the ground is generally most conducive to breathing easily and creating a good contact with the earth. In addition, a lying position is most people's habitual sleeping position. Granted, this is a shift in consciousness, but not the one we have in mind with the exercise!

5. *Breathing Pattern.* Unless otherwise indicated, the breathing pattern for these exercises is in through your nose and out through your nose.

6. *No marathons.* Observe the time periods. They are important in all exercises, especially those in which there is a meditation period or a *release phase*. The reason for this is, again, the need to ground and integrate what is drawn into your energy system when you do the exercise. In addition, when an exercise is to last a pre-determined amount of time, it means there is a mechanism in place for coming back from whatever you encounter in the exercise. This can be of great help in gaining the confidence necessary for entering areas of consciousness that might otherwise be daunting.

7. *Do all the steps.* Be careful to observe and do each step of the instructions. If you do not understand an instruction it is better not to do the exercise at all, rather than doing it and doing it wrong. Simply drop the exercise that is giving you trouble and move on to an exercise that is clear to you.

8. *Keep a journal, either written or tape-recorded.*

9. *Honor the context.* Finally, here is a request which I make to all my workshop participants, one which I also make to you: Please keep these exercises to yourself. They have come to you in the context of this book which prepared you to work with them. Unless you are willing and prepared to do the same for those with whom you would share this work, don't piecemeal it out.

Each of the exercises we work with can have very strong effects. If they are done regularly over a period of time, they will tend to draw you into what I call a "trajectory of effects," that will influence your personal self-healing process, and can be tracked on many levels. (For more about the kinds of effects you can expect from energy healing practices, see Chapter Fifteen.) The only way to responsibly prescribe such an exercise to another person is to make certain you are familiar with how it affects you over a period of time.

## A VISIT WITH A PAIR OF SCOTTISH HEALERS

Though I had read about such things as earth currents and power spots, I will never forget my first vivid encounter with the forces that move through the planet. On a trip through Wales, my wife and I were invited to visit the home of a Scottish couple, Angus and Winifred. The two of them lived outside the Welsh town of Abergevenny, near Mt. Skerrid. Once we reached the town, we stopped to call for directions to their house. A red phone box stood at the corner of the square. I popped the last of my 1ten-pence coins into the slot, unsure of how much I needed for a simple local call.

Angus, the husband in this pair, was in his seventies. His particular love was the lore of power spots and earth currents. Typical of some seventy-year-old Scottish mystics, he loved to hold forth at every opportunity, a pedantic index finger pointing to the skies, especially on subjects of an arcane nature. As it turned out, Angus was one of those generous souls who could hold forth on any subject whatsoever, no matter how little he knew about it. After explaining to him that we were in town and now needed directions to their house, he proceeded to give me, over the phone, the entire history of every landmark along the way.

"And thair, James, on the left you'll see a mighty alder ..." and he launched into a monologue about when the troops of so-and-so passed through during the Battle of Abergevenny in 1263, and so-and-so was hanged from its branches. On and on, he narrated an unending litany of glorious triumphs, ignominious defeats, and historical turning points of the hallowed terrain we were about to traverse en route to his house, but as yet he hadn't told me how to get there.

Meanwhile, I knew that the pay phone's warning signal was about to sound, telling me to insert more coins into the pay phone. I also knew I had no more appropriate coins in my pocket. Try as I may, there was no stopping Angus, so I left the phone dangling in the phone booth while he droned on and on, and went in search of proper change.

"And in the fateful year of eighteen hundred and ..." Angus's stentorian voice followed me as I ran across the square to the only shop that appeared to be open at that hour. It was an ironmonger, and even now, after having been inside this establishment dedicated entirely to ironmongery, I still couldn't tell you what that is exactly. It was a junk store, basically, filled with odds and ends in haphazard heaps that appeared ready to avalanche to the floor at any moment. I closed the door softly and peered into the dimly lit room. There, in the unnatural dusk of the shop, an elderly man sat behind the counter, watching me, but saying nothing. No relation, obviously, to Angus, who I knew was still orating into his phone, oblivious to my absence.

This was 1984, the year of the newly-minted one-pound coin in Great Britain. Unfortunately, the phone boxes had not been retrofitted to accommodate the rather thick new coins, something I figured out while waiting for Angus to tell me where to go after I reached the mighty alder. I slid two of the hefty one-pound coins across the counter toward the ironmonger.

"Good afternoon," I said to the man. "Could you please give me change? I need it for the phone box across the square."

We Americans take change-giving for granted, but here in Abergevenny, Wales, it wasn't so simple. The ironmonger said nothing as he gazed at me through thick glasses. The man, musty and ancient like the relics for sale in his shop, must have realized that he was having an encounter with a foreigner. He looked at the two one-pound coins in front of him and then back at me, contorted his face into a pained, "I smell excrement" look, and said in a slow, measured, loud voice, "Sir! I wish you to know that I am both a Royalist and a Traditionalist and I do not recognize these coins as money. If you have a proper banknote, I shall consider giving you what you request."

The man had his boundaries all right. Being neither a Royalist nor a Traditionalist myself, and never having been confronted with one before, I was stopped cold by this reply. I then told him my wretched situation. "I've left Angus, or his voice at least, hanging out there in the phone box and I still don't know how to get to his house, and now I've run out of coins!"

"Angus?" the ironmonger Royalist and Traditionalist asked, "Angus the Scotsman? Just turn left at the alder and carry on a mile or two. It's a low stone house by itself on the right. You can't miss it." I thanked him, left the shop, and got into the car, not stopping at the phone box. The phone's receiver dangled by its metal cord, still swaying with the verbiage that swelled through it.

Winifred greeted us at the door and swept us into the room where we would be spending the night. Once our suitcases were ensconced in the guest room, she met us in the kitchen. On the table were four unmatched cups and a pot of tea covered by a blue cozy. We sat in the tiny kitchen lit only by the waning light of approaching dusk. Some pre-Enya, but vaguely Celtic new-age tones drifted in from elsewhere. Mt. Skerrid, its split peak—according to legend, cloven by the mighty sword of the Archangel Michael—loomed visibly through the window.

Winnie was at least thirty years younger than Angus and abuzz with the story of how, not even a week before, on a dark, howling night, a knock was heard, and there on their very doorstep stood none other than the great Sir George Trevelyan, author of *The Aquarian Vision*, who commanded them to follow him to a secret site on sacred Mt. Skerrid. There, he ordained them the stewards of the mountain.

Then she remembered that we had just arrived. "We're so glad ye could come. Ye must be exhausted, the both of you, driving all the way from St. David's."

"It was a pleasant drive."

"Och, a grueling one, if ye ask me. I'm nae much on the roads, myself. Now take Angus—he's been on the telephone with someone for quite a while and he ought to be oot soon—he's one to take off an' explore. He and Sir George go off for days, seein' to this or that, makin' sure all's in order on the sacred mountain. Good stewards o' the airth, the both of 'em." She put her cup down and stood up from the table. She had on heavy woolen socks with brightly colored separate toes.

"Wait right here, I'll go tell Angus ye've arr—"

Angus stood in the doorway. Like many Scotsmen above a certain age, he looked like he had endured a great deal of raw weather. He had an intense, dark, gathering storm for a face with eyebrows like clusters of auburn brambles clinging to wind-blown coastal cliffs. After little more than a handshake and a nod of greeting, he laid a large paw on my shoulder and marched me out of the kitchen and into the living room. At Angus's prompting, I walked a diagonal line across the low-ceilinged room and in the middle felt an extremely odd sensation, as if I were passing through a zone of warped space. He informed me with obvious pride that this was a *ley line*, or current of the earth's energy, running right through their very own living room. It was quite palpable, and it was my first conscious experience of such a phenomenon, followed by an explanation typical of Angus.

"James," he explained, "thair's a world o' communicatin' bein' done by the planet wi' her very self, an' 'tis my unshakable belief that the airth in her great intelligence, uses all means to do so. Take yer mighty cathedrals, for example, with their lofty spires up in the sky. Doan they look for all the world like radio transmitters? And if you were to tear 'em down—deconstruct them, if you will—ye'd find a great number of 'em sittin' right on top o' pagan temple sites, some o' them made of the very materials that went into the pagan temples thairselves, stolen o' course by the new conquerors, thus was it ever. Now, James, your pre-Christian heathens were wily about finding power places upon which tae build their shrines and temples. O' course they were, James. Where else would one place a holy shrine but on a place o' power. Naturally they did because your heathens and pagans were themselves in a mighty communion with the forces and currents of the planet 'neath their feet. We in our modern times, James, we have simply put our churches and cathedrals upon sites already selected for us by Druids who knew a power spot when they saw one."

Angus continued on at length and, aided by thick, dark bread, local cheese, and more than a tot or two of whiskey, I settled in to an evening of lore about the world of earth forces. Since the four of us were at that time all students of the same teacher of energy healing and familiar with practices involving the energy-active positions on the physical body, it was not hard to find countless parallels between the points and line of energy movement in the human body and those in the body of the earth.

Since my encounter with Angus and Winifred, I have come to appreciate the fact that the story of a being—whether that of an individual human being or of our planet—is recorded in the body. This comes to life when you visit other places on the globe, each place with its history and encoded energetic record. The same thing applies to our travels around our bodies and energy systems in inner pilgrimages.

# Section Two

## PERENNIAL THEMES IN ENERGY HEALING

There are broad patterns to energy healing and spiritual process, and it's helpful to know how to identify them. At first, discerning those broad patterns can be like staring, clueless, at a tangle of lines on the puzzle page in a children's magazine. The moment your eye finally recognizes the fly hidden among the random sketchings, however, you're converted. You can no longer not see the fly. Next page, it's not a fly you're looking for, but a dog, so you have to teach your eye a new trick. Once you have sighted Fido, there he is, of course, looking back at you. Turn the page. Can you see the fox? The bird?

In energy healing, you will find, hiding in plain sight, a number of recurring themes, and they're worth paying attention to and learning about. Like the flies and foxes hiding in the puzzle picture, once you spot them they are hard to miss. And once you spot them you can work with them in a purposeful way. These are what I call perennial themes of energywork, since they make their appearance again and again, like crocuses in spring.

In Section One, we already took up two of the ever-cycling super-themes inherent in energywork: spiritual process and the three-fold spiritual path. To these, we will now add thirteen others:

- Calling
- Beliefs
- Holism
- Mindfulness
- Centering
- Grounding
- Expression
- Control
- Balance
- Twin Structures of Consciousness
- Fear
- Resistance, Release and Renewal
- Integration

These themes are all part of the crazy quilt of energywork because they relate to inner plot lines in the story of human unfolding. They have significance on every level of our makeup, from the physical clear through to the psycho-spiritual. They are important aspects of how we humans tick. Like gravity—I'm reminded of the cartoon character Wily Coyote who would race full speed off the edge of a cliff and keep going, running on thin air, but only until he looked down—these perennial themes are the kind of thing you can ignore, but only briefly.

The perennial issues of energywork in this section are crystallized from my personal and professional practice. Working with them has expanded my ability to work beyond the particular protocols and modalities in which I was trained. As a result, I also find that I am able to work with a much wider range of people. I strongly believe that the perennial themes I encounter in energywork are also universal human themes. When I attend to them, I find the common ground I share with everyone.

You can use the major energetic and psycho-spiritual themes in this book as ways to organize the impressions that come to you in the course of your healing work with another person. As you get to know these perennial themes in a personal way, they will give shape and sequence to the way you approach treatments. All these themes are connected with one another, of course, and often there is a specific theme or two sticking out like a red sweater at a funeral. Though your partner may not come out and tell you that he or she is having trouble with grounding or expression or something else, you will, with time and practice and the inner work you yourself do, be able to spot these perennial issues as they arise. Sometimes you become a detective, and your knowledge of perennial energetic and psycho-spiritual issues amounts to a list of "usual suspects," providing clues to what unfolds as you work with a partner.

These are revolving themes that sometimes segue neatly one into the other, but usually not. Sometimes several of them show up en masse in a constellation—a bouquet of perennials. Without doubt, you will identify your own subspecies of the ideas on the list I have provided, as well as other varieties of your own discovery as you include the energetic in your practice.

What emerges is not a new modality of therapy, but a holistic, energy-active orientation that applies, ultimately, to all the various approaches to healing. That is to say, bodywork modalities such as massage in all its forms, Rolfing, craniosacral work, aquatic bodywork, and the various forms of body-centered psychotherapy, to name just a few, can become energy-active modalities when they are integrated with an understanding of principles of energy and consciousness and when they address the perennial psycho-spiritual themes that arise when we move into the energetic.

What follows is an examination of these themes and ways of addressing them personally and in energy-active bodywork. As these are revolving themes, be on the lookout for each of them embedded in discussions of other themes. At times I will refer to specific modalities of bodywork, such as massage, Zero Balancing, or craniosacral work when I feel that these have a particularly exemplary or elegant approach to one or more of these themes. I don't ever mean to imply that other modalities do not offer exemplary and elegant approaches to these themes; these just happen to be modalities I know something about. So please don't be offended if you don't find me talking about your specific modality. The point here is to get as unmodality-bound as possible and point to universal principles whenever possible. Once the cat is in view, and once we agree that we are talking about the same cat, I think we will see that there are many ways to skin it.

# CHAPTER FIVE

## CALLING

*You should be aware of the seeds of feeling in your heart and take care of them. And try to express the feeling sincerely and honestly.*

Iizuka Shokansai

What is this thing we call a calling? Is it a pathway that opens before you, a road to something you know you have to pursue? What began as a hunch turns into curiosity and a fascination and then into something personal and compelling. The other word for a calling is "vocation," and the classic conception of it is that the voice of God has called you to something in this life. When you go so far as to see what you do as a calling, it is no longer a casual undertaking, something you could just drop tomorrow and still feel more or less the same about everything. Something would be missing if you didn't follow and cultivate it; indeed, if you don't follow your calling, your calling might start stalking you.

When something is a calling, there are often strong forces carrying you in a specific direction, and they aren't always easy to handle. Some of the greatest creative works have came about through persons who were ambivalent, to say the least, about expressing their gifts, and even felt plagued by them. One such case was the Russian composer Sergei Prokofiev, who gave us *Peter and the Wolf* and the *Lieutenant Kije Suite.* He was constantly falling in and out of favor with the communist government, and it is said that while other composers had to wait for inspiration, Prokofiev had to cope with it. His muse was on his back around the clock, and it seems he had little choice in the matter of whether or not to create his music.

Because energywork is a way of touching into spiritual process, what surfaces in personal practice often relates to a person's

*It's not a matter of when you reach the kingdom of heaven, but when the kingdom of heaven reaches you.*

Samuel Lewis

*There are very few human beings who receive the truth, complete and staggering, by instant illumination. Most of them acquire it fragment by fragment, on a small scale, by successive developments, cellularly, like a laborious mosaic.*

Anaïs Nin

*When someone asks what there is to do, light the candle in their hand.*

Rumi

emerging qualities, talents, and callings. The emergence of a calling and the expression of spiritual qualities are life-changing processes and, not infrequently, they clash, dramatically, with the established order of your life. Here is where the tools of energy healing are in their true element and the energy healer who follows the signs of this emergence in others often finds herself in the role of spiritual midwife.

Some of us get clues about our path and calling from an early age because of talents that are obvious. For many of us, recognizing our calling is a product of hindsight. A calling might announce itself quietly and then unfold slowly over the course of a lifetime, leading us down a series of different paths which eventually braid themselves together. What I do now as a writer, teacher, and therapist bears little external resemblance to the life I led as a member of a spiritual order or as a language teacher in Europe, and yet all of these persons are somehow part of me. Who knows? Maybe I have more phases and callings ahead of me about which I have no idea! As we ripen into old age, hopefully we look back on the phases of our life and spot the trail of crumbs we have followed, the common threads and themes, our abiding passions, and what we have actually given birth to in this life.

There are usually choices involved in how you express a quality or talent—someone blessed with a natural gift of fine-motor skills might become a great surgeon or a great safecracker! Natural talents usually need to be schooled in some way in order to find a means of coming into this world through you. The very root of the word "educate" means to "lead out." The essence of education is not primarily the taking on of new knowledge, but rather the process of helping latent qualities and potentialities to come out into the light of day.

INNER PILGRIMAGE #6: *The Pilgrim's Secret Training: Getting Guidance About Your Path*

How do you receive guidance about something as subjective as your calling? One approach is to get curious about it, invite it, and then start paying attention to what happens. Inspiration can come to you in all kinds of ways. Still, small voices have biblical credentials, and sometimes a small knowing inside you crescendos and leads you to some action. Your pathway in life is often revealed in bits and pieces on a "need to know" basis. As a result, it is necessary to check in regularly with the deep source of your calling for an update on your path. Who knows? The apple that fell on Newton's head may be getting ready to fall on yours.

The following inner pilgrimage is about receiving guidance from the part of you that knows about your calling, a deeper sense of what is yours to express in this life. To access this guidance, your inner pilgrim will use a symbol, an energetic tool that speaks the language of energy and consciousness. Here is a meditative practice that will let your inner pilgrim explore how this works.

Using Symbols in Energywork

Symbols are tokens of something greater than themselves, and can open you to guidance on your path. They can drop into your meditations and dreams, speaking in a kind of energetic shorthand as they point beyond themselves to a vast, ever-evolving cosmos, one that has you in it. Symbols have long been used intentionally in meditative practice to connect our ordinary consciousness with other dimensions of life. A symbol is a piece of a picture that helps you contact the *rest* of the picture. When you place such a symbol in your energy field and allow your consciousness to respond to it, access to otherwise closed rooms in your inner temple can open to you.

Let's apply this practice to the path of the pilgrim in you.

Preparation: Choose a Symbol

Is there a symbol in your life, one that relates in some way to your spiritual growth or to the opening of your consciousness? If you already have such a symbol, that would be the one to use. If not, spend some time reflecting on what images carry such a connotation for you. One candidate might be a religious or spiritual symbol you feel a personal connection with. Another might be a symbol or picture that represents your path in some way. It could even be the logo on your business card if you have chosen one that symbolizes your life's path or calling.

Exercise Steps

1. Set your intention for this inner pilgrimage. Ask for guidance on your life's path.
2. Choose the symbol you wish to work with. Stay with the same symbol throughout the whole exercise.
3. Move your awareness to the area *above your left shoulder at the level of the side of your head, just above the top of your ear.* This is a specific energy-active position in your aura that relates to your gifts and their conscious entry into your life. Let your feeling of contact to the symbol build up for a minute.
4. Visualize the symbol you have chosen and place it in this position.
5. Disconnect your awareness from the symbol and move slowly with your awareness, over your left shoulder, into your Heart Center. Rest there and let the feeling of that contact build up—one minute.
6. Now, move with your awareness slowly, on your skin surface, from your Heart Center to the Pineal Extension Point in the middle of your forehead. Rest your awareness there and allow the movement of energy there to draw you into the activity of your Pineal Center. Let this contact build for a minute.
7. Now complete the triangle by slowly moving with your awareness back to the position above your left shoulder, and reconnect with the same symbol.
8. Rest your awareness in this position with the symbol and then repeat this process, creating this slow triangle a couple of times, beginning and ending each time with your symbol. Spend a minute with your awareness in this triangle.

9.  Disconnect from the symbol and the triangle. Sit quietly. Simply allow whatever wants to come forward in your consciousness to do so. Take about ten minutes for this meditation.
10. End the exercise.

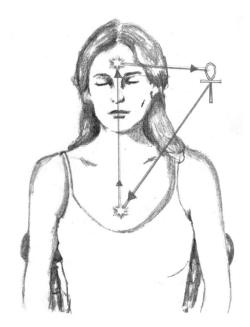

A compassionate connection with other people and the world around you allows energy to move into your Heart Center from areas of your aura connected to your deep calling. This exercise follows one of the ways that energy moves: from the position over your left shoulder into your Heart Center.

INNER PILGRIMAGE #7: *Your Inner Advisory Board*

Part of learning energywork has to do with making use of the energy centers around your body. This takes practice and at first it seems that, besides connecting with them and being aware, you are not being asked to do very much at all. As you work with it, though, you will find an increase in your ability to dive more deeply into the energetic activity within and around you. When you can consciously connect your awareness with these major organizers of your experience with some degree of confidence, these practices become a springboard into what is going on behind the scenes in your own psyche.

As your energy centers heal and come into balance, they will reveal to you their individual characters, their points of view, their different needs, and their ways of putting things together. You can make use of these different points of view by consulting each of your major energy centers in turn on questions of concern to you. This might be about a decision you need to make, something in your world that needs resolution, or insight about your calling. It's like having your own inner advisory board.

The idea behind the following practice is to introduce a question—the same question—into each of your major energy centers in turn and adopt an attitude of listening to what comes back. Simply put, this is a differentiated method of allowing your intuition to speak to you. Bear in mind that what comes into your awareness will be in the language of your inner world, the language of your soul, the same language spoken in your dreams and in other nonordinary states of consciousness. Sure, you might get a message that tells you in so many words to "take the job," or "throw the bum out!" You are much more likely, however, to find symbols, sensations, images, memories, and impressions of various kinds coming into your awareness in response to your question.

Setup:
- Sit comfortably, so you can breathe easily.
- Formulate a question about something you currently need some insight on (preferably *not* fortune-telling questions about stock market tips or which horse is going to win in the third race!). The simplest formulations are the best. Your non-conscious mind already knows the core question behind any subject you might bring up, so just use key words.

> EXAMPLE: If you are in some uncertainty about a work-related decision, your career, your vocation or calling, or a life decision of some kind, just a couple of key words are enough to tickle that core question into activity. It can be enough, for example, to simply use the words, "My work as a healer," as a way to activate your deep psyche around the question that is in you.

Steps:
1. Bring your awareness into your Perineum. Allow your contact to deepen.
2. When you have a feeling contact with the energetic activity at your Perineum, simply ask the question you have formulated. Keep it simple. See if you can place the question, so to speak, in the energy center.
3. Let go of the question and listen. Allow anything—thoughts, images, feelings, memories, etc.—that wants to come forward into your awareness to do so. It may or may not seem to have anything to do with your question. Just let it all come. Don't analyze what comes. Give this a couple of minutes.
4. Release your awareness from your Perineum and move to your Sacral Center in the center of your sacrum and repeat this procedure, using the *same question.* Give this contact a couple of minutes.
5. Repeat this procedure, using the same question, in turn with your other major energy centers, allowing two minutes with each:
    - *Hara Center,* which you can connect with by bringing your awareness to a point three finger-breadths below your navel and then relaxing it, allowing the energy movement there to draw you into itself;
    - *Solar Plexus Center,* three finger-breadths above your navel;
    - *Heart Center,* in the center of your chest;
    - *Throat Center,* at the front of your throat, slightly below your Adam's apple;
    - *Pineal Center,* which you can connect with at the Pineal Extension Point at the center of your forehead;
    - *Crown Center,* slightly forward of the very top of your head and a bit up in your hair.
6. Release yourself from the exercise and take some notes on what your inner advisory board has told or shown you.

Even if it makes no sense to you in a logical way, at the end of the process you will likely have a collage of words, images, feelings, and other impressions that came forward into your consciousness when you introduced the question into each of your energy centers. This composite message might be immediately obvious to you. Just as likely, however, you might need to let it simmer before you see the direction in which your inner wisdom is trying to point you.

This is an example of differentiated meditation work in which you are opening the way for communication with your non-conscious. As you develop this tool, the pilgrim in your body will have this inner advisory board or council of elders as an ally.

*Phases in Learning Energy Healing*

A calling likely to be present in many of the readers of this book is in the direction of energy healing. Like any calling, it has its own particular features and presents you with the need to cultivate specific qualities. Let's look at the path that leads from an initial interest or attraction to energywork to a mastery of the skills of an energy healer, keeping in mind all that has gone before about how a calling and one's spiritual gifts are nurtured.

Much of energy healing practice is self-taught, but not all of it. The learning of energy healing necessarily places a lot of emphasis on the experiential and nontraditional modes of gaining knowledge and experience. The education of a healer consists of input from many different sources, however, including traditional ones. Traditional learning comes from what has been handed down from past generations, from the accumulated lore and wisdom of our human culture. Each time you have learned something from another person, or taught someone something, you have engaged in tradition, and chances are that what is handed on to you today was most likely built upon the efforts and realizations of those who went before those who taught you.

In this day of online correspondence courses in which you might never lay eyes on your teacher, it is easy to forget that there was a time when the teacher-student relationship was regarded as the very vehicle for learning not only the external skills, but also the interior contours of a calling. Traditional paths of learning, in which an apprentice works directly with a master, continue to this day in many skilled trades.

Traditionally, a person entering a skilled trade spends years as an apprentice at the knee of a master, actually living in the master's house, sometimes doing household chores in addition to the rigors of learning the trade. The apprentice lives in close proximity to the master and a bond forms between them. The idea was that there was something to be gained by being physically near the master, something that becomes invested, little by little, energetically, in the apprentice. The skill being imparted is not merely a transmission of information or technique but of a certain virtue and state of consciousness passed wordlessly from teacher to student. The student is exposed to all phases of the craft, from its spirit and origins to its technical nuts and bolts, secrets and tricks of the trade, and the business of doing business. When apprentices fall ill, or need to rest, some old traditions understood this as the craft entering the apprentice's body. Mastery is not an overnight process, and the notion of a student "getting it" in a two-week crash course is rather absurd. The master transmits to the student the tradition of a lineage to which he or she belongs, either formally or informally, along with personal variations and adaptations. Past teachers and practitioners who have labored in the same fields are invoked to help the student understand that she is partaking of a tradition, that she is part of a community.

At some point in the life of the apprentice—in some traditions after having produced an apprentice piece—a moment comes when the master says, "You are ready." It is time to leave or be kicked out of the nest. Traditionally, the apprentice in this stage of development is called a *journeyman*. The student is no longer directly under the wing of the master. As the name implies, she takes off into the world and tries her wings, gains invaluable direct experience, hones her skills, makes all the necessary mistakes, and sees where she is, and where she ain't, in her own mastery. It is a time for ripening. The student is then admitted to the guild and becomes a full member of the lineage, sworn to uphold its tradition and rules. Traditionally, the way of becoming a master is to be acknowledged by others who have achieved mastery. It takes one to know one. Token of this step is a masterpiece.

*The Sorcerer's Apprentice*

> *We are more endangered by too much energy too soon than by too little too late, for we understand too little the wise use of power.*
> Amory Lovins

The earliest teaching story I can remember about what can happen if subtle energy domains are opened prematurely involved a sorcerer's apprentice named Mickey Mouse. Walt Disney's *Fantasia* was released in 1949, the same year I and many of the members of my slightly post-traditional generation were born (I think the gods showed remarkable foresight in getting to us early with this teaching). In it was a wonderfully detailed cartoon and music sequence based on Goethe's poem *Der Zauberlehrling*, "The Sorcerer's Apprentice." It captures the classic situation of the spiritual neophyte.

The story is this: no sooner does the sorcerer go to take a nap, leaving his wizard's hat temptingly behind, than his apprentice decides that he will try his hand at "commanding the spirits." A little power goes immediately to his head, of course, and we watch an ego-inflated Mickey drift off into a grandiose dream in which he is directing the heavenly bodies. When he comes crashing back to earth, he is helplessly adrift in the chaos he has unleashed, frantically thumbing through the magician's handbook for an incantation that will subdue the spirits that he had invoked.

We pass many times through phases of learning as we move into the mastery of any skill or the expression of a spiritual quality. A master of anything has all the phases of her learning wrapped up inside her like so many babushka dolls. She remembers the joy of her early beginner's luck, a time when she was so unaware of her incompetence that little successes just seemed to fall into her lap. She may have even told herself, "There's really not all that much to this!" Then she remembers that, by and by, she began to encounter people who really knew what they were doing, and she still cringes sometimes at the memory of how very much she didn't know.

That acute awareness of her incompetence, she recalls, was the very goad that made her seek instruction and actually undergo some discipline. By and by, she learned and grew and reached a point where she was competent—more than competent—and she knew it. Each move, each turn, each handhold, each step, was completely under her control.

But situations arose which challenged her little mastery. They didn't fit the template she had worked so long to perfect. People began finding her whose needs demanded something beyond her competence. She remembers the tears and the sleepless nights as, little by little, she moved toward an invisible edge. She remembers the day she let go of all that she had scripted for herself. All the rudiments and scales she had practiced so assiduously fell away, and for the first time in her life she became the music. The steps she had meticulously choreographed mysteriously disappeared, and she just danced. Her technical perfection and all the modalities she had learned gave way to the spirit of healing. She looks back now, and thinks to herself, *that must have been when I got my wings.* She is now as unconscious of her great competence as a flower is of its beauty. Her mastery is unique to her and exists as a gift to this world.

Learning energy healing takes us through similar stages and phases of growth. As with any other skill there are many levels of mastery in energy healing, as the techniques of your work give way to the art of being with another person in a healing and present way. Technical skills blend with the feeling you have for what you are doing and become part of your expression of your healing gift. Let's look at four distinct phases of mastery that show up cyclically in healer education.

Tooling Up

Many energy healers work intuitively with a minimum of technical knowledge, and their lack of formal training presents no barrier to their effectiveness. For most of us who venture into this territory, however, the natural gifts we bring with us are often in need of schooling. I personally believe that, as NPR news analyst Cokie Roberts once said, "There's something to be said for knowing something." Many people can feel energy and its movement, for example, but most of us have to go through a phase of learning in order to sort out the various impressions we receive. Our sensorium needs to be trained to deliver information that can be acted on, even though acting on it often means simply paying attention, being present, being mindful.

Learning exercises and treatment forms is clearly part of a kind of tooling up phase. These include the necessary work of:

- Learning to sense the movement of energy and understand its language;

- Learning to influence the energy field in a trustworthy and useful way;

- Locating energy-active positions on and around the body and learning their particular traits;

- Learning about energy phenomena, especially as they relate to healing, release, personal development and non-ordinary states of consciousness;

- Learning protocolized treatment forms and how to use structure, as well as learning to work free-form;

- Learning personal development practices. In addition to providing a means of participation in our inner growth, this is the best, and sometimes only, laboratory we have for learning about energy healing.

We don't tool up only once. Tooling up is pretty neat, pretty fascinating, and there is a big tendency in this phase to lust after more and more techniques. Some students get antsy at this stage and indulge in feeding frenzies, as if they have convinced themselves that if they only knew enough techniques everything would be okay. So they go on binges, haunting esoteric bookstores and reading every book on healing, and attending workshops until they're broke, trying to satisfy a seemingly endless hunger for information. As everyone finds out, however, you can go to school for years and come out heavy with knowledge, but the moment you start actually working with clients, you find out that more is needed.

## Developing Your Own Approach

The tooling up phase sooner or later gives way to the need to work on an approach of some kind. This phase has to do with bundling together the tools you have mastered and skills you have learned and putting them to work in some purposeful way. Here is where you begin (if you haven't done so up to now) to ask yourself, "Why am I doing this in the first place? What is all this good for?" We begin to see that there are many possible interpretations of what energy healing is all about. The skills and techniques that you acquire as you tool up will tend to organize themselves around the stories you are telling yourself and what you most deeply believe about what you are doing. Your approach will inevitably find its center near what you believe is important.

One of the truly nice things about energy healing is that it operates on a variety of levels. Many people, for example, will use their tools in the service of "fixing" the person they are working on, because they earnestly believe that this is what healing is all about. Other persons see energy healing as a means of entering into the psycho-emotional processes that underlie symptoms, and use these practices as a vehicle for healing traumatic past events, providing for release of old experience, and the drawing in of new. Others see energywork predominately as a psycho-spiritual discipline, and still others see it as a means to kick-start meditative experiences or help another person to enter altered states of consciousness and then integrate their experiences with their everyday lives.

Energy healing integrates all the aspects of this continuum, from symptoms and problems to exploration to transcendental experiences, without parking exclusively on any one aspect. I can tend to a client's headache in a way that makes room for emotional release and inner exploration that may even flow into some transcendent experience and a reentry into everyday life with a new feeling. It is all part of the same continuum.

Approach building is just as fascinating as tooling up, and it often has more power to it. There comes a time, however, when you have grooved in your basic set of techniques so that they become seamless and effortless, and your approach becomes a part of your approach to life in general. Then, marvelously, when you relax the need to tool up or build an approach of your own, the whole project takes a new turn.

## Healing Relationship

When you work with another person, it can be said that healing work takes place in the zone between you and your partner, which Diane Tegtmeier, author of *Relationships that Heal:*

*Skillful Practice within Nature's Web*, calls "interspace." As your need to gather more and more new tools and techniques relaxes, and as you evolve something of a personal approach to your work—in short, when you reach a level of confidence that allows you to relax with what you're doing and be yourself—there comes a point when the healing relationship you have with your partner comes into the foreground. This expresses itself in bodywork in the unspoken, unseen negotiations between you. It shows in the way a new client will check you out—maybe completely unconsciously—before a word is ever said to see if they feel safe with you. When there is true subconscious cooperation between you and your client, the healing process takes on a certain spontaneity.

I occasionally work with individuals whose energy sensitivity is far more acute than mine. Their ability to take in impressions is both a blessing and a curse for them, because the more impressions they take in, the more they have to process somehow. These highly sensitive persons respond consciously to very small impulses, and they have taught me that nothing is insignificant in energywork.

Conventional bodywork can completely miss areas of need in highly sensitive persons if it ignores the energetic. They won't feel served. Often it is enough to set the stage, create a trustworthy space for the person to be in, and their process will unfold with only minimal external intervention on your part. The establishment of this safe space or *energetic kiva*, is what provides them with an environment in which they can walk the three-fold spiritual path, slipping a bit more easily into other states of consciousness and then returning, ready to meet their world again. In many people, this ability is quite developed, and all they need is that extra bit of energetic support. The container of the healing relationship between you and your partner is often where that can happen.

A fascinating illustration of the workings of healing relationship is in Nicholas Evan's book, *The Horse Whisperer*, in the description of the healing space that grows between Tom Booker, a healer of horses, and Pilgrim, an aptly named horse that has been savagely injured. There is a scene, rendered wonderfully in the Robert Redford film, that contains all the elements of the creation of healing space. In this scene, Pilgrim gets spooked and bolts, and the horse whisperer takes off after him, following but never forcing himself on the frightened animal. Little by little, he skirts the horse's visual field, keeping a respectful distance. Day turns to evening as the horse whisperer crouches, patient as a tree, across an open meadow from Pilgrim, their eyes trained on each other. A palpable energy moves in the space between them. They wordlessly negotiate their space and, by and by, fear subsides. The zone between them opens and the horse approaches. Finally, Pilgrim is standing in front of the horse whisperer, less than an arm's length away. Still, the man does nothing until finally, the horse nudges him with his snout. Only then does the horse whisperer reach out and slip the rope over his head and lead him back to the corral where the healing work can continue.

Like the best bodyworkers and healers I know, the horse whisperer moves in a dance between being and doing. His mastery of technique is so seamless that you don't even notice it. His approach is so uncomplicated as to be virtually invisible, but through it all it is his empathy and ability to be unflinchingly present with Pilgrim that stitches man and horse together into a unified fabric.

There is more than one healing relationship going on when you work with another person. The obvious one is the healing relationship between you and your partner. The other, less obvious one is the relationship both you and your partner have with the wisdom residing deep within each of you. Your effectiveness as a healer depends on the interaction between the healing qualities active in you and that same area of quality that is latent in your partner. This does not happen through words. In fact, it doesn't even happen between you and your partner without first happening between you and *yourself* in your own personal inner work. Facilitating a healing process in another, if it is to go beyond a merely technical level, begins with you.

As the healing relationship grows between you and your own inner world, the healing qualities set free in the process transmit wordlessly to others and stimulate similar qualities in them. They sense it, and they respond spontaneously. If I were to give a name to what makes this possible it would be compassion, your feeling for the other person. The reason is simple: whatever you feel your calling to be, its expression into this world involves your Heart Center, and it is the nature of the Heart to reach out and set up an energetic exchange between you and other people and the world around you. When compassion—a feeling for the other person—expresses through your Heart and the way it touches others, it acts as a vehicle for your deeper qualities, the ones associated with your calling, to move outward, into the world. The compassion that fills the space between you and your healing partner is what makes it a healing relationship.

*Developing your abilities in healing is learning about people, not about a technique.... The use of healing qualities is really the use of feeling for the other person.*

Bob Moore

Dancing with God

We have been examining phases of learning energy healing, but in truth, these phases can be found in the learning of practically any discipline, since the mastery of one phase tends to segue naturally into something beyond itself. These stages repeat themselves; we never stop learning. Only novices in a discipline delude themselves with the notion that they've "got it." Masters, on the other hand, regardless of the discipline, are humbled by how much they don't know. In healing work, you can have all kinds of tools and skills at your disposal, and you can have evolved your own approach to using them, but the techniques and approaches by themselves can get pretty boring if they are not in the service of the fundamental healing relationship between you and your partner. And yet, even the healing relationship will ask for something more, something beyond itself.

Approaches are bigger than individual techniques and tools, and the healing relationship with another person is larger than any particular approach, but what is larger than the healing relationship you have with your client? To get at a real answer, we need to clear out our limited categories of thinking and understand that each of us is part of a greater whole. When we give a treatment, for example, we are not only treating an individual, but we are touching a part of a far greater body. The person we lay hands on is a cell in the body of their family, their group, society, and nation, the human race, the living planet, indeed the person you touch is a cell in the greater body of all sentient beings and all creation. Only the limitation of our hearts and our imaginations prevents us from experiencing this.

Your ability to be conscious that you are touching into this hidden wholeness as you do your work—both in your inner work with yourself and in healing work with others—opens the door to the fundamental spirituality of energywork. Healing work, with its multitude of techniques and methods and the special partnership that develops between you and your partner, can become a connection to the universal principles that guide Creation, the unseen give and take of energy and life-force, the operation of Love on a grand scale, a dance with the Source of Life.

In moving toward a practice and teaching of energy-active bodywork, we need to provide educational settings in which these four phases can be honored. Students of bodywork will not stop needing solid fundamentals of anatomy and physiology, therapeutic massage and bodywork, business and an ethics of truly skilled healing relationship. But those who are attracted to energy-oriented bodywork and therapy are in need of an education that prepares them for spiritual process as well. This is because the tools of energywork are derived from age-old spiritual practices, the ancient technology of consciousness, aimed toward nothing less than receiving what Joseph Campbell called "the inexhaustible energies of the cosmos," something which has implications far grander than even our contemporary notions of "optimum health."

# CHAPTER SIX

## SELF-KNOWLEDGE
### SNEAKING UP ON YOUR BELIEF SYSTEM

Stanislav Grof, the Czech-born psychologist who developed Holotropic Breathwork, once said that the first barrier to entering altered states of consciousness is physical, and that the second level is *philosophical.* He was attesting to the power of our beliefs and their power to determine what we experience. Since our beliefs shape the very way we see the world and what we experience consciously, the issue of beliefs is a perennial theme in the pilgrimage of energywork.

*Beliefs: A Perennial Theme of Inner Work*
Internal lives of healers vary. A casual observer walking in on a healing session would witness variations on themes of touch, manipulation, massage, a panoply of hands-on and hands-off maneuvers—things that, in most cases, can be described on a technical level. What they would not see so easily is the wild variety of ways in which practitioners see themselves, what they believe about what they are doing, and the particular frameworks, stories, paradigms, beliefs, and models they are maintaining, consciously or unconsciously, as they do their work. Where one therapist thinks of the spine as a physiological assemblage of bones, soft tissue, fluid, and nerves, another might see it as God's walking stick. While one healer might see her job as restoring healthy blood flow to a set of muscles so her client can be relieved of his pain and get back to normal, another healer, using more or less the same external forms and techniques, might understand that she is reprogramming her client's DNA, charging her client's light body with color and sound, or channeling energy from the Pleiades. And each one of those stories would itself be pegged to background stories, beliefs, and perspectives of its own.

Your system of beliefs affects how you work in healing. The reason is that your skills and techniques will tend to organize themselves around how you see yourself and what you most deeply believe about what you are doing. We bodyworkers, therapists, and counselors have a responsibility to find ways of examining our core beliefs about ourselves and what we do, and about our role in the healing process, because they affect those we treat.

*Jeremiah the Healer: A Small Project for Examining Beliefs*
I once knew a healer named Jeremiah. He looked a lot like Sai Baba, a tall, good-looking man with dark skin and a generous bushy Afro. Jeremiah got quite a reputation as a layer-on of hands, in part because he was effective, in part because he would fall asleep when he worked. He would place his hands on his partner's body, and thirty minutes later (or longer), Jeremiah would wake

up and the person would feel better, much better. When you asked Jeremiah how he worked, this is what he would say:

> I put my hands on,
> an' start to pray,
> then I fall asleep,
> an' get out the way!

What basic beliefs can you hear in Jeremiah's explanation of his healing work? After all, he is tipping some cards with his little rhyme, revealing something of how he sees his role, and showing something of how healing works, according to him. Try this: use your imagination for a moment and ask Jeremiah a few questions about what he does. Grill him, pin him down. Take a few notes on your inner interview with Jeremiah, the sleeping healer.

*Getting at Your Own Beliefs*

Because the energetic dimension is not a part of most people's everyday conscious world, we do not have anything approaching a cultural consensus about it. When you become involved with energywork, you venture out over the edge of what most people take to be real. There are moments when you realize that, belief-wise, you have snuck away from the crowd and you're suddenly on your own. It's a predicament many energy healers face: you have to get comfortable with these beliefs of yours without a supportive mass mind propping them up, and that means first becoming aware of them. An effective way to become conscious of your own beliefs—not just the ones you can name off the top of your head, but the deeper, less conscious ones, too—is to try and articulate them to another person who is willing to listen. If you have ever tried to tell the story of your inner life or write something like a spiritual autobiography, you may have found that articulating something as close to the bone as your deep personal experiences has a way of moving your whole inner process. Inevitably, you run into the contours of what is real for you, the bedrock of your inner world. And when you take an inventory of your beliefs there are some questions that need to be asked:

*Are your beliefs really yours?* Or are they are part of the mass mind, things that everybody assumes automatically, without reflection? Or have they been borrowed from someone else? Reflect on whether your beliefs came to you from your parents, from school, from your religious instruction, your guru or spiritual teacher? Contrast this with what you believe because it is part of your own direct, personal experience. These are likely to have a different power.

*Are your beliefs progressive?* That is to say, do your beliefs change and grow as you change and grow? This may be the best way to find out if a belief is truly your own, or one that you have accepted from an external source. One of the great problems associated with having other people's experiences (which is basically what you are doing when you accept uncritically an external belief structure) is that you have no means of progressing a belief that is not your own beyond a certain point.

Finally, *which of your experientially-based beliefs have you actually acted on?* These beliefs have power in your life.

Here are some questions for your reflection, designed to give you a way to drill into your beliefs about healing:

Questions for Reflection

- According to you, what is the goal of healing work? Why do it?

- What is "healing," according to you?

- How does healing work, according to you?

- What do you call yourself and your role in the work you do? Try to get at how you think of yourself as you work, and how you came to that belief.

- Describe your work in some detail. Tell what you actually do. While you're at it, try to get at what turns you on about what you do and what you feel is important in your work.

- How did you come to this work? Is your work connected to your sense of a calling? Describe the path you have taken so far to come into the work you do. Was there a moment when you identified this as the work you want to do?

- Talk about what has influenced you, turned you on, inspired you. Talk about peak experiences, teachers, moments when you have seen your path.

- What kind of clients do you work best with? What kind do you work least well with?

- What are your doubts about your work?

- Describe the role of resistance, sexuality, and emotions in your work. Go into how you have come to your position on these issues.

- What would you like to learn; where would you like improve?

- Is your healing work a spiritual practice for you? Describe.

- What is the source of your work? If you work with energy, how do you connect with the source of the energy you use?

Getting to know your own beliefs is really about getting at what is real for you, and it is important preparation for working with others. A by-product of digging into where your beliefs come from is that you gain respect for the beliefs of other people, and for their way of putting the world together. This will make a deep listener out of you. One of the greatest skills to be learned in the art of energetic healing work is that of working with the beliefs of the other person, and not overriding them with your own. Many people, for example, are going to jump ship if you mention reincarnation as a possible context for what they are experiencing in this life. The very same person, however, might be very open to understanding that he is carrying something of his entire line of ancestors in every cell of his body, in his DNA.

*Pilgrim's Progress: Spiritual Map Making*

> *Tulip Elegies-II*
>
> *Geese bleat over the roof, conversing*
> *somehow with stars as we drowse*
> *beneath constellations of beating wings.*
> *Rearranging staggered lines they steer*

*a sunward pattern, calling out
as they fly, naming the long way.*

*Below, under shovels of dirt
the dead move imperceptibly,
turning into other shapes of life.
Tulip bulbs shift under dark horizons
of winter and wedge against years
of decayed shale. Shoots form within,*

*still trapped, and a miniature blossom
waits in each bleached kernel. Last
spring
winged leaves fed this future and
wilted.
Now, unmoved by geese or moonlight,
bulbs listen through solstice nightfall
for the searing call of one hot star.*

Denise Low

*So is the kingdom of God as if a man should cast seed into the ground: and should sleep, and rise night and day, and the seed should spring and grow up, he knoweth not how. For the earth bringeth forth fruit of herself: first the blade, then the ear, after that the full corn in the ear.*

Mark 4: 26–28

## Seed—Root—Sprout—Flower

A lot of our growth is unconscious. We grow for years in the unreflecting state of childhood. Puberty barges in as a riot of growth as young people trip, unaware, over their budding strength and beauty. The skills and qualities we now take for granted were planted long ago by the dark of the moon. The seeds we throw over our shoulder today will soon be growing behind our backs, lying in the ground until conditions are right. One day, a sprout pokes its head through the surface of the ground.

Paying close attention to something as it grows is a participation in events that usually take place when nobody is looking, like the flowering of certain desert cacti, which open only once and then only at night. There are milestones and landmarks along the path of each of us, but often only a careful examination with the help of hindsight will reveal what they are.

Many of life's landmarks are on everybody's maps and timetables. I learned to walk, started to shave, and had a mid-life crisis pretty much right on schedule. Many of the contours of my life, though, can be mapped only by me. When it comes to consciously charting your inner life and spiritual growth, the usefulness of other people's maps tapers off sharply. That means you have to craft a map that serves your needs and, more to the point here, the needs of the spiritual traveler inside you. Here are a couple of mapping projects for the pilgrim in your body.

MAPPING PROJECT #1: *Spiritual Autobiography*
Maps organize your experience. They are tools for reflecting on where you are, where you've been, where you're heading. Different maps show different features of the territory. A topographical map and a political map offer different takes on the same landscape because of their differing ways of organizing information. Personal maps—often in the form of stories—act as divining rods for probing into life's journey. The very act of consciously recalling and collecting together the various stations of your life—the form could be as simple as reminiscing about the houses you have lived in, the cities, states, and lands of your life—can give you fresh clues as to your present "location." When you get together with a group of people and introduce yourself by telling about yourself, where you are from, what you do, and so on, a certain set of stories emerges. But try switching the focal point and watch how differently personal history is organized. What happens if each member of the group tells the stories behind the scars on their bodies, their children, their divorces? Go to a nursing home and listen to the "organ recitals," as residents regale one another with the minute details of the operations they've had. The focal point that organizes the information is part of the map.

Creating a spiritual autobiography is a way to sneak up on the story of your inner path. It is a challenge that yields all kinds of insights if you rise to it. It is relatively easy to see where you have been, but not so simple to recognize what it is that has moved you. Enter the project with curiosity about the river that has carried you from one station of your life to the next, and see if you can discover the grace working behind the scenes.

Jump in. Give it cache and a snazzy title, maybe *The Secret Spiritual History of Pilgrim X*; or *My Spiritual Autobiography and the Story of my Unfolding as a Healer, Teacher, Artist, Leader*, etc. In it include:

- Events and experiences which have lead you to your belief system concerning the spiritual dimension of life;

- Peak experiences;

- When have you become aware of your particular spiritual gifts?

- What have been the elements of your growth as a healer, teacher, artist, leader, etc.?

- When were you introduced to tools having to do with conscious development—for example meditation, prayer, or healing exercise?

- Create a section called "My Secret Training." Look at the circumstances and predicaments in your life, especially the times of crisis. *What have the turns in your life forced you to learn?*

- What is it that has pushed or pulled you into new phases of your life?

- What themes, challenges, and lessons recur, and what patterns emerge?

MAPPING PROJECT #2: *Synoptic Personal History*

When I lived in Germany, I had a doctor named Dr. zur Linden. During one visit, as a "prescription," he gave me an assignment: a *synoptic medical history*. He gave me a huge sheet of newsprint and showed me how to make a number of columns in which to line up the critical events in my life alongside a timeline with events in the world at large and my health changes. On my next visit, yellow highlighter in hand, Dr. zur Linden poured over the chart I had produced. In no time, he connected a number of inner and outer events in my life, and these connections were the source of a cascade of insights for me. I became aware of the importance of context: the significant events, repetitive patterns, and changes of my life did not occur in a vacuum!

You can take this kind of approach as you create a map of your pilgrim's quest in this life. If you take the challenge of actually sitting down and creating a synoptic history of your inner and outer life, carefully telling your life's story, or writing a spiritual autobiography, you may well find that the process activates you in unexpected ways. Half-forgotten scenes from your earlier life might come bubbling up as you perform such acts of memory. At times, the telling of your story becomes a probe into hidden beliefs and codes at work in you behind the scenes. As with your spiritual autobiography, it might reveal a kind of secret training that you have been receiving for a long time.

On pages 74 and 75 you will find a sample synoptic personal history to give you an idea of how this looks, plus a blank history chart to get you started. Look at the section with the heading *Events in My Life*. These events are not just outer ones, of course, and neither are the ones under the heading *Personal Conflicts* in the next column. Here is where you will want to draw on the backstory you created in your spiritual autobiography.

Beliefs play a unique role in the development of your gifts. Your experience and your beliefs are joined in a chicken-and-egg relationship: what you experience is highly influenced by your beliefs, and, conversely, your most solid beliefs are formed, inevitably, by your experiences. If you are an energy healer, you will surely see how unconscious beliefs affect those who come to you as clients.

This chapter concludes with a couple of anecdotes about beliefs.

# Synoptic Personal/Spiritual History

A mapwork tool for seeing coinciding events in your life.

**SAMPLE:** The idea here is to line up, chronologically, the significant events of your life.

| Time Line | Events in the World at Large | Events in my Life ✛ | Personal Conflicts | Health Changes |
|---|---|---|---|---|
| 1945 | Hiroshima, End of World War II | | | |
| December 1947 - 1949 | War over, American post-war baby boom starts | My parents got married/ I was conceived/born. | | |
| May, 1951 | | My younger brother was born. | Remember getting my head stuck under the backyard fence as I was trying to get out. | Headaches? |
| 1952 or 1953 | Eisenhower is president. America's post-war optimism, amidst McCarthy-era anti-communist hysteria. "I like Ike" buttons at home. | Tonsilectomy: parents trying to get me into car to go to the hospital/I'm screaming to my grandmother to save me. | | |
| 1954 | | Pre-school. My grand-father dies. | | |
| November, 1960 | Paranoia about the Soviets. JFK elected president | I'm in the 6th grade. I have a best friend who I just idolize. | My mother is ill all the time. I feel like an outsider in my class. My friend has other friends. | I have a cold all the time. |
| Autumn, 1962 | | My mother dies. I'm in the eighth grade. | Can't talk. Remember looking down so much that I would walk into bigger kids w/top of my head. | I have a cold *all* the time |
| Christmas, 1963 | JFK assassinated a month ago | My 13th birthday, onset of puberty | Constant unrequited crushes on girls. Vivid fantasy life. | |
| 1964 | The Beatles are on the Ed Sullivan show. | Always loved listening to my mother's music. Now I find my own. | | |
| Summer, 1964 | | Trip with Dad and my brother Bruce to California. First time at ocean. | | |

✛ Here, you want to use things you have comeup with in the writing of your spiritual autobiography.

74

# Synoptic Personal/Spiritual History

A mapwork tool for seeing coinciding events in your life.

| Time Line | Events in the World at Large | Events in my Life ✢ | Personal Conflicts | Health Changes |
|---|---|---|---|---|

THE IDEA HERE IS TO LINE UP, CHRONOLOGICALLY, THE SIGNIFICANT EVENTS OF YOUR LIFE.

✢ Here, you want to use things you have come up with in the writing of your spiritual autobiography.

# FROM THE STORYBOOK
## TWO ANECDOTES ABOUT BELIEF

### I.
### SIGNS AND MIRACLES

*When President Calvin Coolidge was asked if he believed in baptism
by total immersion, he answered, "Believe in it? Hell, I've seen it!"*
Related to me by my father, Hunter Gilkeson

There are times when the last thing a man wants to hear from a woman is, "I don't feel noth-ing!" One of those times is halfway through a five-day energy healing class he is teaching, and the woman is one of the students. While everyone else in my energywork class seems to be getting it—that is, they were having enough success at consciously connecting with their own energy field and the energy fields of their treatment partners that they didn't have to take my word for its existence—this one woman isn't.

Energy sensing, linking consciously with the energy system, can be a stumbling block for beginners. The people who do the best with it right off the bat are the kinesthetic types. They seem to be able to feel the subtle energetic movement in their own bodies as soon as you point it out to them, and when they put their hands on another person they feel it there as well. Energywork is just one of those things you can't go into head first, and here is this poor woman, trying to go in head first, unable to feel anything at all and getting more and more frustrated as the week progresses. Not a good sign.

She's tall and good looking, very intelligent in a serious, analytical way, definitely not a kinesthetic type. It's her first time in this country. Her heavily accented English is the kind spoken by people who learned it because it was required of them when they went to school but who found it totally boring, something to be endured. Suddenly, here she is, in a country where that's all they speak and, lacking all experience in an English-speaking country, she's totally out of her element linguistically with everything she hears and every time she opens her mouth. The result is a vaguely Transylvanian, comedic Count Dracula accent, like Natasha in the old Rocky and Bullwinkle cartoons.

Something tells me that she is judging everything we do in class in terms of its immediate applicability to the kind of physical therapy and massage she is involved with in her home country. Worse, she seems to want me to sell her on energywork, prove to her somehow that the subtle energetic world is real and worth paying attention to. As a teacher, this is a point where, if you don't watch out, a power struggle can start and you risk falling into the trap of abandoning the basically feeling nature of the undertaking and try instead to convince a skeptical person by means of some digitized, logical argument. I hate that situation. I would rather preach to the choir any day. But there she is, not even remotely a member of the choir, with her hands on her partner, struggling along in all good faith to feel *something*, anything, so she can be convinced she's not wasting her time. So I keep trying.

I lightly touch the back of her hand. "Okay, totally back off on your pressure, and try to invite the sensation into your hands. Try to just let it come to you."

"And *what* I am supposed to feelingkh, please?" Her hands are rigid and wooden on her partner. She's totally in her head.

"Nothing specific … it's like … *listening* with your hands," I tell her with the wan hope that she'll catch the brilliance and originality of this simile.

"Listen? With *hands*? I am sorry, I do not understand you. Repeat, please, what you have said." The idea is suddenly way too complex to take in; if you don't really have the language, the overwhelming tendency is to take everything literally. We're stuck.

Finally, in exasperation, she throws up her hands. "I don't feel nothingkh! For what is this good?" I'm not sure I know.

By now, the rest of the class is distracted. She's just being honest, and she is not the type to just smile and pretend she's getting it when she isn't. I feel I have to find a way through this knothole because it's starting to siphon off some of the good feeling that has prevailed in the class up to this point. Half joking, I make a suggestion. "Maybe you should pray for a miracle."

She passes this proposition through the dictionary in her head. "You mean I should make so … pray for miracle?" She takes her hands off her partner, puts her palms together, fingers up, prayer style, and casts her eyes upward toward the heavens. She's checking to see if she has understood what I'm saying. The notion obviously tickles her. "Okay, I pray for big miracle. You pray, too, for miracle," she says to me, "so I will believe, okay?" Apparently, her little outburst of a few moments before and my playful suggestion that she pray for a miracle have helped her to lighten up. All of a sudden, there is something delightful about her. She's laughing about it. That's good.

"Okay," I say. "We both pray for big miracle."

At break that afternoon I walk in on a strange scene. A sparrow has flown into the school's dining room and is having all kinds of trouble flying back out. Some of the windows are open, but the bird is unable to find them, crashing instead into the panes of the closed ones in its frantic attempts to escape. After each frustrated attempt, the poor bird flutters back out into the room and tries again, smashing with fragile fury into another closed window pane.

As I stand there watching, I recall that when I lived in Germany, I taught myself to energetically "herd" wasps out of the house when they got in and couldn't get back out. In southern Germany, when the plum trees ripen and there is all kinds of canning activity going on inside the houses, it is not uncommon for these little wasps to fly in through the unscreened windows and collect in the kitchen, drawn by the sweet vapors of the maroon-colored plums being processed into preserves.

Unlike their cranky North American relatives, these German wasps are docile, sweet-natured creatures. I learned to use my hands to move waves of energy at them, gently splash them with energy, and coax them toward an open door or window to fly back outside where they belonged. Piece of cake, actually, once you get the hang of it.

This memory comes to me as I watch the frightened little bird trying to escape from the dining room, and I wonder if I could energetically herd it toward an open window as I learned to do with the German wasps. Why not? I open one of the windows as wide as it can go and then get the sparrow between me and the open window. I extend my arms and begin to massage the space between us, splashing the bird with gentle, but insistent ripples of energy. She feels it and begins to respond. Together, we inch toward the open window. By and by, she lands on the window sill. Slowly—no quick moves—my hands come closer and closer to her, but instead of darting out the window like a German wasp, she freezes, goes completely inert and rolls over onto her back with her little sparrow feet sticking up in the air. Gently, I scoop her up in both hands and drop her out the window. She falls a few feet, then rights herself in midair and flaps away. I turn and see my unbelieving student standing in the doorway, wide-eyed, mouth open. Apparently, she has witnessed the whole scene with the bird.

"Now I believe you!" she says, laughing. "This is my miracle!"

She had a wonderful, ironic sense of the whole thing. She became very animated and got a lot of mileage out of recounting the "miracle" with a combination of pantomime and hands-and-feet Dracula English for the other members of the class. The whole thing turned out well. Her belief system got the seeing-is-believing booster shot it needed, and she went on to witness a couple of other small miracles and even started to enjoy the class.

For my part, I told them about energetic wasp herding in Germany. I also told them that some time after figuring out how to move the plum preserves-loving wasps around with waves of energy, I went into my bedroom and found a hornet in there. I got behind it, extended my hands and began to move closer, splashing it with waves of energy, intending to coax it out the window. Hornets, however, have a much more cantankerous temperament. This one felt me coming all right, but instead of lifting off and drifting obediently toward the window like the wasps had done, it turned toward me and began to wave its vibrating antennae in *my* direction. I stopped in my tracks. The hornet lifted off and landed a foot or so closer to me. I took a step backwards. The hornet waved its antennae some more, and soon it had me backed up to the open bedroom door, and out I went.

## II.
## ANGELIC VOICES

Music educator Nora Berzheim told me a story about Michael Vetter, the German teacher of overtone singing, which sheds an interesting light on the issue of belief. Michael's specialty is instructing his students in the art of using their voices to produce sounds that fan out into harmonics. If you have heard Tibetan chanting or Tuvan throat-singing, you know the curious and special quality of this style of singing. A single singer can set the atmosphere in a room to ringing like a bell, vibrating with a chiming reverberation. One of the by-products of learning to produce overtones is that your ear becomes attuned to the overtones in everyday sounds.

The story goes like this: Michael Vetter goes to visit his dying mother. Many members of the family are gathered around her as she lies there, passing in and out of consciousness. No one expects her to survive many more days. It is winter and the house's steam radiators hiss, crackle, and creak as the heat passes through them. Vetter's sensitized hearing is drawn into the "song" of the radiators, and by and by he can hear their overtones. He finds he can attune to one overtone, and then the next. In this way, he is able to "climb the harmonic ladder." It helps him pass the time.

Presently, the family members in the room begin to stir, and quite unexpectedly, Vetter's mother opens her eyes, suddenly bright with joy. She tells them she was drifting in a reverie when she heard the singing of the angels. She knew they were singing for her. What her son "knew" to be the overtones of the radiator, she "knew" to be the singing of the angels. She assures everyone that she is going to be all right. To prove it, she goes on to live several more years.

# CHAPTER SEVEN

## HOLISM

*Imagine all things and creatures as the cells of a single living being.*
*All are but parts of one stupendous whole,*
*Whose body Nature is and God the soul.*

Alexander Pope

There was a woman named Sarah who came regularly for sessions with me. She had been severely injured as a young child—run over, intentionally she believes, by a family member. Sarah had a remarkable ability to vividly articulate body memories recovered during energy healing sessions. In one session, she found herself identifying strongly with all the female children throughout history who had been rejected, punished, even killed, because they were not born as boys. Whether or not that was the specific motivation of the family member who injured her, Sarah felt a grief that went beyond her own personal biography, place, and generation. She described the sensation, paradoxically painful and comforting at the same time, of feeling like a cell in a vast body, and her heart went out to this particular group of people of which she found herself to be part. At the end of the session, she agreed to devote some time and energy—in the form of prayer and other spiritual work—to the healing of this specific set of people.

Sarah's experience sheds light on one of the great perennial issues of energywork, namely holism. Finding out that you are part of something much bigger than you thought, discovering that you are a cell in a greater body, shatters the belief that you live only as an isolated individual, unable to draw on, or contribute to, anything greater than your solo self. It is a fundamental piece of spiritual awakening.

Native people acknowledge their participation in the web of life with the words, "All my relations," as they enter ceremonial space. They are acknowledging that each of us is a body contained within other, greater bodies. You might be accustomed to thinking of yourself as just good old you, independent and splendidly isolated from all others. But look again: you are also part of a family, a genetic line, a tribe, a race, an ethnicity, a nationality, a language group, a set of people with a common experience, perhaps a religious persuasion, a minority status, a profession or career path, a particular generation marked by a certain common history, challenges, and experiences. Ultimately, we are all part of the greater whole of humanity and the family of all sentient beings. Each of these greater bodies is evolving and growing, just like we are as individuals. Our healing and growth as individuals plays a role in the healing and growth of these greater bodies, and likewise, the evolving health and wellness of these greater bodies is part of our individual wholeness.

*The whole is more than the sum of its parts.*

Aristotle

*Miasms*

Sarah had awakened to one of her miasms, or fields of experience that she shares with a specific set of others. (Here, I am taking some liberties with a term used in classical homeopathy, and I will explain the term in a moment.) She understood that she was part of a greater whole. This kind of experience comes into view so strongly in energetic healing because when we move into the energetic aspect of our makeup, we move into the holographic level of how we are organized. Our whole being is present and accessible in each of our parts.

When we apply this perspective to the things that happen in energy healing work, a couple of related things come into view. One is the fact that we can treat an entire individual, energetically, through any part of his or her body. The other is the fact that holism doesn't stop with us as individuals; you can treat a larger organism—a family, for example—of which the individual is a part, by treating the individual.

The original doctrine of miasms in homeopathy had to do with Samuel Hahnemann's (the father of homeopathy) belief that those whom he treated were all connected, genetically, to one or the other of the great plagues that had ravaged Europe throughout history. According to this view, each individual therefore partakes of something of the pathology of that plague. He saw and treated his patients not as isolated individuals, but as individuals who were part of a greater whole.

As a corollary to this view, he believed that even if an individual patient exhibited only a few of the plague's symptoms, that person ought to be treated for *all* the plague's symptoms. In more modern terms, we might say he saw the individual who was sick with the plague as a holographic fragment of the plague. In a certain sense, he was attempting to treat the *whole epidemic* through an individual piece of it; he was using the individual as a "handle" on the greater whole.

Modern homeopaths debate the validity of Hahnemann's doctrine of miasms. They want to know if there are only the miasms he named, and whether or not each and every one of us are linked to one or the world's plagues. Not being a homeopath myself, I don't care if Hahnemann covered all the bases or not, and I will leave them to their debate. But do I know a holistic concept when I see one. What I take with me from the whole discussion of miasms is this: we are each whole systems within ourselves *and* we are also part of a greater whole, indeed of many greater wholes. Here is where the idea of miasms is useful when it comes to holistic thinking.

The realization that we are all part of something vastly

greater is a part of spiritual awakening and the kind of experience Sarah had, in which her injuries triggered an awareness of herself as part of a greater body, is not uncommon in energywork. Again, this is because of the holographic nature of energy and consciousness, and holistic approaches to healing and growth—if they are truly holistic—will, by their nature, address this. If you are using energy healing in some form, you are already using tools that trigger a holistic response. Your conscious participation starts with your appreciation of this phenomenon.

The exercises to follow will contribute to your awareness of the holistic nature of energy and consciousness. Here is an inner pilgrimage that involves a greater body we all share:

INNER PILGRIMAGE #8: *Expanding Awareness of Two Heavenly Bodies*
*Preparation:*
- As with all of these exercises, it is a good idea to read through all the instructions before starting.

- MUSIC: Have some music at hand, so that you can turn it on during the second part of the exercise. In my experience, it is best to use music that doesn't have a big throbbing rhythm. Nature sounds and adagios work well for what we are about to do.

Part One: Visualization and Awareness of the Planet
1. After you have settled in and are sitting comfortably, take some time to sink into the feeling that you are sitting on the planet, held in place by gravity.
2. Visualize and feel your location on the planet. Take a minute to relax into this awareness.
3. Imagine that you are slowly, gradually lifting off in a hot-air balloon. "Zoom out" and view your location from above. Go only as high in your visualization as you need to in order to see where you are in relation to the mountains, plains, lakes, forests, oceans, and other geographical landmarks.
4. Visualize the states or countries around yours, and the continent you are on. See if you can sense them. *Feel them.* Don't worry about the geographic accuracy of your visualization. Stay as much as possible with the feeling of what you are doing. Give this process two or three minutes.
5. Slowly stretch your visualization and awareness out over the earth's surface up to the North Pole, and then …
6. Stretch your awareness to the East …
7. … then to the West.
8. Slowly expand your awareness down to the South Pole.
9. Move your visualization and awareness slowly on the earth's surface to the other side of the planet from where you are.
10. In this way, examine the whole surface of the earth. Examine the land and the oceans.
11. Slowly move your awareness down into the earth. Examine the inside of the planet. Use your awareness to penetrate through the layers of rock and plumb the underground oceans until you find the molten core of the planet.
12. Bring your awareness slowly out to the surface. Examine the whole planet at once.
13. Release this visualization and simply sit with whatever comes up within you.

Part 2: 360-Degree Listening

1. Make a feeling contact with your Throat Center. A good contact position is on the front of your throat, just below your Adam's apple.

2. Allow a couple of minutes for the contact to intensify.

3. Release your contact with your Throat Center and turn on the music with the volume medium to low.

4. Focus your listening on your left side. That is, try to hear everything that is to the left of your body. Spend a minute listening to the sounds to your left.

5. Now slowly move your listening around you, behind your body until you are listening to what is behind you. You might feel as though you were listening with the surface of your skin. Listen to what is behind you for a minute or so.

6. continue moving your listening around you until you are aware of the sound to your right. One minute.

7. Slowly move your listening around you in the same direction until you are listening to the sound in front of you. One minute.

8. Continue with the slow movement of your direction of listening until you reach the position on your left side where you started.

9. Slowly move around your body one more time with your listening. This time keep moving instead of stopping until you reach your left side again.

10. Stop moving your focus and simply listen. At first, you might feel like you are doing this with your ears, or that this is something you are primarily doing at the level of your head. As the exercise progresses, however, you'll start doing this with your whole body. *Whole body listening.*

11. Sit with this for ten minutes.

12. End the exercise.

*Holistic Appreciation*

We have curious abilities when it comes to our senses. We are geared for both specific and holistic sensing. We have the ability to sense all kinds of things in our environment very individually and very specifically. You can teach yourself to pick out the song of a single bird out of the morning cacophony of feathered conversation in a forest. I remember my feeling of accomplishment the first time I managed to single out and follow the viola part in a string quartet. We can also use these same senses of ours to expand our awareness into the hidden, but accessible, wholeness of which we are a part.

Your deep understanding that you are part of a greater whole is enhanced by using your senses in meditative practices. Here are a few more exercises to help your senses extend and increase your appreciation of the essential holism of life. The first of these holistic appreciation exercises is one I taught myself at the retreat center where I live and work. The natural pools there flow with hot and cold water from springs that come straight out of deep subterranean aquifers. The water is both fresh and ancient.

INNER PILGRIMAGE #9: *Touch Water*

1. Submerge your body in water. While it is great to do this in the ocean, in a lake, river, or natural spring, you can do this at home in your bathtub. (If all you have is a shower, it's time to activate your imagination!)

2. Feel the water on your skin. Feel it touching the entire surface of your body. Stay for a moment with the experience of the water touching you all over. Let it in.

3. Now *reverse the experience*: now it is you who are touching the water. Touch it and feel that connection, not just with your hands but with every part of your body. Close your eyes and spend a couple of minutes touching the water with your entire skin surface.

4. Extend your senses into the water around you. Let your senses blend and elongate into the molecules of the water.

5. Call to mind that this very water that you are touching is but a tiny portion of the vast body of water that circulates throughout the earth.

6. Feel your way into that vast body of water. Extend your awareness out into the ocean or lake or river you are in. Extend it into the stream coming to you through the faucet of your bathtub (or up through the nozzle of your shower) into the pipeline from the reservoir that is fed by wells and springs coming up from ancient aquifers, underground lakes, and streams. Reflect on how all water is interconnected throughout the earth, existing in all its various states, from the water in your body to the flowing water of the planet's rivers, oceans, lakes and streams, to the water contained in glaciers and polar icecaps, and to the water of the endless cycles of vapor and clouds and rain. Water, water everywhere!

7. Through the water that is surrounding and permeating your body, reach out and touch *all water.*

8. Spend five to ten minutes with what comes up in you as you do this.

9. Take note of your experiences.

INNER PILGRIMAGE #10: *Touch Air, Breathe Sky*

1. This is a good one to try with no clothing on. Sitting or lying comfortably, feel the air that is touching your skin surface. Let it touch you all over. Stay with that sensation for a minute.

2. As in the previous exercise, reverse the sensation. Now it is *you* who are touching the air. Touch the air with your entire skin surface. Spend two minutes touching the air with your skin surface.

3. Bring your attention to the tip of your nose. Imagine for a moment that you are a tiny being, perched there, at the tip of your nose. From this vantage point, follow the movement of air into your body and back out.

4. Feel what happens as the air comes into your body, touching your inner spaces.

5. Move your awareness back to the surface of your body and again touch air.

6. Call to mind that you are touching a miniscule portion of the vast sea of air that makes up the atmosphere of our planet. You are breathing in bits of sky, aren't you? The very same air that is touching you is also touching everything and everyone on the surface of this planet. You are at this moment touching the same vast body of air, a piece of the same sky, as someone in Wichita, Kansas or Kuala Lampur! As consciously as you can, Touch this air that we all share.

7. Spend five to ten minutes with what comes forward in your consciousness. Don't analyze what comes.

8. Take note of your experiences.

INNER PILGRIMAGE #11: *Touch Earth*

You do this exercise the same way as you touched air and water:

1. Sit, stand or lie down comfortably.
2. Shift your awareness to what is supporting your body. Can you feel the Earth holding up the house or chair or tree that you are sitting in, or lying on?
3. *Reverse the sensation.* Now it is you who are touching earth. Send your awareness down into the earth. Can you extend your awareness deep into the earth and feel the enormous living globe we live on?
4. Tune in to *all that is solid,* all that is structural of the earth.
5. Spend five to ten minutes with what comes forward in your consciousness.
6. Take note of your experiences.

INNER PILGRIMAGE #12: *Touch Fire*

Same idea here, but instead of sticking your hand in the campfire in order to touch fire, try this:

1. Sit outside in the full sunlight with your eyes closed.
2. Feel what happens as the layers of your energy field peel open and allow the yellow, fiery energy of the sun to enter.
3. Imagine that you can pick out a single photon of the sun's light, one tiny particle of light. Remain focused on your little photon for a few moments before releasing it.
4. When you have released that single photon, widen your sight to the whole field of sunlight you are sitting in, all the trillions of photons around you.
5. Through these photons, Extend your awareness to the sun's energy as it enters all living bodies it touches. Stretch your awareness to the *fire within all substance.*
7. Spend five to ten minutes with what comes forward in your consciousness.
8. Take note of your experiences.

INNER PILGRIMAGE #13: *Of Roses, Dogs, and Gold*

This time, try linking your awareness with a substance, plant, animal, or mineral, and see if you can connect your awareness with its "larger body." This is much more than an abstraction or an exercise of your imagination and your ability to visualize, though it might start that way. In doing this, you are learning to shift your awareness from the seemingly isolated individual plant or animal to the greater whole of which it is a part at the energetic level. When you do that, you are teaching yourself to touch its *essence.*

As homeopath Asa Hershof says, "A rose is very rosy, and a dog is very doggy." The individual rose is part of the larger body of "rosedom." It partakes of "roseness," the same way that dogs partake of "dogness." And so, if you are connecting in this way with a rose, see if you can extend your awareness to "roseness," or the essence of rose. In this way, you become aware of their greater bodies and experience what it is that makes a rose distinct from a dog.

Let's try this idea out with something with a substance that has a distinct quality.

1. Find a piece of gold. It might be a gold ring on your finger or a piece of jewelry, a gold coin, or one of your great uncle's gold teeth, may he rest in peace, that you are wearing on a string around your neck.

2. Hold that piece of gold in your hand. Examine it closely with your eyes. Take in its color, its texture, its feel and qualities. Rub it. Taste it. Smell it. Take in its vibration with your senses. When you do this and truly get a feeling contact with your piece of gold, you are taking a vibrational sample of gold.

3. Put the piece of gold aside.

4. Now close your eyes. From the vibrational sampling you just gathered, create a field of gold vibration in the space in front of you. This is visualization, and then some. You are getting at the field of gold vibration, the particular frequency of gold, the energetic pattern of gold.

5. Spend some time with this field of gold vibration and see if you can feel it, the same way you did before with water, air, earth, and fire. In this way, you are touching all gold.

6. Concentrate this field of gold above your head.

7. Starting just above your Crown Center, bring this gold vibration down all around your body. You might imagine a whole paint bucket of liquid gold being slowly poured on your head and allowed to cover your entire body. Sit for a minute in this golden energy.

8. Now let go of this contact and choose one of the following words:
   • Protection
   • Attraction

9. Make a *feeling contact* with what the word you chose stands for to you

10. Release the word contact and take a period of five to ten minutes and allow what wants to come forward into your awareness to do so.

11. Take note of your experiences.

These exercises will expand your appreciation of holism and the larger body that you inhabit. The pilgrimage of energywork leads our inner spiritual traveler, step by step, out of the illusion that we are separate from the rest of life. At the level of energy and consciousness, we live as babushka dolls[12] nestled within each other, as Alexander Pope put it, "parts of one stupendous whole."

_____

12   Come to my Web site at http://www.jimgilkeson.com/ to see the beautiful babushka dolls painted by Pilgrim artist Aimee Eldridge. Instructions on how to find the Pilgrim Extras on my Web site are on the final page of this book.

## CHAPTER EIGHT

### CULTIVATING MINDFULNESS IN ENERGETIC PRACTICE AND SUBTLE BODYWORK

*Stay close and do
nothing.*
Attributed to
someone at the
San Francisco Zen Hospice

In energywork, you get to find out what happens when you make an energetic connection with yourself or another person and then pay attention in an engaged, openhearted way to what arises. In these practices and treatments, you spend a lot of time listening. You listen with your hands, with your whole body, with your heart. At first, this can seem tedious because it is almost the complete opposite of doing. But then you catch on to just how much takes place all by itself when you practice mindfulness in energywork, when you turn your caring awareness—attention with no strings attached—toward the small events that make up a meditation or healing session.

*Caring Attention =
Life Force + Consciousness +
Feeling =
Healing Potential*

In Buddhist and Vipassana meditation, mindfulness refers to a set of techniques in which you deliberately become non-judgmentally aware of your thoughts and actions. This sort of practice is imminently transferable to energywork and subtle bodywork when we apply the same strategy to what we perceive with our inner senses and with our hands. The use of mindfulness practice has been explored for years with wonderful results in Hakomi Body-Centered Psychotherapy, to name one example. Its efficacy in managing pain, stress, and depression have been well documented by researchers like Dr. Jon Kabat-Zinn, whom many people know from the PBS series *Healing and the Mind*.

Mindfulness opens up a wider field of consciousness

around what you're attending to. If your various techniques and modalities are the tools you wield, this mindful awareness is the room in which you work. In this environment, paradoxically, you are neither trying to make something happen nor are you trying to prevent anything from happening. Learning to be mindful in energywork is learning to be interested in life the way it is, things the way they are. It lies at the heart of listening and in the art of asking questions. I am reminded of the title of a new book by *Fresh Air* host Terry Gross, widely known as a great interviewer whose gift is her ability to elicit interesting, natural responses from her guests. Her book's title is *All I Did Was Ask,* and this says it in a nutshell. When you hear her talk, what comes across is a genuine interest, an unfaked, unmorbid curiosity about her guest. Who wouldn't open up and reveal themselves?

The same thing happens in your own personal inner work and in subtle bodywork. Mindfulness and true interest, even a kind of watchful, compassionate curiosity, help the other person to be more of who they are—though a word might never be spoken out loud. There is a process at hand, and you are watching it, listening to it, with interest as it unfolds; trusting it, though you really don't know the outcome. The trick is to become a benevolent stalker of the process at hand, awake, connected, interested, and mindful. Robert M. Pirsig, author of *Zen and the Art of Motorcycle Maintenance,* wrote about how to treat what comes to our attention when we meditate or inquire into something, and it applies to what comes up in our inner work and when we set our hands on another person in healing work. Here's what he had to say:

*It was a wonderful session! You knew exactly what not to do.*
Beverly Kune

> Just live with it for a while. Watch it the way you watch a line when fishing and before long, as sure as you live, you'll get a little nibble, a little fact asking in a timid, humble way if you're interested in it. That's the way the world keeps on happening. Be interested in it.
>
> At first try to understand this new fact not so much in terms of your big problem as for its own sake. That problem may not be as big as you think it is. And that fact may not be as small as you think it is. It may not be the fact you want but at least you should be very sure of that before you send the fact away. Often before you send it away you will discover it has friends who are right next to it and are watching to see what your response

is. Among the friends may be the exact fact you are looking for.

*Veterinarian Hands*

In energy healing, we aren't out fixing people, but rather meeting them at the deepest available level. It is out of that deep, intimate meeting that all else arises. If we are going to split hairs, there *is* an agenda in energetic healing work, but it is a very wide open, spacious agenda. We are not trying to determine specific outcomes or take away a symptom or make the other person "better" according to some standard or norm, but rather to connect compassionately and deeply with the process at hand and let things unfold as they unfold. You stay in the saddle and trust the horse to know the way back to the barn. Given space and a bit of support, human consciousness heads all by itself toward balance, healing, and wholeness. When you trust that, you can then be there to facilitate, which, as the word says, means to "make easier" the process. It's unheroic, but it's still a lot.

In therapeutic work, regardless of what style or modality you practice, when you get the *subconscious cooperation* of your treatment partner by creating a mindful, compassionate interface through your touch and presence, you are aligning yourself with the person's deep inner wisdom. If you don't have that alignment and cooperation, the whole undertaking suffers. When this all-important connection with your partner's deeper self is reached, you will likely find her falling into trust under your hands, like a horse that instinctively relaxes under the hands of a practiced veterinarian. When you meet your partner with "veterinarian hands," it sends a signal to the wisdom deep within her that you are trustworthy and willing to accompany her into places in her body and psyche that are wounded and fragile. Her inner wisdom will become active in some way, now that someone is actually following what's going on, perhaps providing the next tiny movement in her body, the emergence of a critical hidden memory, the connection of crucial dots of insight in her mind, the resolution of some unfinished business or the tipping point into needed emotional release. Whatever the manifestation, follow and support it, listening deeply as you go.

This is especially important where there is trauma. Going into a guarded place in your partner's body means also going into a guarded place in her psyche. Subconscious cooperation has to be earned. You have to be authentic in your desire to be present without imposing an agenda. If you are working to be gentle and noninvasive, and this doesn't truly extend to the attitude you carry, you'll be found out. The guarded psyche in your partner will pick up on this. Often, it gets back to your deeply held beliefs about what you are doing. If there is a hint of the kind of attitude that has to spring into action like a religious zealot in a barroom, roll up its sleeves, spit in its hands, and proclaim, "Okay, we're gonna whip you into shape in no time!" this can cause more sensitive and tender processes to go hide behind the moon. This kind of fixing attitude that some healers adopt, even though they might have no active agenda about it, will be detected and reacted to and can cause a shutdown of the process, at least temporarily. Alternatively, when you offer deep listening presence, your simplest therapeutic activities can have beautiful results. Your skilled touch becomes an arena in which the "work" is performed, not by you, and not by the surface consciousness of your treatment partner, but by forces much closer to the Creative Source residing within each of you.

Let's move now to some practices that will exercise your ability to come into this mindful state as you work with yourself and with a treatment partner.

INNER PILGRIMAGE #14: *The Starfish Exercise*

We'll start with a small exercise that helps the communication between your hands and your heart, a good step toward veterinarian hands. On the way, you will be working with the energy centers in your hands, your Heart Center, and also with the tiny energy centers in your fingertips.

Steps:

1. Sitting upright, make sure you are grounded and centered.

2. Bring your awareness into the center of your left palm and relax it there. Allow the energy-active position in your palm to become active and draw your awareness into itself. Give this a minute.

3. Release this contact and move your awareness slowly into your Heart Center. You can either move on the skin surface of your arm or in a slow, conscious line from your left Hand Center to your Heart Center. Allow this contact to deepen. Remember to let the energy center do the work of drawing your awareness into itself. Your job is to maintain a loose, relaxed focus. Give this Heart Center contact a minute before moving on.

4. Now release this contact and move your awareness, slowly, consciously, into the center of your right palm, again either on your skin surface or in a slow, straight line. Allow this energy center to respond to your awareness while you stay relaxed. Let this contact deepen for a minute.

5. From your right palm, move now back to the center of your left palm. Move slowly and consciously in the space between your hands. (If you move slowly, you'll find out that it is anything but empty!) Let this contact deepen for a minute.

6. Repeat steps two through five. Build the triangle one more time.

7. Sit for a minute and feel the triangle (Hand Centers and Heart Center) that you have traced.

8. Now move your awareness into both your right and left Hand Centers at the same time and allow that contact to build up.

9. From both of these active Hand Centers, slowly move your awareness outward, on the skin surface of your fingers and thumbs, to all your *fingertips at the same time.* Let the tiny energy centers in your fingertips respond to the presence of your relaxed awareness. After a minute or so, slowly move back to the center of your palms and let your awareness sink in there. Let this contact deepen for a minute.

10. Move with your awareness on the skin surface, back and forth between your hand centers and all ten of your fingertips. Take a moment each time to let your contact with your Hand Center and your fingertips deepen.

11. After three or four "commutes" between your Hand Centers and your fingertips, arrive back at your Hand Centers, release your contact, and sit quietly for five minutes, allowing whatever wants to come into your awareness to do so.

12. End the exercise.

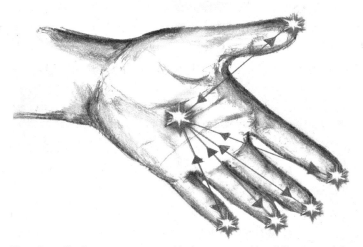

The strength of energy movement between your Hand Center and the little energy centers in your fingertips is enhanced with this exercise. This is a great exercise for healers who use their hands, because your Heart Center comes into a circulation with both hands.

This practice is a good way to open your hands energetically and bring them into alignment with your Heart Center. This is crucial when touching others, and a good step in developing "veterinarian hands." In line with that, let's move now to a couple of practices that teach you to move into a useful healing connection with a partner, and in the process find the right level of contact.

PARTNER TREATMENT #1: *"May I Come Closer?": An Exercise for Developing Deep Energetic Connection with a Partner*

In mindful, sensitive healing work, it is important to start out on the right foot when it comes to connecting those with whom who we work. The following practice helps you establish a trustworthy energetic link with your partner and open the pathways of silent communication between you. This promotes the kind of subconscious cooperation that will support all of your healing work. The fruit of this practice will be an increase in your mindfulness and your ability to find an effective interface and connection with your partner. We'll begin with the basic practice and then differentiate it.

Steps:
1. Start by momentarily disconnecting from your partner. You might take a step back from where your partner is sitting or lying. Close your eyes and take a *mental snapshot of your own body.* Do the same thing with your feelings and attitudes of the moment. This is a good way to increase your clarity when you finally enter your contact with your partner. It helps you to avoid the problem of over-blending and the resulting tendency for an unwanted transfer of energy from your partner.
2. With your partner either sitting or lying comfortably, begin by placing your hands at least two feet off your partner's body (palms facing your partner).
3. Though it is a nonphysical form of contact, try to feel that you are touching your partner, because, in reality, you are.
4. When you have contact, silently ask the question, "May I come closer?" and wait for an unspoken response under your hands. This might come as a feeling of opening or

relaxation in your partner's field, or a feeling that your hands are being magnetically drawn closer to your partner's body.

5.  Wait until you sense your partner's silent permission and then move your hands a bit closer and again ask the same silent question, "May I come closer?" See also the note below.

6.  Continue this silent question even after your hands are resting on your partner's body.

7.  With your hands resting on your partner's body, ask the question again, "May I come closer?" Listen with your hands to the unspoken response coming from your partner.

8.  Repeat this a number of times with your hands on your partner's body.

9.  Allow the energy of your hands and your sense of contact with your partner to gently penetrate deeper into your partner's body a little at a time.

> NOTE: Of course, you might not get a big resounding "Yes!" each time you ask, "May I come closer?" It is definitely possible to get a response that feels like "No!" or "Stop right there, please. Don't come any closer." In that case, don't jump ship, and by all means don't take it personally. Simply keep your hands and your mindful awareness right where they are. Most often, the resistance you encounter is not about you at all, but rather your partner's energy system saying, "I need you to be right there, where you are," or, "Please back off a bit." In either case, stay connected to your partner, but don't move in any closer. Instead, make the best, most mindful contact you can right where you are, and then when you feel a change, silently ask the question again, "May I come closer?" and see what happens.
>
> It could easily be that it takes some time for your partner's system to get used to you being there. Don't force anything.

Questions for You

1.  Did the act of internally asking permission to come closer make you more mindful of your partner?

2.  Did you sense a response from your partner when you posed the question silently?

3.  What differences did you feel as you moved slowly closer, asking permission each step of the way?

4.  Did your partner answer with a no at any point? What was your response?

5.  Did the no turn into a yes at some point?

6.  What happened when you finally made physical contact your partner?

7.  What was it like to slowly move deeper into your partner's body with your consciousness and the energetic penetration of your touch?

Levels of Touch

The previous exercise can help you to appreciate what can be gained by moving slowly and mindfully into your contact with your partner. Now it's time to differentiate your touch.

The teachings of Fritz Smith, MD, the developer of Zero Balancing, have provided me with two very useful insights into subtle touch that have shaped how I work in energy healing. The first of those insights is that some of the most important healing occurs when mindful, caring touch is brought to the juncture of the structure of your partner's body and the energy that flows through it. This means touching in such a way that you can place your awareness on *both structure and energy at the same time.*

The other insight is that our bodies and energetic systems organize themselves around the clearest and strongest impulses that they encounter. Falling on your tailbone, for example, definitely sets a strong and clear impulse. So is a surgical incision. So is a cutting comment from someone you love. No sooner is such a clear impulse set than your body and psyche begin to reorganize around it. What this suggests is that we can deliberately offer our treatment partners new, healthy impulses to replace the older, traumatically charged ones. In touch work your mindful, caring contact at the interface of structure and energy provides your partner's organism with a clear, strong new impulse around which it can reorganize. Here are some suggestions for putting these ideas to work as you approach your touch work, regardless of the bodywork or energywork modality you might use:

- *Touch Bone:* Once you have made your initial contact, slowly increase your pressure until you can feel your partner's skeleton with the bones of your skeleton—this is typically the bones of your fingertips, but the same applies to whatever part of your body you are using—for example, the bones of your forearm or elbow. See if you can be aware of both the structure of your partner's skeleton and the energy conducted by her bones at the same time, using no more force than what is necessary to connect consciously with the bone. Bring your awareness into this bone-to-bone interface between your partner's body and your body—and in so doing, become extraordinarily aware of where the bones of your fingertips end and your partner's skeleton starts.

- *Touch Soft Tissue:* Here, your contact is with the soft tissue of your partner's muscles, nerves, tendons and viscera. Where you had your connection with your partner's skeleton in the previous example, you now are working at the interface of structure and energy at the level of her fascia. This is the connective tissue that wraps and connects every fiber, bone, and organ in your body in a single contiguous piece. The fascia is a conductor for all kinds of impulses throughout your body. As a result, when you touch fascia with clear intention, you create an interface with a major communication system.

- *Touch Skin:* The skin surface is the meeting place between the inner and outer layers of the etheric, the part of the energy field that immediately surrounds and penetrates your physical body. The etheric is the storehouse of the subconscious, and it creates a bridge of communication between your body and the other dimensions of consciousness. Touching at the level of the skin surface in this way is another example of connection where structure meets energy. Again, you bring your mindful awareness to that point of contact.

- *Touch Aura:* Here, too, we have an opportunity to use subtle touch in a place where structure meets energy, albeit on a more subtle level than we had with our partner's skeleton, fascia, and skin surface. The main prerequisite is that you be able to consciously sense what you are touching. In your partner's aura, you will find that its subtle structure will present itself to you, as well as its energy movement.

PARTNER TREATMENT #2: *Differentiated Listening*

Here is an adaptation of an evaluation practice used in craniosacral work. The idea here is to school your ability to shift your attention among various aspects of the energy movement under your hands. This is a bit like teaching yourself to pick out individual instruments in a band or orchestra and following them for a while through a piece of music. Not only is this a way to allow differentiated impressions to come to you from your partner, it is a good method of staying energetically engaged and deepening that connection. This will also help you to stay "in the saddle" if your attention starts to wander.

Steps:
1. Choose a pair of energy-active positions, one on each side of your partner's body. A good choice for this deep listening exercise would be your partner's Shoulder Points, located at the corner of your partner's shoulders, where her collarbones meet her shoulder blades. Move into your contact gradually (you might want to repeat the practice of "May I come closer?" to make your contact): simply place the center of your palm lightly on each of these positions. This allows the energy centers in your palms to interact with your partner's shoulder points.
2. Once you have made a good energetic connection with your partner, spend a bit of time simply paying attention to the natural exchange of energy between your hands.

Here are few tasks to perform with your awareness as you "listen" with your hands. In essence, they amount to asking a number of questions of your partner's energies and then sensing what comes back to you. As you shift from one question to the next, you get a slightly different angle or perspective on the same basic energetic event. It is important to remember that none of this is about comparing your partner's energy activity to some kind of norm or about superimposing how you think their energy movement ought to be. It is about staying connected and aware of what's taking place, all by itself, under your hands. Remember, you are neither trying to change what is happening under your hands, nor are you trying to keep anything from changing. Keyword: mindfulness. Try this:

After making a good energetic contact with your partner's shoulder points:
1. Compare the energy activity at the right and left shoulder points, one with the other.
   • How *alike or unlike* are they?
   • Is one *stronger* than the other?
   • Are they doing the same "dance?" Is one trying to do the rumba while the other is doing a waltz?
2. See if the energetic activity on one side connects, or interacts, in some way with the other side. Ask yourself:
   • Are they *in synch or out of synch with one another*?
   • Do they pulse together, ripple, or ping-pong back and forth?
   It could be that they aren't talking or dancing with each other when you first arrive. Stay tuned and mindful and see if they don't begin to "find" each other as your sensing progresses.
3. Now switch your awareness to the sensation of energy movement under your hands and ask yourself: "How *vital* is the energy activity?" See what impressions come to you about your partner's vitality. This can give you a read on how much vital energy is available for your partner's healing process. When there is lots of life force available, your partner is more likely to move through her process more quickly than if she is depleted.

4. Switch your awareness to the speed of the energy pulsation under your hands and ask yourself, "How *fast* is the energy activity?" Again, the idea here is not to measure the speed of the activity or compare it to a norm, but rather to place your awareness on this specific aspect of the energy movement.

5. Ask yourself, "How big and expansive, or small and contained, is the movement?"

6. Ask yourself, "Where is this energy *concentrated*?" Check to see if there is a noticeable concentration of energy:
   - In your partner's bones: do they feel heavy or charged up?
   - In her soft tissue: are her muscles tight, held or charged up?
   - At her skin surface: does her skin surface feel active or charged up?
   - Off her body: do you run into concentrations of charge or activity in her aura?

7. Ask yourself, "What is this energy like?" Here, you are opening yourself up to the qualities of your partner's energy. Go ahead and let your subjectivity have its say! Is it lively and free, gray, feeble, bright, scattered, muddled, murky, clear, salty, bossy, stuck, open, empty? Does it feel like snow sifting silently through soft, sensuous azure-colored silk scarves, or does it feel like a dead dinosaur rotting at the bottom of a frozen lake? You're not necessarily telling your partner all the wonderful subjective impressions you come up with; the idea here is to open the door to qualities the way they come while continuing to stay connected and keep listening.

8. Ask yourself what kind of composite "snapshot" of your partner's energetic movement you gained from your differentiated listening. What changed all by itself in the act of listening?

*"Alien Communication": Meeting, Mirroring, Matching, Mimicking in Energetic Bodywork*
Energy-active bodywork takes place in a cocoon of mindful presence. You not only listen with your ears, but with your whole sensorium, which is to say with the entire sensory and intuitive world that brings impressions into your awareness. When you have truly connected with your partner, follow her spontaneous, involuntary movements. These are part of the language of her subconscious. If she scratches her nose, great, but that would be a voluntary, intentional movement and not the kind of movement that is meant here. Spontaneous movements might be gross movements of her gross anatomy, but quite often they are the tiny internal micromovements that she might be barely aware of. Following these tiny movements is a way to enter a subtle process of communication with your partner. This is how you learn to speak the language of mirroring, mimicking, and following movement in your partner's body and energy field. This seems to be one of the most basic ways that we humans (and other sentient beings) have of communicating.

Imagine yourself confronted with an extraterrestrial who has stepped out of a spaceship and is now standing in front of you. Not threatening, not fear inducing, just another sentient being, like you, who is in your presence as you are in its presence. When you have gotten over the initial shock and oddity of having an alien standing in front of you, the thought comes that the alien must also be having some of the same feelings of strangeness at finding itself confronted with the likes of you.

So there you are. You both see each other. You both wonder if you can communicate, but you have no common language. What next? Slowly, for lack of anything else to do, you raise a hand, and as you do so, the alien slowly raises a hand. You let your hand down, and down goes the alien's hand. Up goes your hand again. This time you stick your index finger in the air, and in response the alien does the same. This time the alien tick-tocks his finger back and forth, and in response you tick-tock yours too. You are both charmed, utterly taken with the novelty of this

94

and before you know it, you find yourselves playing together, making tick-tocking fingers, peace signs, and childish shapes of animals from your respective planets. A rudimentary trust grows between you; the alien takes a timid step toward you and, in the magic of the moment, you forget to be afraid; you also take a step toward the alien. By and by, you touch hands, palm to palm, and begin to move together. Bit by bit the two of you meet and get to know each other in a dance of mirroring and mimicking each other's moves.

Something like this fanciful scenario takes place between you and your partner when you do subtle bodywork. One of the safest, most effective ways to gain the subconscious cooperation of a partner is to take up a relaxed touch contact and follow the internal micromovements of his or her body. These tiny spontaneous, involuntary movements create a doorway into processes below the threshold of consciousness. To contact these tiny movements and gestures, and move with them in such a literal yet elegant way is to take up a dialogue with your partner that doesn't depend on words. In that encounter, you allow another side of your partner to speak in a language that is both subtle and direct. To skillfully dance with this deeper dynamic can often lead to moments when you partner's subconscious, like the alien you've learned to dance with, realizes that you are actually catching on to what it is trying to do. This is like the shocking moment when both you and the extraterrestrial realize, "Oh my God! It's trying to communicate with me!" When you neither force yourself on your partner, nor abandon her, but rather make yourself available at the cusp of structure and energy through touch, you are in position to support and facilitate what is trying to happen under the surface. The subtle movement is not just physical, but also in the psyche, which is very connected to your partner's natural subconscious tendency toward healing, balance, and wholeness. By moving with your partner, you are demonstrating to your partner's subconscious world that you get it, with the result that you are both led into the deeper underlying process.

*When we encounter another through touch we step consciously into nature's web.*
Diane Tegtmeier

PARTNER TREATMENT #3: *Following Tissue Movement: "Alien Communication" with Your Partner*
The practice of following tiny movements in your partner's body shows up in many subtle bodywork forms. The idea receives a lot of emphasis in craniosacral work, for example, because it focuses on the slow, barely visible dance of the skeleton and the fluid and energetic tides within the head and spine. As we follow subtle movement like this, we are doing it where the

body's structure meets the vital energy that enlivens it. Engaging your partner's body and closely following its micromovements in this way, sometimes mirroring, matching, mimicking, but in all cases *meeting* it, is part of what it means to use the physical body as a "handle" on a larger, deeper process. Let's try it.

With a partner who is either sitting or lying comfortably:

1. Take a moment to center yourself.
2. Slowly place your hands on your partner's body. You may want to use the practice of "May I come closer?" to establish a good energetic contact.
3. *Touch bone.* By that, I mean make your physical contact deep enough that you can feel your partner's skeleton with the bony structure of your hand. Your touch should be deep enough to feel the bone without losing your sense of energetic connection. After your initial contact, quite often you can lighten your touch. This takes practice, but you'll know it when you've got it.
4. Relax and invite the subtle movement of your partner's skeleton into your hands.
5. Follow the movement physically, and track it with your awareness. See if you can do it without forcing it to do anything. Yes, the fact of your following, matching and mirroring what your partner's body does will tend to enhance and slightly exaggerate the movement. That's okay. It's like a conversation between two people: the movement in your partner is like one person making a statement, and the other responding with, "Oh, really? Tell me more." This gets you deeper into the underlying process.
6. Give this process ten minutes.
7. Release your contact and take note of what happened. Compare notes with your partner.

The practice of mindfulness is the key to developing a listening, nonjudging heart and relaxed, alert awareness that serves every phase of the inner pilgrimage. In addition, it is essential for developing trustworthy "veterinarian hands" for doing energy-active bodywork. Let's turn now to another perennial theme of energywork, one that works hand-in-glove with the principle of mindfulness.

# CHAPTER NINE

## CENTERING

*Behold, I am here, Lord.*
Ananias,
the initiator of Saul of Tarsus[13]

Centering is any intentional practice that brings you into a mindful state. When you find your calm center, you reconnect to your essence and your source of energy, clarity, and peace. Practices may be as simple as placing your attention on your breath or a sacred word and then returning there ever so gently whenever you notice your mind wandering. It can be done while sitting in meditation or when you are active. Centering may also be another way of expressing the need to be right where you are, and to do what you do from your heart and the core of your being. Examples of centering practices are found in Buddhist Vipassana and Christian contemplative traditions.

One of the great obstacles to centering is our tendency to leave pieces of ourselves strewn about the emotional and psycho-spiritual landscape. Look at what happens to people's hearts, for example. Janis Joplin urged her lover to "take another little piece" of hers. Tony Bennett left his in San Francisco. The problem only begins with where we leave our hearts. Over the course of a lifetime we get involved, energetically and spiritually, with all kinds of people, ideas, passions, projects, hopes, fears. These are errands from which our energies often need to be called back into the present moment.

Having your energies scattered out like this—and therefore unavailable to you—is like initiating a number of automatic withdrawals at the bank, and then forgetting about them. Time passes, and then one day when you are about to launch a new project, you take a good look at your bank statement and realize you're broke! Then it is time to stop this unconscious leakage of your resources. In the case of your vital energies and your spirit, it's time to reel them back in. This is so important because many of the challenges in your life, especially those having to do with your healing and personal development, demand that you have your energies available to you in the present moment.

INNER PILGRIMAGE #15: *Calling Your Spirit Back (The Basic Exercise)*
In *Energy Healing: A Practice to Inner Growth*, I described a deceptively simple exercise that

---

13    The scene is described in the ninth chapter of Acts. Ananias is told by Christ to find Saul, who has been blinded by their encounter on the road to Damascus. Ananias then goes and lays his hands on Saul, whereupon the "scales fell from his eyes," an esoteric reference to initiation.

I consider a great prelude to any kind of energetic or spiritual practice. I called it *Mindfully Disconnecting From What Has Your Attention*. The exercise consists of sitting in a meditative state of mind, simply taking note of where your attention goes all by itself, then intentionally disconnecting from whatever is holding your awareness, and drawing back to yourself the life force you have invested in worries, preoccupations, habits, fears, old injuries and injustices, old loves, something someone said yesterday, anticipation of a vacation, worries about money, and all your other kinds of internal projects.

Here is the basic exercise for mindfully disconnecting from what has your attention and calling your spirit back to yourself:

1. Sit quietly and notice where your attention is. Watch where your attention goes. Don't try to change it. Don't try to keep it from changing. Give this a couple of minutes. Just observe. Don't judge.

2. When you see where your attention and energy are invested, try this: say, within yourself, "I call my spirit back." You have the authority and the power to do this. disconnect from this focus and draw your attention back to your body. This is a place to use creative visualization. Here are some suggestions:

   - Imagine an electric cord plugged into the image or thought which has your attention. Now unplug from that image and pull the cord into your body.
   - Imagine a rope tied with many knots around what has your attention. Now see the knots loosen, untie, or slip apart. Pull the rope into your body.
   - Imagine a tentacle, like those of an octopus, with suction cups latched on to something. See the suction cups detach. Draw the tentacle back to you.
   - As you repeat this practice of noticing where your attention is and then calling your spirit back to you, take note of where it returns to on your body.

3. Repeat this five or six times.

   NOTE: Like any other exercise or practice involving our energies and spirit, this takes practice, honesty, and time. Do not naïvely assume that "pulling the plug" a few times in a visualization means that you have resolved a long-standing issue. In most cases, our spirits have been scattered to the four winds over a long period of time, and we call them back little by little, one grain at a time.

As you call your spirit back and actually find it returning to you, you will also find a return of your vitality and clarity of purpose taking place. Other things might also happen: it's not uncommon for a significant return of spirit to yourself to trigger a season of reorganization and a sorting out of big and small things in your life. Once, in a healing session, a woman told me that her sacrum didn't feel like it was hers. She had been working with this practice of calling her spirit back in general, and I suggested that she do it with this specific part of her body. In the course of calling her spirit back to her sacrum, she awoke to the distinct sensation that she had her mother's sacrum instead of her own, whereupon we set out to retrieve her sacrum and put it back where it belonged. What started out as a fanciful visualization practice took a real turn as she realized how she had been carrying her mother since she was a little girl. By and by, she called her spirit back and sent her mother's sacrum back to her, where it belonged, and felt a new strength return to her.

Calling your spirit back to you and, in the process, cultivating your center will also give you some important clues to what is going on with the pilgrim on your treatment table, in your counseling office, or in casual conversation. In my practice, when a healing partner is unable to find the juice required to meet the challenges that life is presenting to her, I get curious about where her energy is going. I look to see if she is constantly being dragged out of her center, into the past or the future, into repetitive patterns or obsessive thought-spirals about old pains, external events, and other people. It indicates the need for her to come to center and find her way back into the present.

Being mindful and centered in yourself is the first thing you can do for the spiritual traveler who comes to you for help. It will add clarity to the words you speak, deepen your listening, and bring the indispensable quality of presence to your touch. In healing work, the clear intent and mindful presence in your touch can provide your partner with a whole new point around which to reorganize. Your practice of centering is a key.

*Beyond the Basic Exercise*

You can use the basic pattern of the above exercise to call your spirit back to your body, or any part of it. It is a good thing to do when you are injured or ill, or in the time after an operation. The basic exercise of calling your spirit back to you can also be done with each of your individual energy centers. It makes sense to do this because each of these centers of energy and consciousness registers and stores experiences in its own way. Directing your attention to one of your energy centers, and allowing this contact to intensify, may well show you where you have been hanging out spiritually, behind the scenes. The themes and issues of each energy center will suggest ways in which you have extended, and over-extended yourself. And they offer important clues to how we send our spirits and energies out and then forget to call them back.

Inner Pilgrimage #16: *Calling Your Spirit Back to Your Heart Center*

Your Heart Center is a meeting point between your upper and lower energy centers, and it has its mysterious way of blending together what comes from within you with the world and people around you. Often, the first step on the path of finding your calling—or, more appropriately, being found by it—is to find out where your heart is. Here is an adaptation of our basic practice:

1. Settle into a comfortable sitting position. In the words of poet Mark Nepo, "Inhale, and whatever you're running from, let it catch up with you."
2. First make a feeling contact with your Heart Center. This position is in the center of your chest. Remember, it is not enough to simply think about or even visualize an energy center. Here, you are making a feeling contact with this area at about the level of your skin surface. See if you can relax your attention and simply allow your awareness to be drawn into your Heart Center and let it do the work of drawing your awareness into itself.
3. Allow some time for the contact to intensify.

4. Bring to mind one of the aspects of the Heart Center. Words that link you in a feeling way to aspects of a particular energy center can be like stones you can lift and discover what is hiding under them. Here, you make a *feeling contact* with what the word stands for in you. In a practice like this, words can be used to evoke something in yourself, and then pay attention to what is evoked.

 Here are some "stones" to lift up as you call your spirit back to your Heart Center. Try these one at a time and give them a bit of time:
   - Sorrow
   - Joy
   - Connection with others
   - Compassion

5. Choose one of these words and get a feeling contact with what that word or phrase stands for with you.

6. Let this contact draw you into some kind of experience. Give this a couple of minutes.

> NOTE: Bear in mind that experience that comes up might
> be the *opposite* of what you started with. For instance, if you
> connect with your Heart Center, and then choose the word
> "joy" and make a feeling contact with what the means to you,
> you might be drawn into its opposite, "sorrow." This is a natural
> occurrence, since your Heart Center contains both polarities,
> and both are there to be explored. You don't have one without
> the other. Let this happen.

7. Call your spirit back to you and see if you can feel where in your body the energy returns to.

8. Allow some time for whatever wants to surface within you without judging what comes.

9. After about ten minutes, return to a normal sense of your body and end the exercise.

This exercise is an example of centering yourself and calling your spirit back to yourself in a very specific way. As we move on to more of the perennial themes of energywork, watch for variations of the practice you have just done with your Heart Center using your other energy centers.

# CHAPTER TEN

## FOUNDATION AND
## THE DOORWAY DOWNWARD

*Many people remember the newspaper comic strip B.C., by Johnny Hart. One of my favorite B.C. cartoons starts with one of the characters looking up at another character who is busy laying bricks while suspended in the air.*
*"What are you doing?" asks the one standing on the ground.*
*"Building a wall," says the other. "Why do you ask?"*
*"Just curious. All the pros start at the bottom."*

If there are *super-perennials* among the perennial themes of energywork, grounding is one of them. It begins with the need to be at home in your body and in a good energetic exchange with the earth, extends to your physical and psycho-spiritual foundation, and reflects into your environmental and social sphere. In this chapter, we're going to examine what this means for you and, if you work with others, for your treatment partners.

*Becoming a Grounded Person*
In classes, I sometimes hear beginning students say things like, "I felt strange while I was giving that treatment. I guess I forgot to ground myself." This gives the impression that grounding is something you do once in a while, just before you give someone a healing treatment, and the rest of the time it's kind of optional. This is a bit like the person who folds his hands and gets off a quick prayer or two a few minutes before dying, but otherwise lives without much conscious spirituality at all. There are problems with this approach, both to spiritual life and to being a healer.

Grounding is about much more than a set of tactics for *earthing* yourself, though that is an important and necessary starting point. Your involvement with exercises and practices that enliven your connection with your lower body and the earth will definitely help you feel more rooted and stable, but they are the beginning, rather than the end, of the story of grounding. Behind the scenes of all the conscious work you do to ground yourself, there are other, bigger stories unfolding. One of them is your relationship to everyday life and your ability to be present in what you do. Another, the biggest of them all, has to do with the long work of settling deeply into your true identity. Becoming a grounded person means having found yourself in the ground of all being, the ongoing work and realization of a lifetime. Stepping in this direction involves one of the great paradoxes of spiritual life: when it comes to opening your consciousness to higher dimensions, it is often the case that *down* is *up*.

*Downward Mobility*

For any number of reasons, many of them having to do with the way we are trained during childhood in matters of sexuality, hygiene, self-image, and modesty, a lot of us have a hard time bringing our awareness below our beltlines in more than an external, superficial way. When it comes to energetic movement, emotional expression, and sensitivity, many of us are significantly absent from our lower bodies. When this absence is combined with ideas of spirituality that tend to glorify only transcendence and the functions of the upper centers of consciousness, it can create a disconnection from much that is vital and juicy about being alive. This disconnection comes at the expense of a conscious inner life that extends to our lower energy centers, and it can unnecessarily hinder our sense of joy, grounding, sexuality, creativity, and relatedness to life. The importance of inhabiting your lower body applies doubly to you if you feel called to learn the essentials of energy healing.

*All this preoccupation with the upper chakras casts a shadow over the lower chakras, which are then sometimes forced to skywrite their plight in dreams of orgies and overflowing toilets.*

Energy Healing:
A Pathway to Inner Growth

Counterintuitive though it may seem on the surface, a spirituality without the "base note" of your lower centers of consciousness quickly becomes otherworldly and disconnected from everyday life. If you discover that your lower centers—Perineal, Sacral, Hara, and Solar Plexus—have been relegated to stepchild status, either because of a bias in your ideas about spirituality, or simply because you know instinctively that they will challenge you if you go there, I hope the exercises in this book will give you a means of meeting that challenge. Your spiritual life will benefit greatly from work with your lower centers. With this in mind, let's begin our practice of calling our spirits back into our entire lower body, starting with a deceptively simple inner pilgrimage.

Inner Pilgrimage #17: *Calling Your Spirit Back Below Your Beltline*

1. Sit comfortably in an upright position. Make sure you are not cramped in any part of your body and can breathe easily.
2. Drop your awareness into your lower body, below your navel. Feel your lower abdomen from the inside. Extend your feeling to your pelvis, sacrum, coccyx, and all the organs inside. Include your pubic bone and genitals, perineum, and anus.

Relax the best you can in this awareness of your entire lower body.

3.  Simply breathe consciously, practice mindfulness, and allow the feelings that arise within you to come into your awareness. *You are not trying to make anything happen, and you and not trying to keep anything from happening.* Allow the feelings, images and thoughts to come without editing or judging them. They might be emotional, sexual, childish or unusual in nature. Just let them be that, if that is what they are. Give this about five minutes.
4.  Release yourself from this contact and end the exercise.
5.  Try this practice of sitting with your relaxed awareness in your lower body every day for a week. Start with five minutes and gradually extending the period to ten minutes per sitting.
6.  Take note of what comes up in you.

This simple exercise can get the ball rolling toward increased aliveness in your lower body. If you have been living most of your life in your head and upper body—and that means most of us—truly coming consciously into your lower body, even for a minute, will feel like going skinny-dipping in the unknown. When you have worked with this exercise for a while and get so that your lower body and energy centers really wake up and smell the coffee, you will feel the return of your vitality and creativity as well as the quickening of your spirituality and intuition.

INNER PILGRIMAGE #18: *The Etheric Diaper: A Lower Body Pilgrimage*
The idea of this inner pilgrimage is to bring about a harmonious energetic activation of your lower body. We will start by bringing awareness to our lower centers of consciousness, and then introduce a specific color into these centers.

> PLEASE NOTE: This exercise can be quite activating (that's the point!), depending on the quality and depth of the energetic contact you are able to make with your lower body and the areas of your psyche associated with it. Like any energy exercise, this one will tend to bring things into your awareness that have been in the background, maybe for a long time. This works best if you go slow and observe the times designated for each step.

Preparation: Setting Up the Exercise:
*   Read through all the following exercise instructions and make sure you understand them clearly.
*   Sit upright, either on a chair or on the ground. It's okay to use a cushion.
*   *Locate your seventh thoracic vertebra.* This is the vertebral connection for your Solar Plexus Center. Make sure you know where it is because we will be using it in the exercise. This isn't hard to do. Just put your finger on the highest point of your upper abdomen, on the soft tissue just below the bony structure of your sternum, between the sides of your ribcage. The seventh thoracic vertebra is in the middle of your back, straight back from this position
*   *Color:* We will be using a reddish-yellow color in this exercise. If you have access to it, the exact color for this is Pantone #122 reddish yellow. If you don't have Pantone color

sheets, find a photo of a California poppy, which approximates this color. Or, better yet, if you happen to have a live California poppy, you can set the real thing in front of you. You'll refer to this reddish yellow color during the exercise.

- *Music:* Have some music ready to play at the end of this exercise. Find something that you like to move to.

Part 1: Circulation

1. When you are comfortable, move your awareness to the contact position for your Solar Plexus Center. This is located three finger-breadths above your navel on the front of your body. As in all work with energy-active positions on your body, you will want to make a relaxed, loose contact with this position. It helps to direct your breathing into the position. When making a feeling contact with an energy-active position, you keep your attention loose.

2. Allow about two minutes for this first contact to intensify.

3. Now, begin a slow circulation as follows: slowly move your awareness on your skin surface down the midline of your body in a swath a couple of inches wide: over your navel, lower abdomen, pubic bones, over your genitals, perineum, anus, up the back of your body, and over your sacrum and lower spine until you reach your seventh thoracic vertebra in the middle of your back.

4. Pause a moment at your seventh thoracic vertebra, allowing that contact to build.

5. Now, branch your awareness out in both directions, following the line of your ribs around to the front of your body, ending where you started at the Solar Plexus Center, three finger-breadths above your navel. Rest there a minute.

6. Repeat this slow circulation a couple of times, moving your awareness on your skin surface. Finish at the Solar Plexus Center position. Spend five minutes with this circulation.

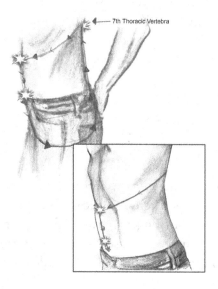

This exercise activates and blends the activity of your Solar Plexus, Hara, Perineal, and Sacral Centers.

Part 2: Add Color
1. (The reddish-yellow color should be in front of you, where you can see it, in the form of either a colored sheet of paper or a California poppy.) Disconnect your awareness from your Solar Plexus and open your eyes.
2. Look at the reddish yellow color and link your awareness with it. In this way, you take a vibrational "sample" of this color frequency.
3. Close your eyes now and visualize a field of reddish-yellow color in front of you.
4. Wrap your entire lower body in this color. Put on reddish yellow "etheric diapers."

   NOTE: When you use color this way in your energy field, *it will probably change to another color* at some point. Let that happen.

5. Give this some time and then repeat this step a time or two by reconnecting with the reddish yellow color and again "diapering" your lower body. Spend about five minutes with this phase.

Part 3: Call Your Spirit Back to Your Lower Body
1. Disconnect your awareness from the color and the circulations.
2. Call your spirit back to your lower body. You do this exactly the same way you did with your Heart Center in the previous chapter. The simplest way is to internally use words to the effect of "I call my spirit back." It helps to use visualizations like the electric cord unplugging and returning to the vacuum cleaner, and then see where on your body you feel energy returning to you. This can be very helpful in understanding your process.
3. After calling your spirit back to your lower body a number of times and noticing where the energy returns, sit quietly. Give yourself a period of five to ten minutes to allow whatever wants to come into your awareness to do so. Here, it is important not to judge or analyze what comes. Just allow yourself to feel what comes. Let the imagery and thoughts and sensations to move through. Pay attention and stay connected in a feeling way.
4. Disconnect from the exercise and put on some music and dance or move your body.
5. Take some notes on your experience.

It's time now to explore two energy-active positions in our bodies that are constant players in the project of becoming a grounded person.

*Perineum: The "Doorway Downward"*
One of my favorite characters in the energywork scene is the French-Canadian qigong master, Daniel Tallifer. He truly understands the first rule of teaching, which is "First, entertain." His classes are great fun, and they often begin with a session of perineum self-massage (which would look pretty outrageous to an uninitiated casual observer), followed by a round of tightening and releasing this muscle located between your anus and genitals in order to step up awareness and energetic activity there. Actually, people really like to massage and squeeze their perineums; they just don't always know it when they first start. During the exercise, Daniel urges participants to really *tighten* their perineums ("Just a bit longer, please … *crack a nut!*") and then release the

muscle. It just goes to show that you can get folks to do just about anything if you are a rascally guy with a French accent.

At some point in the proceedings, Daniel demonstrates what it is like to be rooted to the ground by inviting the largest man in the group to try and push him over. Once, a man about twice Daniel's size came forward and leaned into him, giving it all he had, to no avail. Daniel simply directed the energy of the man's push down into the ground. The more the man pushed, the more Daniel relaxed and allowed the force to move through him. He was rooted like a tree.

This is all very impressive and entertaining to watch, and once you get the hang of it, it isn't all that difficult to learn to relax into this kind of rootedness and become very hard to push over. The serious heart of this has to do with the fact that with some practice the energy-active center at the perineum sets us up with a vital energetic exchange with the earth. As we root ourselves more and more reliably, we are better able to draw the earth's energies upward, into our bodies. In addition, our Perineal Center becomes the *doorway downward* that enables us to release energy downward, into the earth. All of these blessings—the comfort, support, and safety of a conscious, living link with the earth—are among the fruits of grounding. Your repertoire of energetic and spiritual practices is incomplete if it does not include some basic ways to work with your perineum and Perineal Center. Here is a simple bouquet of exercises for your perineum and Perineal Center that includes a few winks from qi gong master Daniel (*Merci, mon frère!*):

INNER PILGRIMAGE #19: *Finding the* Doorway Downward
Part 1: Self-Massage for Your Perineum
There are a couple of ways to go:

- *The Direct Approach:* Standing with your feet about shoulder-width apart, bend your knees slightly. With the fingertips of one or both hands, massage your perineum, the muscle between your anus and genitals.

- *Use a Tennis Ball:* Sit on the floor with a tennis ball under your perineum. Roll on it with tiny movements and allow it to massage the muscle of your perineum.

*Five Zones*
Whether you use your fingertips or a tennis ball, try to give your perineum a good, thorough massage. There are five zones of your perineum to which you will want to pay particular attention:

- Front, toward your genitals

- Middle

- Both sides, to the right and left of the center

- Back, toward your anus

Spend several minutes with your perineal massage. Like any muscle, your perineum will benefit from increased fluid movement in its tissues. Circular movements with a fair amount of pressure will reward you with a feeling of increased vitality.

Once you have completed your self-massage of your perineum, it's time to increase the tone of the muscle.

Part 2: As Daniel Says, "Crack a Nut!"

Steps:

1. Stand with your feet about shoulder-width and bend your knees a bit, making sure your feet are well rooted.

2. Drop your awareness down into your perineum.

3. Breathe in sharply and hold your breath; as you breathe in, tighten your perineum, too. Hold it.

4. Take in more air and hold it; tighten your perineum some more. Hold it.

5. Do it one more time. More air … and yes, "crack a nut" with your perineum.

6. Now release the air in your lungs and release your perineum. And very important: Direct the energy of this release downward, into the earth, not upward into your head.

7. Repeat Steps two through five a number of times.

8. Stop and relax. Enjoy the energy movement in your body.

Part 3: Bounce It All Down

By now, your perineum should be pretty toned up and energetically active. The idea here is to bounce your energy down into the ground, down your legs, and out your heels and feet, and down through your perineum in the direction of your energetic South Pole. Here we go:

Steps:

1. Still standing with your feet about shoulder-width, bend your knees a bit, making sure your feet are well rooted. Begin a small bounce-bounce-bounce with your body. have most of your weight on your heels. Feel the vibration of the bounce through your entire body. Get everything moving!

2. *Visualization:* Bring your awareness to your perineum and visualize a doorway downward opening at your perineum, legs and feet. This doorway downward is how energy moves down, down, down, through your body, into the earth. Everything that your heel-bouncing shakes loose—tensions, pains, thoughts, emotions—drops down through the *doorway downward* into the earth.

3. Bring your awareness and the vibration of your heel-bouncing into each part of your body in its turn, to let it discharge its emotions and excess energy through the *doorway downward*.

   - Your toes and feet
   - Ankles (all your joints will be grateful for this)
   - Lower legs
   - Knees
   - Thighs
   - Groin on both sides
   - Genitals, testicles, ovaries
   - Pubic bone
   - Pelvis and sacrum
   - Lower abdomen

- Lower back
- Navel
- Upper abdomen
- All internal organs in your abdomen
- Rib cage and lungs
- Fingers and hands
- Wrists
- Lower arms
- Elbows
- Upper arms
- Shoulders
- Neck and throat
- Lower jaw
- Tongue
- Mouth and lips
- Teeth (make 'em rattle!)
- Face (it's amazing what we hold in our faces)
- Skull and brain
- Scalp and hair
- The thoughts in your head
- The energy around your head (shake it all down)

4. Stop bouncing and settle.
5. Stand or sit comfortably and enjoy the sensations in your body.

Part 4: Call Your Spirit Back to Your Perineal Center
Steps:
1. Sit down and settle in.
2. Bring your awareness to your Perineal Center and allow that contact to relax and deepen. As you do this, your awareness will be drawn into the activity of this energy center. Stay with this contact for a minute.
3. Release this contact and drop with your awareness down to your energetic South Pole which will feel like it is about three feet (one meter) in the floor or ground below you. Relax your awareness into this contact and give it a minute.
4. Move your awareness back and forth a number of times between your Perineal Center and your energetic South Pole, stopping briefly at each of these positions to allow your contact to deepen.
5. Return your awareness to your Perineal Center.
6. Call your spirit back to your Perineal Center, using the same steps as you used in previous exercises.
7. Release this contact and sit quietly, allowing what arises within you to do so—ten minutes.
8. End the exercise.

Getting to know your perineum physically and energetically can be one of the great surprises in learning energywork. For the pilgrim in your body, this journey to the South is a source of strength, support, and great healing.

*Holy Bone:* Os Sacrum

Let's turn now to one of the most fascinating positions in our bodies, the sacrum, a critical juncture of structure, energy, and consciousness. For me, the fascination begins with how it is named.

We who live in the West have inherited a scientific language of the body from our European forebears of the Renaissance. Discounting parts of the human body named after their discoverers, we have an anatomical language, much of it derived from Latin and Greek, that opens a little window on a bygone worldview. Quite often the shape of a body part suggested its name. All the anatomical names with the suffix *-oid*, for example, tell us that it is "like" this or that. The *rhomboid* muscle is shaped like a diamond, rhombus-like. The *ethmoid* bone right behind the bridge of your nose is perforated with holes, giving it a name which means "sieve-like." The name in Japanese for the beautiful *sphenoid* bone behind your eyes literally means "butterfly bone." It gets its more prosaic name in the West from its wedge-like shape. Ovaries are named after eggs (*ovum* in Latin) and the word "uvula," the name of the tiny pendulum of flesh at the back of your mouth, is Latin for "little grape." The pituitary gland sits regally ensconced in a cradling structure in the *sphenoid* bone known as the *sella turcica*, Latin for the "Turk's saddle." The long bones in your hands and feet are called *phalanges* because they line up side by side like the phalanxes of a military formation. Your collarbone is also called the *clavicle*, which comes from the Latin word for "little key," and your *scapula's* name has the same root as the word "scalpel," which comes from the Latin word for "blade." *Coccyx* is Greek for "cuckoo," and those who named it for us obviously saw that little bird's beak in the shape of our tailbones. At the other end of your backbone, up in your cervical spine, names are both mundane and divine: your second cervical vertebra, the *axis*, is named for its job (it turns), while your first cervical vertebra, the *atlas*, is named after a Greek god whose job it was to hold up the world.

In these bodies of ours, with cuckoos at one end and Greek gods at the other, it is usually easy to associate the names we have received from these early anatomists with some kind of meaning. But one anatomical name that defies immediate pigeonholing is the sacrum, or its full name in Latin, the *os sacrum* or "holy bone." What were they thinking when they named this bone? Instead of jumping to immediate conclusions about where this name might have come from, let's first see what we can learn by working with it in the context of energywork. Let's see if we can discover for ourselves what a holy bone might be.

Since we are interested in both structure and energy, our work with the sacrum is important. It is the physical keystone of your lower body as well as a foundational keystone in your psycho-spiritual life, as it is also the anatomical seat of your Sacral Center. In energy-active bodywork we are addressing neither exclusively the physical nor the nonphysical, but rather the place where the two meet.

Like any part of your body, your sacrum is infused with the concerns of the energetic activity centered there. In order to carry out its energetic mission, your Sacral Center's job is made infinitely easier by a physical sacrum that is healthy, structurally aligned, and able to move freely, according to its natural rhythms. Structurally, if your physical sacrum is out of place, turned, torqued, twisted, stuck, or otherwise unhappy, everything else, including your spine, neck, jaw, and head will have to compensate. Since the dural tube, that tough, slightly elastic membranous sheath around your spinal cord, is attached inside the second segment of your sacrum, a twist in your sacrum also puts a twist in your dural tube, and the influence of that goes right up into the membranes inside your head. For these reasons, working on your partner's sacrum is a key to helping in cases of back pain, sciatica, and headaches, to name a few.

In terms of energy and consciousness, if your grounding function and foundation are hindered, for whatever reason, the rest of your world has to compensate. The most basic aspects of your life are a commentary on what might be called your *root situation*. Here are a few of these considerations:

- Whether or not you consciously inhabit your body
- Whether or not you have a home, a livelihood, a means of support, a sense of meaning and stability in your life
- The degree to which you can express who you are in your everyday life
- Your sense of the geographical place in which you live
- Your sense of place and direction in this world

It's not hard to see, therefore, why your Sacral Center will begin to fret and send symptomatic signals when basic needs are not met. One effect of this is that it is difficult to truly express your spiritual gifts and qualities if you are not somewhat stable in this world.

Susan, a woman from Oregon, passed through a necessary but painful period of what might be called a *root situation-related depression*. She had been working toward her nursing credentials when she began learning shamanic practices from her Native American teacher. In the course of that time her gifts as a healer had begun to unfold, but a recent divorce and financial difficulties were also making her life a struggle. Her life became nomadic, and for a number of years, she was often depressed as she felt she was unable—"totally out of position," as she put it—to express her true calling. When her father died, Susan inherited a bit of money, bought a small house, and resumed her nursing studies. Her life regained stability and a daily rhythm, and she now directs an alternative health modalities department in a large university research hospital.

As is the case with all your energetic centers, your Sacral Center needs opportunities to recollect itself and regroup. Calling your spirit back to your Sacral Center can be an important starting point for getting in position for expressing your calling.

INNER PILGRIMAGE #20: *Calling Your Spirit Back to Your Sacral Center*
When you work with an energetic center, you also deal with the issues that belong to that center. Conversely, even if you find it difficult to consciously locate one of your energy centers, it is still possible to work with it by attending to its concerns. For instance, when you make positive changes in your *root situation*, you also strengthen, balance, and heal the etheric structure of your Perineal and Sacral Centers. If you have done the previous exercises, you have already paid some attention to your Perineal Center. Now it's time to turn to some of the most important Sacral Center issues because it is in those very issues that you will probably find bits of your spirit hiding out, waiting to be called back.

*Location:* I use the center of the physical sacrum as a landmark for consciously connecting to the energy of the Sacral Center. If you think of the sacrum as a downward-pointing triangle, it would be the center of that triangle. Remember that the physical landmarks I describe aren't one and the same with the energy-active positions themselves, but they are excellent access positions for catching a ride on the energetic movement into the center of these positions. In this case, the center of the sacrum is an effective starting point from which to allow your awareness to be drawn into the activity of the Sacral Center.

I am used to simply getting what I would call a *feeling contact* with the center of my sacrum, then relaxing or *loosening* my awareness, so as to be drawn into the center of the energy position. With practice, there will come a moment when you *know* you are in the activity of the energy center and you will be able to go where that activity takes you.

The Exercise:
When you are sitting in a mindful state:
1. First, make a feeling contact with your Sacral Center. Remember, it is not enough to simply think about the energy center. Here, you are making a *feeling contact* with the center of your sacrum. See if you can simply allow your awareness to gather itself there. If it helps, place your fingertip on the center of your sacrum for a moment, move your awareness to where you feel your fingertip, and then remove your hand from that position. Try not to concentrate, or fix, your attention. Instead, keep your awareness *light, relaxed, loose, and a bit fuzzy*.
2. Allow a couple of minutes for the contact to intensify.
3. Bring to mind *one* of the emotional aspects of the Sacral Center:
   - Success
   - Failure
   - Meaningfulness
   - Meaninglessness

4. Take up a feeling connection to one of these words and what it represents for you. Let this contact draw you into some kind of experience. Don't judge what comes up in you. Remember that when you pick an aspect of an energy center, you also activate its opposite. Every coin and every energetic quality has two sides.
5. Call your spirit back to you—you can use the words, "I call my spirit back"—and see if you can feel where on your body the energy returns.
6. Give this about ten minutes to allow experience to come up in you. Even if nothing comes into your awareness during this time, try to sit quietly, listening deeply, feeling the space within you.
7. End the exercise.

Here are some other words and phrases that relate to your Sacral Center. They amount to a root situation inventory and can be worked with in the same way as you did with the four words above:
   - Expression of my being, my gifts
   - "Who I am"
   - Your own name (the one your parents gave you)
   - Sense of belonging/exclusion

- Family
- Community
- Teams
- Survival
- "My place in this world"
- Stability
- "My home"
- "My livelihood"
- "My body"
- "My direction in life"
- Having your feet on the ground.

*Ten Reasons to Work with Your Lower Energy Centers (Especially if You Work with Clients)*

1. The energy centers in your lower body create your grounding and your connection with the earth and with *everyday life.*

2. Your lower centers of consciousness are able to ground what you draw into your consciousness via your upper centers. This means they allow you to *contain and embody* what comes to you from higher dimensions of consciousness. If you want your sense of spiritual connection to perk up, work with your lower energy centers.

3. Your lower centers act as a *pole to which your intuition flows.* Again, if you want your intuition to increase its activity, work with your lower centers of consciousness. Otherwise, insights might come, but often, without adequate grounding and containment, what comes to you tends to be a flash in the pan.

4. Your ability to *express* yourself depends, in part, on the health of your Sacral Center, as it is energetically paired with your Throat Center in the Circulation of Expression.

5. Your lower centers are emotional and, as such, they are sources of great power when they are healthy. Conversely, they are sources of internal obstacles when they are repressed and unable to release their emotional charge.

6. *Presence:* If you sometimes find yourself spacing out, or having trouble staying in your body and in the present moment, it is definitely time to learn how to work with the energy centers in your lower body.

7. Your *creativity* is linked to your lower energy centers. Accordingly, much of what blocks your creativity will be associated with these centers, too.

8. *Grounding:* If you work on other people, your ability to ground energy will be called on again and again. The energetic unit formed by you and your partner creates an amplified need for grounding, especially when your treatment partners have emotional or other kinds of releases of excess energy from their bodies.

9. *Grounding again:* Working with your lower centers helps you keep your feet on the ground and not get bowled over when energy is intense.

10. And, again, *keeping your feet on the ground:* Working with your lower centers helps you to stay out of some of the traps of ego-inflation that can show up when developing healing qualities.

*Working With Others*

Your own grounding is the key to helping a healing partner to ground. This is not meant to imply that you have to be perfectly balanced, centered, and grounded before you ever set your hands on someone else. Each of us is a work in progress. Still, the effort and care you put into getting to know your own lower body and your lower energy centers from the inside and cultivating an ongoing appreciation for the life you live there will become one of your greatest resources when you work with someone else.

Lack of grounding is one of the most common energetic maladies. In the case of persons who already have their feet on the ground, it's often enough to just jog their grounding function in order to reactivate it. For some people, personal habits, lifestyle choices, and environment can make a difference in their grounding. Such things as drug use and lack of healthy nutrition and sleep can be among the factors that hinder good grounding. I once worked with a man who was having a terrible time feeling grounded and anchored in his body. When I put my hands on him in a treatment, the first image that came to me was that of a huge quartz crystal. The image was so striking that I asked him about it, and he told me that he had a collection of massive crystals—mostly quartz. He estimated that he had around two tons (!) of quartz crystal in his house. Until our session, he had not made any connection between the high frequency energy field produced by all his crystals and his inability to feel rooted.

Still others have never really been grounded. In them, the process of grounding and establishing a foundation often means dealing with long-standing unconscious obstructions and fears about being in their body and fully incarnated into this life. Healing in this situation can be a long-term project with many emotional and psycho-spiritual dimensions. In all cases, however, there are ways of helping your partner's grounding, and if you work with others, treatment forms like the ones to follow ought to be part of your repertoire.

I used to live in Lawrence, Kansas, a university town with a diverse population of poets, pilgrims and PhDs. Many of my clients were professors, university faculty, and students, and not a few of them showed the energetic consequences of sitting for hours each day at a computer and leading a decidedly cerebral life. I came to think of them as my "cotton candy people" because of the way static energy, like static electricity, would collect in a hazy, smoky aura around their heads and just hang there, like the smog in Southern California that, on some days, doesn't move even when the wind blows in from the Pacific.

Sometimes it was enough, as a prelude to a massage or craniosacral session, to contact their Side-Head Points (two finger-breadths above the tops of their ears) with my hands at the skin surface, wait for a good energetic connection to develop, and then gently stroke the energy down their shoulders and arms to their fingertips several times, and follow that with the same energetic contact at the side of their heads and gently stroke it down their body to their legs and feet. This gets things moving in the right direction to allow the build-up of static energy to once again become *moving* energy, which then has a much better chance of sorting itself out and grounding.

Here is a slightly more elaborate variation of the same idea that makes use of energy streams in your partner's energy system. In the collection of treatments to follow, you will begin by using the tips of your middle and ring fingers and the fingers and the palms of your hands as *energy paintbrushes* and *energy brooms* to sweep your partner's etheric streams clean[14].

---

14    For more personal aura cleaning self-treatments, see the chapter called "Twin Structures of Consciousness."

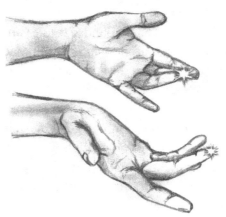

The tips of your middle and ring fingers (your fire and water fingers), used together, are an excellent tool for making a balanced, powerful energetic contact with energy-active points and streams.

PARTNER TREATMENT #4: *Southward Bound—A Handful of Partner Treatments for Grounding*

Preparation:
- For this treatment, your partner is standing.
- Encourage your partner to close her eyes and feel down into her feet and concentrate about seventy percent of her weight in her heels.

Part 1: The Headband
1. Standing behind your partner, reach around her head with both of your hands.
2. Place the tips of both your middle and ring fingers on your partner's Pineal Extension Point in the middle of her forehead.
3. Give this contact a few moments to deepen.
4. When you feel a good energetic contact, slowly slide your fingertips around the sides of her head until they meet at the top of the groove of her neck. Imagine you are stroking out an *energetic headband* around her head. This works best with fingertip contact on the surface of your partner's skin.
5. Continue this slow stroke down her neck, along the tops of her shoulders and the outside of both her arms to her fingertips. After a few strokes, if you feel a good contact, you can do this to good effect *slightly off her skin surface.*
6. Do this a number of times, and as you do it, be sure to maintain a good energetic contact.

Part 2: Down Your Partner's Back
1. Still standing behind your partner, start the same way as in step one, starting with your fingertips in the middle of your partner's forehead. This time, stroke the headband around to the back of your partner's head, but this time, bring both your thumbs into contact with her spine, one on either side, just under the base of her skull.

2. With your thumbs on either side of her spine, use your palms to stroke the energy slowly down your partner's back, over her buttocks and down the backsides of her legs to her heels. You are drawing her energy down from her head to the ground. Do this slowly and consciously several times.

Part 3: The Mask

1. Come around now to the front of your partner. This time place the tips of your energy paintbrushes (middle and ring fingertips) together again at the Pineal Extension Point and allow the contact to intensify.

2. This time, you are going to use your fingertips to trace a *mask* of lines on your partner's face. Keep your finger contact light, your movement slow and conscious. Here is the path you will follow on your partner's face[15]:

3. Start at her Pineal Extension Point.

4. Move down to her Point of Silence (at the top of her nose, between her eyes).

5. From there, slowly trace a pair of "spectacles" around her eyes. Let your fingers meet again at her Point of Silence.

6. From there, trace a line down either side of her nose.

7. At the corner of her nose, "paint" a line around the corners of her nose and in toward the midline, *not quite letting your fingers meet.*

8. Move down to just above her upper lip.

9. Move along the top of her upper lip on both sides to the corners of her mouth.

10. Move around the corners of her mouth and then in toward the midline again, not quite touching.

11. Move down to her chin and then along the line of her lower jaw up to just under her earlobe. Stay there with your fingertip contact and let the energetic contact deepen before moving on.

12. Continue down both sternocleidomastoid muscles—these are the prominent muscles that stand out on the side of your neck when you turn your head to one side—to her collarbone.

13. Stay a moment at this position on your partner's collarbones.

14. You are now at the *stress points*—let's call them *Collarbone Points*—on the top of your partner's collarbones, where the sternocleidomastoid muscle attaches. From here, use your fingertips, or thumbs to stroke out parallel lines, either side of the midline, down the front of your partner's body. Stay about a half inch to an inch either side of her midline and stroke downward to the tops of her pubic bones.

15. Make a detour around your partner's genitals and continue the stroke down the insides of her legs to the ground.

16. Repeat this several times. After a pass or two, you can make your contact just off the skin surface—a half inch or so—if you like. The etheric stream you are working with is both just off the physical body and also interpenetrating with it. If you move off your partner's skin surface, make sure you can actually feel the energetic contact.

17. Take your hands off your partner and have her stand a minute or so to feel her new sense of connection to the earth.

---

15    If you have the means to do so, take a look at this exercise among the "Pilgrim Extras" on my Web site (some things are just easier to show than tell). See the instructions for finding the Pilgrim Extras on the last page of this book.

What you have done is to use available energy streams to help "clean house" in your partner's energy field and, very importantly, support the movement of excess energy around your partner's head down to the ground.[16]

PARTNER TREATMENT #5: *Structure and Energy in the Spine: Therapy for God's Walking Stick*
Besides being an important part of your central nervous system, playing a core role in literally every function and activity of your life, your spine is a flashway of consciousness and energetic impulses. Working with the spine in treatments is a wonderful way to help your partner become more grounded. Here is a safe, simple, but very effective way to give your partner's grounding function a jumpstart. The physical landmarks you will be using for this treatment are your partner's spine, sacrum, legs, and feet.

Preparation:

- Make sure your partner is comfortable. Have your partner lie face down, preferably with his face in the face cradle of your massage table so that his head and neck are not turned. You might also want to see if your partner would like a pillow under his feet.

- Take a moment to increase your grounding by moving your awareness into your lower body and energy centers. Bear in mind that when you work on a partner lying horizontal on a table, *you are taking on the grounding for both of you.*

Treatment Steps:
1. Place one hand on your partner's sacrum and the other at your partner's medulla, just below the base of your partner's skull. At this position, your hand will be covering your partner's neck, including the vertebral connection of her Throat Center at the third cervical vertebra.
2. Bring your attention to the natural exchange of energy between your hands and allow this energy movement to work. Give this initial contact a couple of minutes.
3. With one hand remaining stationary on your partner's sacrum, *pick up your other hand an inch or so from your partner's body* and place it about one hand's breadth further down his spine. Picking up your hand and replacing it, instead of sliding it down your partner's spine, allows for some needed energetic expansion to take place in your partner's spine. This helps excess build-ups of energy to release.
4. Allow that new energetic contact to deepen for about a minute.
5. Continue to move your other hand's contact down your partner's spine, one hand-breadth at a time until you have addressed your partner's entire spine. Remember to lift your hand off your partner's body a bit between contacts. Give each new connection about a minute.
6. Now let the hand that has traveled down your partner's spine rest on his sacrum. With your other hand, make contact with his knees, first one and then the other. To do this, simply place your hand on the back of your partner's knee and allow the energetic contact to deepen. The actual energy center at the knee is in the center of the joint.

---

16    For a detailed look at this treatment, come to the Pilgrim Extras on my Web site. (See the instructions for finding the Pilgrim Extras on the last page of this book.)

7. Keep your contact with your partner's sacrum and place your other hand on one of his heels and place your attention on the exchange of energy between your hands. Give this some time to deepen before moving that hand to your partner's other heel and letting that energetic contact deepen. Another energy-active position you can use is the energy center in the soles of his feet.

8. Place your hands on both heels, both foot soles, and spend a minute or so with the contact.

9. End the treatment and allow your partner some time to "simmer."

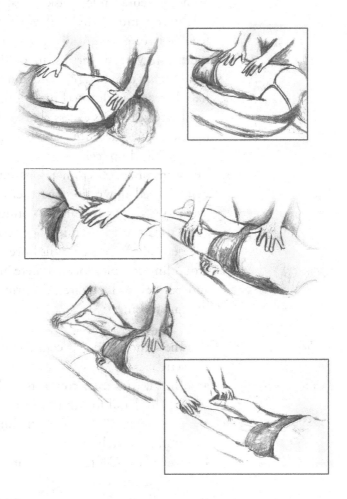

This treatment is excellent for helping your partner to calm down, slow down, and "come down out of their tree." Start by placing one hand on your partner's medulla—at the back of her neck—and one hand on her sacrum, and allow yourself time to feel the natural exchange of energy between your hands. While keeping the one hand stationary on her sacrum, use your other hand to address each segment of her spine (see the detailed instructions) until you reach her sacrum. Then you create a connection between her sacrum and her knees and feet. Allow time for each of these connections to deepen.

*Four Things to Note as You Do this Treatment:*

1. You can also proceed *one vertebra at a time*. One way to do this is to use two fingers—I typically use my middle finger and ring finger—and place them either side of the spinous processes of the vertebra you are touching.

2. Whether you are connecting one vertebra at a time with your fingertips, or a number

of segments at the same time with your whole hand, what you are doing is allowing each area or segment of your partner's spine to relate energetically to his Sacral Center. This allows each part of the spine to discharge excess energy and come into alignment with his grounding function.

3. Some vertebrae might ask for special attention. You might run into individual vertebrae that pulsate, or feel "hot" or energetically jazzed up when you contact them with your fingertips. It could even feel as though the vertebra is moving. When you encounter a vertebra like that, stay with the contact long enough to give it a chance to release its excess charge of energy. When that release takes place, the vertebra will settle down and lose its jazzed up feel.

4. Be aware of spinal connections for energy centers. As you proceed down your partner's spine, you are also providing all of his spinally connected energy centers with a chance to ground themselves by coming into energetic alignment with his lower body and the whole grounding complex located there in his sacrum, coccyx, and perineum. Here are the vertebral connections for the spinal centers:

*Sacrum stuck, beware, the heart will suffocate.*

Tao te Ching

- The Throat Center connects to the third cervical vertebra.
- The Heart Center connects to the position between the third and fourth thoracic vertebrae.
- The Solar Plexus Center links to the seventh thoracic vertebra.
- The Hara Center has a connection to the third lumbar vertebra.
- The Sacral Center, as its name suggests, has a connection to the center of the sacrum.

As you move through these areas of the spine, internally acknowledge where you are in your partner's energy system. Be sure to at least say "hello" in your awareness to each of your partner's energy centers.

5. *You can also reverse the direction of this treatment,* working from your partner's feet up his spine to his head. In this case, you would remain stationary with the hand that is on your partner's medulla, while moving upward, a hand's breadth at a time from her sacrum. The effect is different, of course. In general, working from the

head downward has a calming effect on the energy field, while working upward has an activating effect. Consider starting with the downward direction and then following it with the upward direction.

*An Energywork Tip for Craniosacral Practitioners: Combining Energy-Active Positions with Simple Lumbosacral Decompression*

Craniosacral practitioners know how important it is to take care of the sacrum. It is the keystone of the lower body, and its good alignment and mobility will have a huge effect on what happens elsewhere in your partner's body. The above treatment in which you moved your point of contact, vertebra by vertebra, downward on your partner's spine to his sacrum is a very good prelude to the kind of gentle lumbosacral decompression used in craniosacral work. I find that anywhere in the body, when the energetic and emotional charge held in soft tissue has a means of releasing, then such conditions as compressions and structural misalignments have a much better chance of correcting themselves, and this idea applies here.

Let's take a structurally oriented treatment from standard craniosacral work and combine it with energetic principles to create an energy-active bodywork treatment that also addresses the perennial theme of grounding. If you start with the above partner treatment, you have already set the stage. Now you'll give your partner's sacrum a chance to align structurally and give the energy center at his sacrum an opportunity to balance energetically.

Start by performing an L5/S1 decompression, stabilizing your partner's lower lumbar vertebrae with one hand and putting gentle inferior traction on his sacrum. While you are creating this opportunity for an L5/S1 decompression, other things are afoot as well. Energetic things. Here is a great opportunity to work at the cusp of structure and energy.

1. Stay with the gentle traction on your partner's physical sacrum and, at the same time, shift your attention to include the energetic activity of his Sacral Center.
2. With your other hand, make a good energetic contact with each of the following energy-active positions in turn, and place your awareness on the natural energetic exchange between your hands:

   - Both Hip Points in turn (these are the energy-active positions located on the lower inside of your partner's iliac crest, where the sartorius muscle attaches)
   - Both adrenals in turn (the adrenal glands are energetically linked with the Sacral Center)
   - Liver Point[17] (on the inferior margin of your partner's rib cage at the end of his right seventh rib)
   - Spleen Point (on the inferior margin of your partner's rib cage at the end of his left seventh rib)
   - Both Shoulder Points (located at the corner of your partner's shoulder where the collarbone and shoulder blade meet) in turn
   - Heart Center

Leaving aside the Heart Center connection for the moment, note that when you connect your partner's Sacral Centers with the paired positions listed above, you are forming a downward-

---

17    Both the Liver and Spleen Points will be introduced in more detail in Chapter 13.

pointing triangle. In each case, you are making a connection between your partner's Sacral Center and energy-active positions that play a direct or indirect role in the Sacral Center's balance and well-being. Again, the best way to do this is to make the best energetic connection you can and then pay attention to the natural exchange of energy between your hands.

The downward energetic movement you have created in your partner's body presents a good opportunity to also enhance the circulation of the etheric in his lower body and legs. (Here, "etheric" refers to the layer of energetic movement that interpenetrates with the physical body.) Grounding doesn't go only in one direction. It is not just a matter of tossing down an anchor to the middle of the planet. That is part of it, but the other side of the coin is receiving the movement upward from the earth as well.

The sacrum provides a physical handle on many psycho-spiritual themes and processes, so you are never wrong to give a lot of attention to this center of activity. The vital exchange of energy between you and the earth through your grounding expresses one of the three great polarities that each of us live within, the other two being the exchange of energy and consciousness that exists between ourselves and the Cosmos through our Crown Centers and the exchange that pulsates between ourselves and the living world around us via our Heart Centers.

Energy-active bodywork makes use of the way the etheric flows up, down, and around your physical body. It has its dominant direction of flow, like a wide river, up the front and down the back of the left side of your body, and up the back and down the front of the right side of your body.[18] Let's apply the dominant direction of etheric flow to the process of grounding.

PARTNER TREATMENT #6: *Etheric Circulations for the Sacrum, Hips, Legs and Feet*
The following treatment can be done directly on your partner's body, with or without massage oil or through clothing or a sheet. Let's call it a *grounding loop*.[19] It can look like this:

Part 1: Grounding Loop on Your Partner's Backside
At this level close in to your partner's physical body, the dominant circulation of energy moves *up the back of his right leg to his Sacral Center and then down the back of his left leg*. By enhancing this movement at the skin surface, the Sacral Center is allowed to both ground its excess energy and receive fresh energy. While there is also a flow of energy in the opposite direction, this is the dominant direction of flow. The same basic flow is available to every position in your body, and as a result, this same basic tactic can be used to help other centers and organs release excess energy, ground, and be replenished.

Part 2: Grounding Loop on Your Partner's Front Side
Here your partner is lying on his back. This basic grounding loop entails enhancing the etheric movement *up the front of his left leg into the area of his Hara Center in his lower abdomen, and then down the front of his right leg*. In this simple form of *etheric massage*, move your hands either just off your partner's body or touching lightly at the skin surface. In both of these grounding loops, you move with the dominant direction of etheric flow: up the front side and down the back on

18 *Energy Healing: A Pathway to Inner Growth* has additional exercises to help you get familiar with this flow.

19 To see this treatment, come to the Pilgrim Extras on my Web site. (See the instructions for finding the Pilgrim Extras on the last page of this book.)

the left side of your partner's body and up the back and down the front on the right side.

> MASSAGE NOTE: This will look strange to you at first if you are used to doing massage on the abdomen in a clockwise direction, following the large intestine, because the dominant direction of etheric movement is in the opposite direction. Here, you *consciously shift your focus* to the interface between the etheric and the physical. Your contact is light, either on the skin surface, or just off.

There is no reason such a tactic couldn't be integrated into massage. Can you see how this basic idea could be supplied to other energy-active positions? Think of how you would do this with your partner's Heart Center, for example, or his Solar Plexus Center.

Let's conclude this chapter on grounding with my spin on a kind of application that shows up frequently in biodynamic craniosacral work.

PARTNER TREATMENT #7: *The Starwater Treatment*
Here, you have an opportunity to shift your awareness to a special meeting place between the structure of her body and the energy that moves through it and around it. You might think of this as finding the place where the visible and invisible worlds meet in your partner. This "place" is the cerebrospinal fluid in the head and spine, a substance which A. T. Still, the father of osteopathy, called "one of the highest known elements that are contained in the body." Cerebrospinal fluid makes up part of the medium in which your brain floats. It surrounds the spinal cord inside your spinal column, providing your central nervous system with nutrients, glucose and electrolytes. It provides a fluid cushion to absorb the inevitable bumps and shocks to which our bodies are subjected. In the treatment to follow, you find out what happens when you place your attention on it and mindfully follow its movement and energetic fluctuations.

In our cerebrospinal fluid, we are carrying within us a miniature ocean with its own tides, ebbs, and flows. Cerebrospinal fluid has the same specific gravity as seawater, and it carries in it the oceanic rhythms of the sea. This affinity with seawater invites oceanic imagery. While the filling and emptying phases of the production and re-absorption of cerebrospinal fluid might be compared to the waves on the surface of the

*Starwater*

*Nursing my first baby*
*I drank eight glasses of water,*
*two quarts each day. He grew.*

*I felt like a carrier for water,*
*passing it on through to the child,*
*and some day his child, too,*
*will fatten, remarkable*
*like peaches and muskmelons*
*leaching juice from bare dirt.*

*Astronomers tell us star dust*
*once swirled together,*
*cooled into rocks and water*
*and still circulates,*
*the same matter pulled into stars*
*and Earth and into our flesh.*

*So water travels the skies,*
*stretches into clouds,*
*and falls, moving ever East,*
*circling, the same ancient water*
*caught in the whirlwind*
*binding us all together—*
*gravity, or maybe as we know it,*
*love, or water drawing together*
*all its kin.*

Denise Low
(used with permission)

ocean, there are deeper rhythms that are more like the unfathomable rise and fall of the ocean's depths. Bio-dynamic craniosacralists have a beautifully poetic vocabulary for describing the ebb and flow of this tiny ocean within. They speak of dynamic flows, short and long tides, and the Breath of Life behind the manifestations of the body. Here, hands-on bodywork fully crosses the line into meditation on the Life Force and its rhythms, which are linked to the rhythms of the great cosmos. We not only surf the *cranial wave*, we join with it and become it.

Preparation:

- Remember the last time you were at the ocean. Call to mind that even as the waves come surging into the shore several times per minute, there is also an *undertow*, the backflow of currents into the ocean happening at the same time.

- Now call to mind that these waves and backflows are part of the bigger cycle of the oceans as they rise and fall, ebb and flow, following the cycles of the moon, sun, and stars.

*Position Possibilities:*

- With your partner lying face down, place one of your hands on her occiput (the back of her head) and the other on her sacrum.

- With your partner lying on her back, cradle the back of her head in one hand, and her sacrum in the other.

    Tip: Try lifting up the sheet with one hand and sliding your other hand under the sheet and under your partner's sacrum. That way, your partner won't have to change positions.

- *Occiput only:* Sitting at the head of the table, cradle the base of your partner's occiput in the fingers of both of your hands.

- *Sacrum only:* Slide your hand under your partner's sacrum.

*Steps:*

1. *Relaxed, fluid hands:* Relax your hands as much as you can. You may find you have to adjust the height of your stool and you may have to adjust your hand position so that you are cradling your partner's occiput and/or sacrum in your fingers as opposed to actively holding them in your hands. Your hands will be happier this way, and you will be able to stay with the treatment longer.

2. Now, *touch bone.* That means to use enough finger pressure to momentarily feel the bone of your partner's skeleton at her occiput and/or sacrum. Bring your attention to the bone and the energy moving through your partner's body at the same time. Stay with that contact for a minute.

3. Now, lighten your touch and deliberately shift your awareness from the density of the bone contact to the level of *membrane.* Here, you are tuning in to the membranous sheath that surrounds your partner's spinal cord. Stay with that level of contact for a minute.

4. Now, deliberately shift your awareness to the *cerebrospinal fluid* in your partner's head and spine. By taking these steps, you are shifting from one level of density to another. Note

what happens as you shift between levels of density.

5.  Tune into the slow fluid motion inside your partner's spine, and see if you can track the movement of fluid:

    - Downward from your partner's head, passing slowly into her spine, eventually reaching her sacrum.
    - Then upward until it reaches her head again.

6.  Meditation: See if you can simply join your consciousness with this wave of "starwater." You do what it does. You go where it goes. You become it. Let go. Give this ten to fifteen minutes.

> *Visualization tip:* Start by trying to visualize a very slow moving wavelet, following its crest as it travels the length of this internal waterway. Visualize a long tide as it spreads up a beach. Imagine the leading edge of this tide. Maybe you are surfing it. Try a visualization like these for a minute or so, then let go of that visualization.

> Become as quiet as you can within yourself; enter a state of deep mindfulness and see if you can follow this amazing fluid movement.

We have explored many facets of the theme of grounding. It will provide a key for both your inner work and your work with others. Your appreciation of grounding in all its dimensions will no doubt grow and change with you. Watch for this super-perennial theme peeking through all that you do in energetic work. Your inner pilgrim, and the one in your partner, will be glad you did.

# CHAPTER ELEVEN

## EXPRESSION, CONTROL AND BALANCE

### WHEN HEAVEN AND EARTH MEET—IN US
### (AND WHEN THEY DON'T)

Many years ago—I was in my twenties—I had a vision that gave me an insight into what I was experiencing in my inner world and seeing in the world around me. It was simply this: despite appearances to the contrary, heaven and earth are in the process of coming together. Typical of visions, it was an opening into experiences that I only later tried to roll out in words. In the frame of reference available to me at the time, though, this meant that the invisible world was merging with the visible, the realms of angels and the dear departed with the world of us living humans, the subtler dimensions of consciousness with the denser, more earthly ones. I understood in an intuitive but also visceral way the scriptural references to a "new heaven and a new earth."[20]

As I say, it was a vision, as opposed to a theological formulation, and it has stayed with me. Since that time, I have been fortunate enough to encounter spiritual mentors who have put tools in my hands, given me a framework for finding my path, and then have sent me out the door with the encouragement to find my own path and draw my own conclusions about what I see, including my vision of heaven and earth. In my work as healer and teacher and writer, this vision has shaped my understanding of the way the human energy system behaves, and provided me with a context for energetic exercises and treatments.

What I find is that heaven and earth are represented in each of us in our wonderful system of energy centers, especially in the way the upper and lower ones interact, behind the scenes, in our lives. It might be said that we live at the intersection of heaven and earth, and when heaven and earth meet harmoniously in us, the result is healing. This meeting takes place on all levels of our being, in tiny ways and in big ways, over and over. It is an ongoing process. Heaven is vast. So is earth.

*Circulations of Energy and Consciousness*
When heaven and earth meet in you, it means that your energy system is working as a harmonious, cohesive unit—you're cooking on all burners. There is a blend of activity between your upper and lower centers of consciousness, all playing a role in this meeting between heaven and earth, something that we humans seem to be made for, even though we find so many ways to live outside of that harmony.

---

20    Revelations 21:1

Let's be more specific about this. Each of your upper centers (Crown, Pineal, and Throat) is in a special relationship with one of the lower centers (Solar Plexus, Hara, and Sacral, respectively). Each works together with its partner, and their activities blend. In the same way that all the other C-notes on a piano will vibrate when you strike middle C, the partners in these energy-center pairings vibrate together like different octaves of the same psycho-spiritual and energetic "note." They music they play is the common theme they share in the development and expression of consciousness. The rest of this chapter will be devoted to working with these pairings and their themes. Let's begin by introducing these paired centers and the perennial themes they embody in the circulations of energy and consciousness that they create together:

- The Throat Center and the Sacral Center form the *Circulation of Expression.*

- The Pineal Center and the Hara Center form the *Circulation of Control.*

- The Crown Center and the Solar Plexus Center form the *Circulation of Balance.*

Each of these terms—expression, control, and balance—has special meaning in the context of energy and consciousness and the meeting of heaven and earth within you, and a superficial examination of these words is not going to be enough to reveal what they are pointing to. To get below the surface of these ideas, we'll take a closer look at each of these circulations, what keeps them from functioning well, and what it takes to support them. We'll start with the Circulation of Expression.

### *The Circulation of Expression and the Three Constipations*

As an energetic and psycho-spiritual theme, *expression* is about more than your ability to open your mouth and say what's on your mind and in your heart. That is certainly part of it, but there is more. Often, a good way to grasp the importance of something is to look at what happens when it's *not* working. In the case of expression, there are three dysfunctions that I call the "three constipations." I'm not referring to a Motown singing group that didn't quite make it, but rather to three major areas of life—all interrelated—that suffer a certain kind of constipation when expression is blocked or withheld. I run into these three constipations all the time in my work with those who come to my practice, and an understanding of them has helped me to appreciate the vital role played by the Circulation of Expression in our lives on all levels.

Before we look at each of these constipations in turn, I would like to call attention to the important role played by the Sacral Center in expression, something that might not be obvious when we think of expression exclusively as a Throat Center function. In the last chapter, we took an in-depth look at the importance of your grounding function and your *root situation*, and the key roles played by your Perineal and Sacral Centers. To review briefly, your root situation includes:

- Your comfort in your own body

- Whether or not you have a home, a livelihood, a means of support, a sense of meaning and stability in your life

- Your sense of identity

- Your place and direction in this world

If your root situation is hindered, for whatever reason, the rest of your world has to compensate, and one of the first casualties is your ability to express your deepest self through what you bring into this world. The Circulation of Expression lives in the resonant relationship between your Sacral and Throat Centers, which need each other in order to thrive. Though different, your Sacral and Throat Centers are joined like a tree that grows, blooms, and bears fruit, and the ground in which it is rooted. The earth may seem to hold herself in during winter and times of drought, but in her natural cycles and seasons, when conditions are met, she expresses herself in the wild variety of life that springs out of her. And just as a tree needs the earth in order to grow and bloom, so too does the expression of your being require a foundation. If expression is to be true, it needs to emerge from the soil of your being.

With your work with grounding and the Sacral Center in the last chapter you already started working with the Circulation of Expression. I'm pointing this out because, in what follows, we will take up practices and inner pilgrimages that involve us predominantly with the Throat Center, and I would not want you to think that the Sacral Center is getting short shrift. Know that each time you engage the Circulation of Expression, and every time you consciously engage your Throat Center, you are directly or indirectly also involving your Sacral Center.

Let's look now at each of these constipations in the area of expression.

Constipation in Your Ability to Release Excess Energy

One important aspect of expression is your ability to release energy from your system. In a healthy, resilient person, most of the energy from the small shocks of daily living is released without leaving an accumulation. Try this: hold out one hand, palm down and give the back of your hand a good whack with two fingers. (Don't hurt yourself; just give it enough so that you feel it.) When you do that, you are throwing a quantum of energy into the tissues of your hand. You'll probably find that the mild stinging sensation gives way to a tingle and in thirty seconds or so, it has probably vanished altogether. What you are witnessing is your body's ability to release and disperse the energy of a mild shock.

But let's look at an energetic scenario that most people can relate to. Suppose you have an impact—it could be physical or emotional—that is more severe, so much so that it gets through your defenses. Examples would include being hit by a baseball flying at full speed, witnessing violence, or taking in a cutting remark from someone close to you. In these situations, two things happen: first, the energy of the impact enters your system from outside, and second, you have your internal reaction to the impact. Taken together, this means that there is suddenly a bundle of extra energy to deal with in your body.

Now suppose that instead of shouting out in pain or crying or shaking or any of the natural, spontaneous things we do to dissipate a shock to our systems, you stoically clamp down and hold it in. You may have all kinds of wonderful-sounding reasons for holding back—maybe you tell yourself that it's unwise or unsafe to get angry at Aunt Harriet for her insensitive remarks, or you feel it would mean you were a wimp if you screamed out in pain when a brick falls on your foot—but, regardless of your reason for holding back, the fact is that all this excess energy has to go *somewhere*.

What normally would have come out in sound, tears, or anger is instead pushed down into your system and in many cases winds up lodging in the tissues of your body. When you habitually hold onto the energies that would otherwise move through you in a release of some kind, you run the risk of a kind of energetic constipation. This often involves holding in your sound, which involves your Throat Center. This is why sound is so useful in bodywork. The skillful use of music, gongs, singing bowls, and voice are not only a wonderful means of carrying your consciousness into higher dimensions, but they also provide an ideal means of opening channels of movement for pent-up energy from the tissues of your body, so they offer a level of relief from this overload.

## Constipation in Communication and Relationship

In its most basic terms, communication is about sending and receiving something, and it involves the Circulation of Expression. It might be words or gestures, even telepathy, but somehow something gets to move or vibrate in the space between us. I was a disc jockey with my own radio show for a couple of years. When I first started, I had the eerie feeling that my words and the music I played were just beaming out into empty space, and there was no one on the other end receiving it. It wasn't until someone actually called the station during my program and asked for more information about a piece of music I was playing that I realized I was *connecting* with someone else. Strangely, from that time on, I could feel the presence of the listeners when I spoke into the microphone and played music. A conscious relationship had started.

The words on this page, sent by me and received by you, are carriers of meaning and experience. And I don't have to wait until you send me a letter or email to receive something back from you. Already your response is vibrating within you and a resonance is growing between us. *Hello!*

Your Throat Center plays a major role in relationships since you don't have a relationship without communication of some kind, and that usually involves sound. Among the very first things couples are asked to examine in therapy are their communication habits. To what degree are they each able to express to their partner what is truly in their hearts and minds? Do they feel heard? How well do they listen and really hear their partner? Does their relationship allow not only for their sound, as they communicate with each other, but also for their silence? With questions like these, they are undergoing a check up for the Throat Center of their relationship.

Saying what you need and want, speaking your truth, and being honest are essential parts of living an authentic life. When communication becomes blocked or skewed, or when a person cuts off his true sound, either going incommunicado or communicating in a way that is false, exaggerated, or empty, the result might be called "relational constipation."

*Her husband, Harland, is sleeping like a brick and snoring ... She married him two years ago for love, or so she thought, and he's a good enough man but a devotee of household silence. His idea of marriage is to spray WD-40 on anything that squeaks. Even on nights when he turns over and holds her, Harland has no words for Alice ... This marriage has failed to warm her. The quiet only subsides when Harland sleeps and his tonsils make up for lost time.*

Barbara Kingsolver

127

An interesting phenomenon, well known among craniosacral therapists, is what happens to some people the first time they have their hyoid bone released. The hyoid bone is the U-shaped bone located in your throat, just below your tongue. It serves as an anchor for many of the muscles that make up your throat. All of the bones and soft tissue in your throat are infused with the energies of your Throat Center, and the energetic loading of the hyoid bone has to do with issues of expression. It is not uncommon for persons who habitually hold back on their expression to suddenly find their tongue untied after having their hyoid bone *unwound* in a craniosacral session, which sometimes results in some adjustments in their relationships with those around them when they go home.

Family and social rules play a big role in how we talk to one another. For example, families that no one would ever accuse of being dishonest might have strong, unspoken taboos against saying out loud how you really feel if it would rock the boat or hurt someone's feelings— "if you can't say something nice, don't say anything at all." Families model a certain style of Throat Center behavior to its members, and in the case of families determined to remain "nice" come hell or high water, a lot of authentic expression either has to be heavily edited, or held in and not expressed at all. With this kind of relational constipation, a good deal of vitality and spontaneity is lost as well.

Constipation in the Area of Expressing Your Calling

The Circulation of Expression also has to do with how your being, your calling, and qualities manifest in this world through you. Your Circulation of Expression needs to be in good working order to give voice to what is most deeply in your heart. It might be said that heaven and earth meet in you this way, and when they don't meet, the result can be a stoppage of what might otherwise come into the world through you, a kind of spiritual constipation. When you feel the stirrings of a calling within you, and that calling starts to make demands of you, the health and well-being of your Circulation of Expression takes on major importance. Choreographer Martha Graham said it quite wonderfully:

> There is a vitality, a life force, a quickening that is translated through you into action, and because there is only one of you in all time, this expression is unique. And if you block it, it will never exist through any other medium and be lost. The world will not have it. It is not your business to determine how good it is, nor how it compares with other expressions. It is your business to keep it yours, clearly and directly, to keep the channel open.

Let's move now to a simple exercise with the Circulation of Expression.

INNER PILGRIMAGE #21: *Meditation with Your Circulation of Expression*
Exercise Steps:
1.  Contact your Sacral Center. Do this by bringing your awareness into the center of your sacrum and allowing this feeling contact to deepen. Give this a couple of minutes.

2.  Move your awareness in a slow, conscious arc, away from your body, up to your Throat Center. You might move your awareness out to one side and then up and around your body, or downward and between your legs, and then in a sweeping arc up to your Throat Center; or perhaps away from your sacrum, behind your back, and over the top of your

head. However you do this, try to move your attention *slowly and consciously* when you move between these two positions. When you go slowly and with as much awareness as you can, you'll be surprised how much can happen when you move through the energetic space around your body. Spend a couple of minutes deepening your contact with your Throat Center.

3.  Now move back to your Sacral Center, returning in the *same arc*, out and down your body, and establish a feeling contact there again. Remember to go slowly and consciously.

4.  Repeat this "commute" between the two centers a couple of times. Again, no hurrying. Each time you contact one of these centers, spend a minute letting the contact deepen.

5.  Now connect your awareness with both your Sacral and Throat Centers at the *same time* and feel their interaction. Give this connection a minute.

6.  Release this connection and bring the word "expression" to mind. Try to get a feeling connection with what the word means to you.

7.  Allow a five to ten minute period for a meditation in which you sit mindfully with whatever comes up inside you. Don't judge or try to analyze what comes during the meditation. There will be time for that later if you want it. This meditation is a time for allowing things to arise the way they are in your awareness.

8.  End the exercise.

The circulation of energy and consciousness between your Throat and Sacral Centers is crucial in your development. The deep logic of this relationship says, "Your identity and your physical and psycho-spiritual foundation grow hand in hand with your ability to express yourself and give voice and form to the gifts you have brought with you into this life." A corollary of this is that a person whose root situation is disturbed—examples include all the instances in which a person lacks the basics for survival and stability—will also find it difficult to express their gifts. In working with the exercise above, you will no doubt run into what may be preventing these two centers from communicating easily within you. By and by, as these two energy centers find each other and blend their activity, they will support each other and the various aspects of your life that relate to expression.

INNER PILGRIMAGE #22: *The Throat Center, Sound and Stillness*
With the Throat Center, we are in the world of sound and hearing. Most spiritual paths employ sound in the form of chanting, singing, prayer, music and mantra. The inner, mystical teachings behind all spiritual traditions go further and encourage another classic discipline of sound: deep listening to the music of creation, and beyond that, to what comes *after* sound, namely, stillness. Writer Fran Peavy called it "listening as if there is a thief in the house"

PART 1: Working with the Point of Silence
What follows is an energy exercise that relates to your relationship with sound. It involves what I call the *Point of Silence*. The Point of Silence is accessible at the bridge of your nose, at the position between your eyes. As in all work with energy-active positions on your body, the way you make energetic contact with it is to bring your attention to that point on your body and then

allow your attention to become relaxed and loose. This allows the natural movement of energy at that point to draw your awareness into itself.

The purpose of this exercise is to enter the world of sound in a new way. If you really listen, you will find that there are layers upon layers of sound within you and all around you. Try this:

Exercise Steps:

1. Bring your awareness into your Heart Center and allow this connection to build up for a couple of minutes.

2. Release your connection with your heart Center and listen deeply to the sounds around you and within you—five minutes.

3. Move your awareness on your skin surface, in a slow, conscious line, upwards over the contours of your face, to the Point of Silence, located at the top of your nose, between your eyes. Relax and let your awareness rest there. Give this contact a minute to deepen.

4. Now let go of this contact and move your awareness slowly through your head to the Medulla Position. This is located at the top of the groove in the back of your neck, at base of your skull. Allow this energetic contact to deepen for a minute.

5. Release this contact and slowly move from the medulla position through your body back to your Heart Center and again allow that contact to deepen—one minute.

6. Slowly retrace this triangle—Heart Center>Point of Silence>Medulla>Heart Center—two more times, allowing about a minute of deepening time in each of the points.

7. Release the contact with this triangle and turn your attention to the world of sound within you and all around you—five minutes.

8. End the exercise.

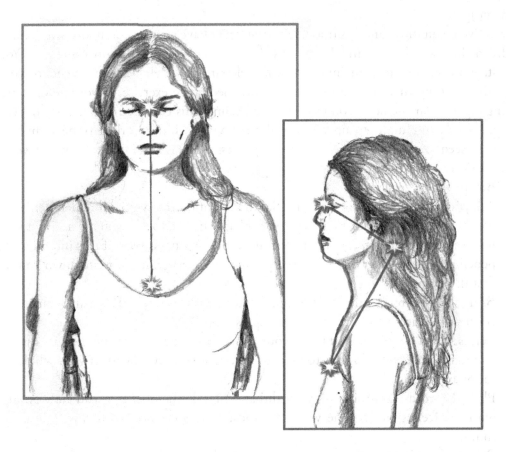

This exercise brings your Point of Silence, your Medulla, and your Heart Center into a balanced connection with one another, allowing them to blend their activity in a harmonious way.

Part 2: Call Your Spirit Back to Your Throat Center

1.  Bring your awareness into your Throat Center and allow the contact to deepen.
2.  Choose one of the facets of the Throat Center and make a feeling contact with what that word or phrase means to you:
    - Letting go
    - Expression
    - Holding back on your expression
    - Stillness (as opposed to holding back your sound)
    - Speaking my heart and mind
    - Living my calling

3.  Let this contact draw you into some kind of experience.
4.  Call your spirit back to you in the same way you have done with your other energy centers, and see if you can feel where the energy returns on your body. If you need to, see the basic exercise in Chapter Nine.
5.  Allow some time for whatever wants to surface within you. Give this phase about ten minutes.
6.  Return to a normal sense of your body and end the exercise.

Dream Setup

Energy-active meditations and treatments like these will have an effect on many levels, including your dream life, which Sigmund Freud called the "royal road to the unconscious." You can set the stage for dreams in your inner work by selecting three elements or events of your day and briefly revisiting them in the form of a short meditative exercise. If you are on retreat or exploring a particular theme of consciousness or healing, this creative triangulation of elements can be particularly useful. It sets up a means of carrying your inner work into the night hours by planting the seeds of dreams that relate to your process. Here is an example from our work with the Circulation of Expression.

Before you go to sleep:

1. Ask your subconscious for a dream. Set the intention that you will remember it. Even if you believe that you don't dream, you probably do, and what you are asking for here is help in connecting *consciously* to your dream life again. As part of this intention, have a pencil and some paper or a tape recorder handy so that you can write down your dream first thing upon waking.

2. Bring your awareness into your Sacral Center for one minute. This starts your conscious connection with your Circulation of Expression.

3. Release that connection and bring your awareness into your tongue. Feel its surface and its interior. Follow it down into your throat. Rest your awareness in your whole tongue for one minute.

4. Place the word "expression" in your throat center. Remember that you are working here with the feeling behind the word. Connect your awareness with this feeling for one minute.

5. Release this connection and go to sleep, and when you awaken remember your dreams. This is the hard part, of course.

6. If you manage to recall your dream, select one thing from it that seems important or unusual and bring it into a short meditation upon waking. In that meditation, ask to be shown more.

*Trust in Life and the Circulation of Control*

Let's look now at areas of energy and consciousness that can be accessed through the particular relationship that exists between your Hara and Pineal Centers, between the middle of your head and the middle of your lower abdomen. I have learned to call this the Circulation of Control, and once again we have another example of language that has more to it than meets the eye at first.

In terms of energy and consciousness, control is about living with the life force that enlivens us, neither repressing it nor allowing it to become the proverbial fire hose whipping around with no one directing the torrents. (Other times, the out-of-control metaphor changes and the fire hose might become a live electric wire, a flood, landslide, or a windstorm.) The relationship between the Hara and the Pineal Centers plays a major role in healing the twin energetic maladies of over control and lack of control. And here again, it is instructive to look at what happens when these two centers are not in harmony with each other, when our heads and our bellies are not talking to one another. The emotional and creative power of the Hara needs the guidance that comes from the connection to higher dimensions of consciousness available through the Pineal Center. This ensures that the Hara won't become an agent of strictly physical and willful control. For its part, the Pineal Center needs the grounding, containment, and centering of the Hara to bring forward its deep insights and bring them to earth. In other words, these two centers need each other.

## Problems and Opportunities

The allure of what is available through activating the Pineal Center is strong; it appeals to the desire, and indeed the need, for visionary guidance in our spiritual lives. The opening of spiritual sight is a wonderful process, but if that opening is not accompanied and tempered by a corresponding activation in the lower centers there will not be a means of drawing in and integrating into one's life what comes through all this openness. As one teacher of mine put it, "I can show you how to open your third eye in about six weeks, but it will take you the rest of your life to truly appreciate what you are seeing."

The Pineal Center draws very fast-moving energies into our consciousness, often accompanied by images and impressions from other dimensions of life. But without a corresponding rootedness in your lower body, the result can be "flash in the pan" experiences, in which a great insight or revelation comes briefly into your awareness only to fade away like a dream. A person with an active but ungrounded Pineal Center will tend to get lost in visions and in more extreme cases have difficulty in connecting with everyday life and other people. The question becomes, "How can I work with my Pineal Center and still keep my feet on the ground?" One part of the answer is to engage the Hara Center, its partner among the lower centers, and bring the two into balance with one another.

The other side of this particular coin is when a person's sense of control comes predominately from the Hara without the insight, inspiration and visionary influence of the Pineal Center. We can all think of people who are unable to believe that anything good can happen if things are just allowed to unfold by themselves, and therefore need to micromanage all the events and people in their lives. The balanced blend of the Pineal and Hara brings in an element of healthy control and makes it possible for us to surrender and trust that, while we do our part, most of life is in higher hands.

Another common disturbance of the control factor is in persons in whom *both* of these centers are very active, but their relationship is skewed and disjointed. The result is an image-filled, runaway Pineal Center accompanied by an uncontrollably emotional Hara Center. The uncontained emotionality of a Hara Center that isn't relating to its partner the Pineal Center can result in a wildly emotional up and down inner life. A Pineal Center that lacks the connection and grounding of its partner can lead to a very volatile third eye—everything clear as a bell one minute, totally confused the next.

Together, these two centers create an important control factor in our energetic systems. Our job here is to engage these centers so they can interact and come into balance with one another. We'll begin by creating a grounded contact with the Circulation of Control and then calling our spirit back to both of these energy centers.

## INNER PILGRIMAGE #23: *Working with the Circulation of Control*

We'll start with the Pineal Center. An easy way to take up contact with your Pineal Center is to use the Pineal Extension Point in the middle of your forehead. To find this position, put the tip of your little finger at the top of the bridge of your nose, right between your eyes. Now stack up the tips of your other three fingers on top of your little finger. Your index finger will be in the center of your forehead. Bring your attention to where the tip of your index finger is touching your forehead. Now remove your finger and allow your attention to relax and gather in that position in a loose, unfixed way. This way, your awareness will be able to hitch a ride on the energy movement, and you will be drawn into the activity of the Pineal Center.

One of the aspects of energy movement at an energy center is expansion and contraction, and this can be quite pronounced at your Pineal Center. Bear in mind that when your awareness is drawn into the activity of this center, you might be connecting with that movement in its expansion phase, in which case you will have the feeling of moving outward, away from the center of your head. If you find that happening, let your awareness be carried along with the energy movement. At some point, the expansion will turn around and your awareness will be carried into the center of your Pineal Center in the middle of your head. It is like catching an outbound bus when you want to go downtown: you know that at some point the bus will reach the end of its route and turn around and head in the other direction. You just stay on the bus. The same strategy applies for any contact with an energy-active position.

In all of these contacts—be they major energy centers, points, or streams—don't be discouraged if at first you don't feel much of anything. The time it takes for these energy-active positions to bloom in your awareness varies from person to person. As with any other skill, it takes practice to bring your awareness to places where it might not have gone before. Once you do make conscious contact, however, it will be much easier for you to find it the next time.

To contact the Hara Center I use a position located three finger-breadths under my navel. To locate it, put your index finger in your navel and then place your other fingers directly under it. Where the tip of your little finger is touching your abdomen is your beginning point. Now remove your finger and bring your relaxed awareness into this position.

## Part 1: Engage the Circulation of Control
*Exercise Steps:*

1. Sit comfortably in an upright position so you can breathe easily. Allow yourself a bit of time to settle in.

2. Drop your awareness into your Heart Center in the middle of your chest, and allow about a minute for that contact to deepen.

3. Release your contact with your Heart Center and drop your awareness into your Hara Center, three finger breadths below your navel. This is your Pineal Center's partner among the lower centers. The better your contact with your Hara, and the more in balance this important center is, the deeper and more balanced your connection with your Pineal Center will be. So give this contact plenty of time to settle in. Give this contact two minutes.

4. Once you have established a good contact with your Hara, now is the time to release that contact and move your awareness slowly and consciously outward from your body about a foot and upward in a sweeping arc to the Pineal Extension Point in the middle of your forehead. Allow that contact to build a minute or so.

5. Disconnect from the Pineal and drop your awareness back into your Heart Center.

6. Repeat this circulation—Heart>Hara>Pineal—a couple of times.

7. Bring your awareness into your Hara Center and rest there.

8. End this part of the exercise by opening your eyes for a moment.

## Part 2: Call Your Spirit Back to your Hara Center

1. Read through the following list of Hara Center-related attributes. Choose one of them to work with and try to get a feeling contact with what that word or phrase stands for in you:

   - Calmness
   - Rage
   - Attraction: for example, how you draw someone to you, or feel attracted to someone
   - Rejection: for example, how you push someone away from you, or feel rejected by someone

2. Give this connection with *one* of these words or phrases a couple of minutes and let it draw you into some kind of experience. Don't judge what comes up in you. Even if, on the surface, nothing appears to be coming up, see if you can just sit with that feeling of "nothing."

3. Call your spirit back to your Hara center and see if you can feel where on your body the energy returns.

4. Repeat this process of calling your spirit back to you a number of times.

5. Sit ten minutes with what comes forward in you.

6. End the exercise and open your eyes.

## Part 3: Call Your Spirit Back to your Pineal Center

1. Take a few minutes after Part 2 before going on.

2. When you are ready to start again, repeat steps 1-6.

3. This time, instead of moving into your Hara, bring your awareness into your Pineal Center. When you do, here are some polarities belonging to the Pineal Center. Select one of these words and get a feeling contact with what it stands for in you:

   - Light
   - Darkness
   - Lightness
   - Heaviness

2. Let this contact draw you into some kind of experience. Again, allow whatever wants to come to the surface without judging it. That is the best way to allow your experience to carry you into something new. Trust the process.

3. Call your spirit back to your pineal center and see if you can feel where on your body the energy returns.

4. Allow some time for whatever wants to surface within you.

5. After about ten minutes, return to a normal sense of your body and end the exercise.

## Meditation on Control

We will be doing this meditation the same way as we did the previous one on the Circulation of Expression. This time we bring together the Hara and Pineal Centers and allow their activities to blend.

Exercise Steps:

1. Contact your Hara Center. Bring your awareness into the position three finger-breadths below your navel and allow this feeling contact to deepen. Give this contact a couple of minutes to deepen.

2. Move your awareness in a slow, conscious arc, a foot or so away from your body, up to your Pineal Center. Spend a couple of minutes with your Pineal Center.

3. Now move back down, in the same arc, to your Hara Center, and establish a feeling contact there again. Remember to go slowly and consciously. No hurrying. Allow your contact with your Hara Center to deepen for a couple of minutes before moving on.

4. Repeat steps two and three a couple of times.

5. Now connect your awareness with both your Hara and your Pineal Centers at the same time and feel their interaction.

6. Release this connection and bring the word "control" to mind. Try to get a feeling connection with what the word means to you.

7. Allow a five- to ten-minute period for a meditation in which you sit mindfully with whatever comes up inside you, neither trying to make anything come, nor trying to keep anything from coming.

8. End the exercise.

*Some Questions:*

- Were you able to make contact with each of these centers as you came to them?
- Was one center easier or more difficult to connect with than the other?
- How about the slow, conscious movement between centers? What did you discover in the energetic space between them?
- What new discoveries did you make in the meditation at the end of the exercise?

PARTNER TREATMENT #8: *The Pulley: A Partner Treatment for the Circulation of Control*

Here is a partner treatment for balancing the activity of the Hara and Pineal Centers. You will be engaging both centers at the same time so that they can interact, first by enhancing the connection between them, then by using *etheric massage* (see below) to create a blend of their activity. Here is how to go about it:

Step 1: Intersecting Lines of Connection Through the Middle of Your Partner's Head

1. Using fingertip contact,[21] connect both of your partner's Side Head Points and place your attention on the exchange of energy between them. These points are located two finger-breadths (your partner's fingertips) above the top of your partner's ears on the sides of her head. Once you have a good energetic contact with these points, give this connection a minute to deepen.

2. Release that connection and connect your partner's Point of Silence and Medulla Position, again using fingertip contact. The Point of Silence is located at the top of the bridge of your partner's nose, between her eyes. The Medulla Position is located at the

---

21    Here, you can take advantage of the natural polarity among your fingers to create a strong, clear interaction between these points by using a positively charged finger on one side and a negatively charged finger on the other. I typically use the tip of my ring finger (negatively charged) on one side and the tip of my middle finger (positively charged) on the other.

top of the groove of her neck at the base of her skull. Here, too, you are paying attention to the exchange of energy between these two points. Give this connection a minute to intensify.

3. Release this contact with your partner's head by removing your hands. The two lines of activity you have activated in steps one and two intersect in the middle of your partner's head.[22]

4. Gently place one hand on your partner's forehead and the other on her lower abdomen. Place the energy centers in your palms on the energy centers there: the Pineal Extension Point is three finger-breadths up from the bridge of your partner's nose and the Hara Center contact is three finger-breadths below her navel. Make the best energetic connection you can and pay attention to the natural exchange of energy to build between these positions. Touch lightly and mindfully, recalling the exercise "May I come closer?" from Chapter Eight.

5. Relax your hands. When you feel you have a good energetic connection with these positions, lift both hands slightly off your partner's body—an inch or so—and feel your energetic connection there. Keep your hands relaxed and fluid. Think of a hovering jellyfish, or seaweed growing from the ocean floor, ever moving with the currents, yet staying in one place.

6. With one hand at your partner's Pineal—see if you can keep your hand energetically open and fluid as it hovers above her forehead—begin by gently activating the energy at your partner's Hara Center. use your hand at her Hara to massage the energy above her belly, moving in a small circle. Move with the dominant direction of etheric flow: up the left side and down the right. Do this for about a minute.

7. Now rest the hand that was circulating the energy at your partner's Hara just off her body—remember to stay energetically connected and to keep your hand loose. This time, massage the energy at her Pineal Center. Here, too, you move with the dominant direction of etheric flow: up the left side and down the right.

8. Alternate back and forth between these centers—one hand stationary, but energetically fluid and connected, the other active with a gentle counterclockwise circulation of the energy.

9. Now you'll create a "pulley" whose wheels are your partner's Hara and Pineal Centers. Connect them by massaging the energy in the zone between your partner's Pineal and Hara Centers. Maintain a good energetic connection and move your hands close to her skin surface in a slow, sweeping motion up the left and down the right sides of her torso an inch or two either side of the midline.

10. When you reach one of the pulley's "wheels" (the Hara or the Pineal Center), circulate the energy a couple of times before moving back to the other one.

11. After moving two or three times around this circuit, gently place your hands back on your partner's body at her Pineal and Hara Centers and once again, pay attention to the natural exchange of energy between your hands. Give this a minute.

---

22   The line connecting the two Side Head Points goes through the pineal gland, while the one connecting the Point of Silence and the Medulla position passes through the pituitary gland. Activating these positions and enhancing their balanced interaction serves the blend of energetic activity between these two important endocrine glands. It also enhances the energetic balance in the center of your partner's head.

12. Release this position and use your hands to connect your partner's Hara first with her left knee and then with her right knee.
13. Now connect your partner's Hara with the sole of her left foot and then with the sole of her right foot.
14. Finish the treatment by placing your palms or fingertips on both her foot soles.

*Furthermore, we have not even to risk the adventure alone; for the heroes of all time have gone before us; the labyrinth is thoroughly known; we have only to follow the thread of the hero-path. And where we had thought to find an abomination, we shall find a god; where we had thought to slay another, we shall slay ourselves; where we had thought to travel outward, we shall come to the center of our own existence; where we had thought to be alone we shall be with all the world.*

Joseph Campbell

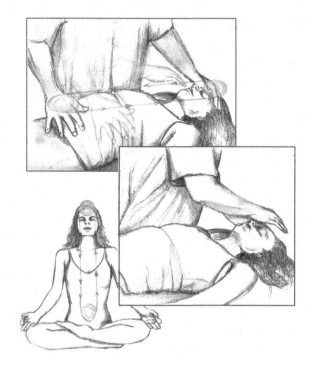

*The Pulley* is a form of *etheric massage* that follows the dominant direction of etheric flow: up the left side of your partner's body and down the front on the right side. The "wheels" of this "pulley" are your partner's Hara and Pineal Centers.

*The Circulation of Balance: An Alchemical Quest*

The pilgrim in your body is on a quest of transformation, and typically one of the first things to be transformed is the pilgrim's notion of what this journey is all about. In stories about spiritual quests, it is not uncommon for the hero to set out with some external or physically defined goal in mind, only to find out that the actual journey, the actual goal, is within. "But I thought I was supposed to _____!" Here, you can fill in the blank with some heroic deed, perhaps slaying a dragon, rescuing someone, or maybe saving the world. By and by, the hero catches on to the changed nature of the undertaking. His journey of a thousand days over unknown terrain isn't "out there"; it's "in here," which can come as a huge letdown for

138

people with careers as heroes in mind. It takes some doing, usually, for heroes to transform into pilgrims and get down to the new job at hand.

The hero-turned-pilgrim had been steeling himself for a clash with irreconcilable, monstrous forces. Now he finds himself dancing with them instead. This dance is depicted variously in mystic traditions as the Marriage of Heaven and Earth, the blend of masculine and feminine, yin and yang, the union of opposites, the alchemical marriage. In her book *Tulip Elegies: An Alchemy of Writing,* prairie alchemist Denise Low had this to say:

> ALCHEMY is about spiritual process, not primitive chemistry or metallurgy. The alchemical tradition is from a time of no distinction between sacred and secular, when the four elements—earth, air, water, and fire—behaved in meaningful patterns. The cosmic egg was still intact. Richard Grossinger writes about a "simultaneity" not unlike Carl Jung's idea of synchronicity; alchemy is: "A method of symbolism working on the simultaneity of a series of complementary pairs:
>
> Sun/Moon
> Gold/Silver
> Sulphur/Mercury
> King/Queen
> Male/Female
> Husband/Bride
> and Christ/Man
>
> The members of a pair work together in a balance, not in opposition."

The relationship between the Solar Plexus and Crown Centers gives us an energetic handle on a third overarching theme, that of balance itself. Balance is a perennial theme in energetic work, but the balance being spoken of here is not about something static or frozen, like a restaurant saltshaker tipped at an angle and poised precariously on a grain of salt. In the world of energy and consciousness, balance is a dynamic, ongoing process of blending and reblending the forces that act upon us and within us. Like the instinctive way your body stays in motion in order to stay in balance when you walk a tightwire, obeying the inner gyroscope of your equilibrium, so too does the world of energy and consciousness within you tend toward balance at every opportunity. To get in touch with this process, we'll approach this Circulation of Balance in the same way we did with the others, beginning with calling our spirit back to these two energy centers.

INNER PILGRIMAGE #24: *Working with the Circulation of Balance*
PART 1: Call Your Spirit Back to Your Solar Plexus Center
1. First make a feeling contact with the Solar Plexus Center and allow some time for the contact to intensify. I use the position three finger-breadths above my navel as a landmark for coming into the energy of the Solar Plexus Center. This is an effective starting point from which you begin to allow your awareness to be drawn into the center's activity. When you make contact with this or any other center, you might feel that you are being drawn into something. (You are!) The sensation might be that of something gathering inside you. Simply pay attention without trying to make anything happen.

2. Bring into your experience one of the feeling aspects of the Solar Plexus Center. As in all our practices in which you use a word to stimulate some inner activity, the idea is to get a felt connection with what the word stands for in you. Here are some good candidates for working with your Solar Plexus Center:

- Fears of all kinds: these would include fear of going crazy or losing control, fear of illness and death, fear of sexuality
- Love
- Feelings of openness and vulnerability
- Feelings of being closed, shut down
- Or see what comes up in you if you get a feeling contact with this little verse by poet Anita Birnberger:

*Guidepost*

*When you don't know*
*the next step to take,*
*take the one*
*you are most afraid of.*

3. Let this contact draw you into some kind of experience. Don't judge what comes up in you.
4. Call your spirit back to you and see if you can feel where on your body the energy returns.
5. Allow some time for whatever wants to surface within you. Resist the temptation to judge or censor what comes into your consciousness. Just let it move through without trying to change it.
6. After about ten minutes, return to a normal sense of your body and end the exercise. Take a few minutes before you continue on to Part 2.

Part 2: Call Your Spirit Back to Your Crown Center

Our system of energy centers mediates the full spectrum of human experience, from the most mundane to the subtlest and most sublime. Up to now, we have dealt with energy centers that have emotional polarities. They have a yin and yang to them, and they deal in aspects of life that have polarities. In the case of the Crown Center, however, we go beyond emotional polarities. For this reason, you won't be using sets of opposites to key into the qualities of this energy center as we have done with the other centers.

*Contact:* An easy way to contact your Crown Center is to first move your awareness to the highest point on the crown of your head. Now move it slightly forward, toward the front of your head, and slightly off the skin surface up a bit in your hair. This is where you can easily be drawn into a center contact with the energy movement of the Crown Center.

*Exercise Steps:*

1. Sit comfortably in an upright position so you can breath easily.
2. Move your awareness to your Heart Center in the middle of your chest, and allow some time for that contact to deepen.
3. Release your contact with your Heart Center and move your awareness into your Crown

Center, just above and slightly forward of the top of your head. Relax your awareness there. Give this contact a couple of minutes to settle in.

4. From this sense of contact, call your spirit back as you have done in other exercises and see if you can feel where on your body the energy returns.
5. Allow some time for whatever wants to surface within you.
6. After about ten minutes, return to a normal sense of your body and end the exercise.

Part 3: Meditation on Balance

Let's turn now to the communication between the members of the Circulation of Balance. We'll be setting this up like we did in the two previous meditations. Here are the steps:

Exercise Steps:
1. Bring your awareness into your Solar Plexus Center, three finger-breadths above your navel. Give this contact a couple of minutes to deepen.
2. Move your awareness in a slow, conscious arc, away from your body, up to your Crown Center. Spend a couple of minutes at your Crown Center.
3. Now move back down, in the same arc, to your Solar Plexus Center, and establish a feeling contact there again—two minutes.
4. Repeat these steps another time or two.
5. Now connect your awareness with both your Solar Plexus and your Crown Centers at the same time and feel their interaction. Sit with this contact for a minute.
6. Release this connection and bring the word "balance" to mind. Try to get a feeling connection with what the word means to you.
7. Allow a five to ten minute period for a meditation in which you sit mindfully with whatever comes up inside you, neither trying to make anything come up in you, nor trying to keep anything from coming up.
8. End the exercise.

INNER PILGRIMAGE #25: *Bringing the Three Circulations Together*

When I teach these exercises in workshops, there is always someone who starts to feel sorry for the poor Heart Center. They hope I haven't been making some terrible mistake by accidentally leaving it out. But they can relax: I'm leaving the best for last.

We have worked with our three energy circulations in isolation from one another in order to get at important aspects of our psycho-spiritual growth and development. Now it's time to bring them together. Here is where we bring in the Heart Center, the lynchpin for all these circulations.

Exercise Steps:
1. Begin by bringing your awareness into your heart center—one minute.
2. With your awareness in your Heart Center, introduce the Twelve-Breath Cycle of energetically balanced breathing that you learned in Chapter Four. As you recall, this cycle consists of three slow, conscious breaths in each of these four modes:
   - IN through your nose and OUT through your nose—three times
   - IN through your nose and OUT through your mouth—three times
   - IN through your mouth and OUT through your nose—three times
   - IN through your mouth and OUT through your mouth—three times

141

NOTE: In the steps that follow, you will be moving your
awareness from one energy center to another in an arc, away
from your body. The direction of this movement will follow the
dominant direction of the etheric, up the left front and down
the right front of your body.

3. Sacral Center: Release your contact with your Heart Center and bring your awareness out away from your body and move it in an arc around the right side of your body to your Sacral Center at the center of your sacrum. Allow that contact to build up for two minutes.

4. Throat Center: Disconnect from your contact with your Sacral Center and move your awareness outward and up in an arc around the left side of your body to your Throat Center on the front of your throat below your Adam's apple. Allow this contact about two minutes to become deeper.

5. Hara Center: Let go of your Throat Center contact and move your awareness now in an arc out and down the right side of your body to your Hara Center—two minutes.

6. Pineal Center: Now disconnect from your Hara Center and move your awareness out away from your body in an arc out and up the left side of your body to your Pineal Center. Let this contact work for about two minutes.

7. Solar Plexus Center: Release your connection with your Pineal Center and move now in the same arcing out to the right side of your body and down to your Solar Plexus Center. Allow two minutes for this contact to intensify.

8. Crown Center: Let go of the contact with your Solar Plexus Center and move your awareness in an arc up on the left side of your body to your Crown Center and allow about two minutes for this contact to build.

9. Heart Center: Finally, disconnect from your Crown Center and move your awareness in an arc back down the right side of your body to your Heart Center. Let this contact be a short meditation, allowing several minutes for whatever impressions, insights and sensations want to come up within you. Take up to ten minutes for this concluding meditation.

10. End the exercise by slowly coming back to your normal body consciousness. Slowly open your eyes and move your body. You might want to take some notes.

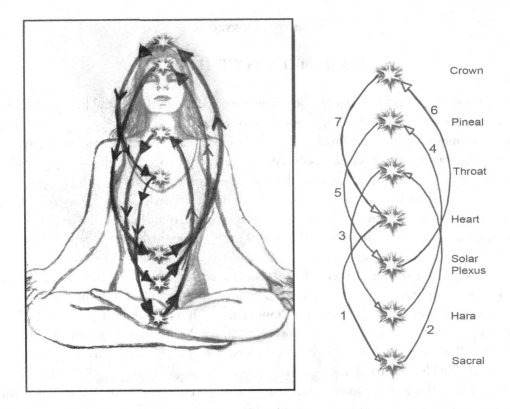

In this exercise, move your awareness into your Heart Center and then to the lower and upper energy center of each of the circulations in turn, then back to your Heart Center.

The inner pilgrimage of energy healing encourages the meeting and harmonious blending of naturally occurring opposites, heaven and earth, within you: the inner and outer, masculine and feminine, light and dark, known and unknown, conscious and unconscious, and yin and yang in your whole system have a chance to interact. That ongoing interaction is constantly giving rise to what psychologist Robert Johnson called our "evolving character." Our work with these paired energy centers is a special example of this: the process of expression is served by the blend of activity between the Sacral and Throat Centers, the process of control by the blend of activity between the Hara and Pineal Centers, and the process of balance by the blend between the Solar Plexus and the Crown. It is in this interaction between the centers that they come into balance with one another.

My personal practice of energywork and my healing and teaching work with others have been helped immeasurably by the work with these paired energy centers and the way their activity joins in the heart. That work has given me some of my best insights into the energetic and psycho-spiritual maladies we humans suffer from when heaven and earth don't meet harmoniously in us. They also give me a vision of the hidden wholeness that is accessible to each of us when they do meet harmoniously. Hardly a session goes by that I don't consult the wisdom of these centers of consciousness.

## MAKING FRIENDS WITH SOUND

My partner Diane and I once took a journey to Abadiânia, in the central highlands of Brazil, to see a famous healer whose base of operations sees the coming and going of hundreds of thousands of pilgrims each year. Abadiânia is the site of a natural vortex of earth energies situated over subterranean quartz crystal beds. All of this energy, together with the highly charged atmosphere of the healing center, makes this location pulsate and hum with subtle vibration. Imagine the ringing high pitch caused by running a moist fingertip around the rim of the largest, finest crystal wine glass in the world. Now imagine that sound raised to a level just beyond normal hearing. That is what permeates the side of town where the healer's center is located; you can't quite hear it, but it's there.

We stayed on the third floor of our *pousada*, or guest house, which faced the center of town. The configuration of the house made our room a sound trap, pulling in every stray sound wave in the area and amplifying it. I thought seriously about climbing out on the balcony and painting a giant ear around our window. No sooner did the sun go down than it seemed that the overall noise level of our surroundings increased dramatically in diversity and volume. Or was it the highly sensitized state of my senses, due to the intensive meditative, healing, and spiritual activities I was involved with at the healing center that caused this amplification? Nights awake in our room, we rode the waves of a relentless sea of sound, the din created by Abadiânia's inhabitants, suddenly numbering in the millions and all of them awake and festive, interspersed with brief furies of wind-pelted rain against our wall, fading to millions and millions of little yappy dogs, birds that sang actual melodies, and the lament of ensembles of roosters and peacocks. Inside our room, the walls and ceiling were alive with creatures that skittered and scratched. There were times of peace, of course, but the noise factor was considerable and intense. In my meditations, I had to somehow make friends with all the sound vibrations in the environment because they just weren't going to go away. That began with finding a way to stop resisting them.

I turned my attention and curiosity toward the chaotic din and started *listening* to the sound instead of shutting it out. I gradually became part of the audience. By and by, the cacophony shifted its character and turned into a huge, crazy symphony orchestrated just for me. I followed the chord changes in the blaring Brazilian pop songs and studied the harmonies. I heard horns playing somewhere and tracked the migrating packs of canines yelping through the neighborhood suddenly, inexplicably, joined by choirs of Benedictine monks chanting from blaring boom boxes. After what seemed like hours, my internal resistance gave way to a burst of glory in which, as singer Paul Simon says, "sound becomes a song." This became my official spiritual entry into my pilgrimage to South America, and after that, the sound was no longer an obstacle to me.

# CHAPTER TWELVE

## TWIN STRUCTURES OF CONSCIOUSNESS

*… like orbiting twin stars, one visible, one dark, the trajectory of
what's evident, forever affected by the gravity of what's concealed.*

Sue Grafton

One of the most common misconceptions about meditation and energy healing practices is that they will mellow you out. Of course, they are a means of shifting your consciousness, finding balance and stillness. Properly applied, they will help you to ground and integrate the life force and wisdom within you. But there are times when the things you do in the name of healing and the expansion of your consciousness propel you, like a TV wrestler getting slammed headlong into the ropes, right into what has been in your way. What writer Nathaniel Mead said about meditation certainly holds true for other forms of energywork: "The attempt to turn a potent consciousness-altering technique into a basic physical therapy and stress management led to a host of upsetting side effects … meditators who began their practice with the idea of reducing stress came face-to-face with their true selves, and the results were sometimes far from relaxing."

There are times in inner growth when the way, both within and without, is blocked or complicated by detours and diversions you never could have foreseen in a million years. Sometimes you just have to agree with whoever it was that said, "The problem with self-knowledge is that, at first, the news is all bad!" Indeed, when you find yourself internally shifting away from the world you have known and taken for granted most of your life and step into the wilder-feeling, more fluid world of spiritual process, there come moments when the only thing you can do is surrender to what is happening with you, blockages, detours, and all. This is the road less traveled in your world, and working through what is blocking your path and resisting your progress makes your path what it is.

In my practice of energywork, both with myself and with others, I run into one degree or another of this phenomenon on a daily basis. I call it the *twin structure* phenomenon: it seems that you don't move into something new without activating a parallel universe of factors, typically the kinds of things that have kept you from that move. The attempt to increase the mobility of an injured limb, for example, often means first meeting and releasing the pain and restriction that is keeping the limb immobile. The attempt to bring consciousness into a part of your body that has been inaccessible to you will, by and by, bring you into an encounter with what has kept it frozen or numb. What frequently happens in the use of affirmations is a good example. Even an affirmation of some quality you would like to embody and express in your life typically brings forward an array of reasons why that particular trait isn't yet in the cards for you.

*If you want to identify me,*
*ask me not where I live,*
*or what I like to eat,*
*or how I comb my hair,*
*but ask me what I am living for,*
*in detail,*
*and ask me what I think*
*is keeping me from living fully,*
*for the thing I want to live for.*

Thomas Merton
(used with permission)

The attempt to move into some new phase of your life is often initially beset by obstacles from without and within.

There are different levels of the twin structure phenomenon in our lives. If you get in your car in the morning and start to back out of the driveway to drive to work and find that you can't do it, there can be many different reasons. Maybe there's no gas in the tank of your car. Maybe there's a tricycle, a fallen-down cottonwood tree, or a family of raccoons in the driveway. Internally, you might find yourself so besieged by reasons why you really don't *want* to go to work, and why it's a bad idea to drive when you should be walking, and on and on, that it paralyzes you. Beyond that, there are the things that you experience *because* you're trying to back out of your driveway— also part of the phenomenon of twin structures. Perhaps your eye is caught and inspired by the beauty of a giant formation of Canadian geese arrowing its way across the sky over your head at the very moment you get out of your car to shoo the raccoons away. Twin structures include all the things that arise as you take action. The encounter with twin structures of consciousness is inevitable as long as we are we are operating within the polarities of existence. It seems that whenever you take action on something, other things start to happen as well. You take action, and the universe moves, as well, as mystic provocateurs like Buckminster Fuller and J. R. Miller point out, at a *right angle* to your line of action.

### Spring Cleaning

The simplest level of the twin structure is the level of the tricycle in the driveway, or the *junk* level. There are things that you simply have to clear out of the way in order to get going with what you're trying to do. In meditation and personal energy practices, the junk level can show up in the form of inner distractions that typically come from the buildup of detritus in your energy field, the stuff you collect in your aura in the course of living your everyday life. If you work therapeutically with others, it's a good idea to be familiar with tactics for minimizing what you collect from other people's energy fields and for shedding what you do collect in the course of doing your work.[23]

Another such obstacle is the residue of emotional energy that has not yet found a way to clear from your system. Chinese

---

23    For more on this subject, see the subchapter "Unwanted Energy Transfer and the Myth of 'Negative Energy'" in my book *Energy Healing: A Pathway to Inner Growth*.

medicine identifies specific organs—heart, pericardium, lungs, liver, spleen, and kidneys—which act, on the energetic level, as emotional filters. That is to say they collect emotional residue in much the same way that the oil filter on your car collects the dirt that otherwise would gum up your oil. The problem is, when the filter gets full, in both cars and bodily organs, it can become a *source* of dirt rather than a collection site for it.

Regular energetic practice will go a long way to preventing the unnecessary buildup of subtle debris in your energy system, whatever the source, but it is a good idea to know how to jump start the process when you need to. Here are a couple of "spring cleaning" exercises for you and your energy field.

PILGRIM'S SPRING CLEANING EXERCISE #1: *The Subway Cure: Sweeping the Etheric Streams Clean*
If you have spent your day in a city, and especially if your time has been spent in large crowds of people—the places that come to mind are subways, busses, trains, department stores—more than likely you have collected your share of subtle energetic debris by the time you get home at night. Then, it's a good idea to do some aura cleansing.

This exercise makes use of the energy streams that act like conduits of energy movement up and down your body, arms and legs. The purpose of this exercise is to literally sweep your energy field clean of built-up debris by using these channels in your subtle energetic field. Remember that your energy field is electromagnetic in nature and, as a result, can pick up charge the same way a magnet does. It is also self-cleansing if given a chance, so what we are doing is supporting it as it does its job.

Here is a simple, effective way to activate the self-cleansing potential of your energy system.

Energy Paintbrushes and Energy Brooms
Let's begin by identifying a couple of ways of using your hands. One way is to make an *energy paintbrush* by using your ring finger and middle finger together. These fingers both have strong emanations of energy, one negatively charged and the other positively charged. Together, they create a blend of forces that is ideal for the purpose of moving stuck energy. Another way to use your hands is to … use your hands. Since we are going to sweep our energy streams clean, we use our hands as *energy brooms*.

> *Energywork Tip:* When you use your hands to sweep energy, keep them loose and relaxed. Additionally, keep your wrists loose and flexible. The positively and negatively charged energy streams in your arms, along with numerous acupuncture meridians, come together at your wrists, and this flexibility will allow the energy to move as freely as possible.

Preparation:
- Do this exercise standing.
- Take off your shoes.
- Get grounded. This is how the energy will be able to move down your body into the earth.

147

Exercise Steps:

<u>The Outside of Your Arms</u>

1. Begin by rubbing your hands together. This charges the energy field around your hands. Bear in mind that when we do energywork with our hands, we are letting the etheric body of our hands interact with the etheric body of the person who we are working with (in this case with ourselves).

2. Reach around the front of your head, and place your right hand on the left side of the base of your skull. Allow a moment for this contact to build up.

3. With the energy broom of your whole right hand, gently, slowly sweep the energy slowly down the outside of your left arm, and off your fingertips. Visualize that you are sweeping water along a gutter, just getting it moving. Do this several times.

> NOTE: Go easy. This is not an exorcism; there is no need to feel that you are flinging evil from you. You are simply giving an encouraging boost to the energy movement which is already there in the energy pathways of your arm.

4. Change arms, this time using your left hand on the right side of your head and down the outside of your right arm. Do this sweep several times.

<u>The Insides of Your Arms</u>

5. Now it's time to sweep the inside of your arms. Place the palm of your right hand on your left side, next to your left breast, just below your left armpit. When you feel a good energetic contact, move your hand up the side of your ribcage, between your breast and your armpit, then down the inside of your arm out to your fingertips. Do this several times.

6. Repeat this with your other side, using your other hand. Do this several times.

<u>The Front of Your Body</u>

7. Put the tips of your ring and middle fingers together—these are your energetic paintbrushes—and place them in the middle of your forehead, that is to say, on your Pineal Extension Point. Give this contact a bit of time to deepen.

8. Using your fingertips on the skin surface, gently sweep down your body. Here is the path they follow:

  • Down your face on either side of your nose
  • Around the corners of your mouth
  • Down the outer line of your throat
  • Down the front of your body an inch or so either side of the midline of your body
  • Around your genitals, and
  • Down the insides of your legs to the ground

The idea here is to sweep *gently*. Think of your hand as a broom gently sweeping water flowing along the gutter on the side of a street. The additional boost helps the water to move the sticks and soil in the gutter. Go slowly, with your awareness in your fingers. Sweep the whole line several times.

## The Back of Your Body

9. Join your two energy paintbrushes again at the middle of your forehead and again let the contact intensify. This time, move them up your forehead, back over the top and back of your head, down the back of your neck and down your spine as far as you can reach. On this sweep over the top of your head, move the fingertips on your right and left hands on the skin surface about three-quarters of an inch either side of the midline.

10. Simply go as far down your spine as you can, then lift your fingers off and reach up your back from below and feel that you are pulling the energy down your back. Unless you are pretty limber you will probably have a small gap between where you left off on the stroke down your neck and spine, and where you pick it up from below. Simply invite the energy to come and meet your fingertips when you reach up for it.

11. Continue sweeping your fingertips along your skin surface, down the length of your spine and sacrum, and down the backs of your legs to your heels into the ground.

12. Repeat these strokes a number of times.

## Solar Plexus

The middle of your body gets a little extra treatment because of the magnetic charge that mounts up in the etheric storage of your Solar Plexus Center.[24] So let's give it a little extra help in clearing itself:

1. Cross your arms over your ribcage. Place your right palm on the left side of your ribcage next to your solar plexus, and your left palm on your right side at the same level. From this starting position, you will have your hands and arms lightly draped, one just above the other, over the middle of your body.

2. Bring your awareness into your hands and slowly pull both hands across your solar plexus at the same time. Bring your hands out to your sides, a foot or so from your body each time. Do this several times, and each time you do it, alternate your starting hand positions. That means that one time your right hand is higher on your body, and the next time your left hand is higher.

3. When you have completed this sequence, sit down and sense your body and the space around it. Visualize clear light filling your body and energy field.

4. Take a few minutes to feel what has taken place in you, and then end the exercise.

PILGRIM'S SPRING CLEANING EXERCISE #2: *Nuclear Waste Clean-Up*

Here is another self-treatment exercise, designed to remove unproductive energetic flotsam and jetsam from your energy field. I give it the name "Nuclear Waste Clean-Up" because I have heard of its use by people who live in the vicinity of nuclear power plants and atomic test sites. I have recommended it for people whose energy fields are getting rid of subtle waste materials in their energy fields after a period of illness or drug use, radiation treatments, or chemotherapy. Even if you don't live with extraordinary toxicity, this is an effective energy field cleanser.

While the previous exercise had to do with sweeping out some major energy streams, this

---

24    In this series, you are using your hands (your energy brooms) to gently sweep energy along the streams in your arms and down your body and legs. For a detailed look at this treatment, come to the Pilgrim Extras on my Web site. (See the instructions for finding the Pilgrim Extras on the last page of this book.)

exercise works by creating a way for subtle particles to be attracted away from your energy field. For this self-treatment, you are going to need some equipment:

- An aluminum pot, pan, or basin deep and large enough to submerge both of your hands, wrists, and arms in it when it is filled with water, ideally the kind used for roasting a turkey in the oven. If no such aluminum vessel is at hand, line the inside surface of a suitably sized vessel with aluminum foil.

- Lukewarm water

- One cup of baking soda

- A towel to dry your hands after the exercise

Preparation:
- Fill the aluminum basin with lukewarm water.

- Pour in a cup of baking soda, and swirl it around until it dissolves in the water.

- Sit down and place the basin in front of you at about knee level. The easiest way is to sit down on a chair and put it on another chair in front of you.

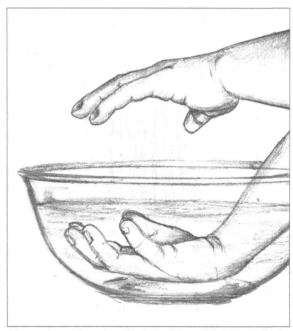

You can use the absorbent qualities of baking soda to draw subtle debris out of your energy field. This is a good practice for general use. It is especially useful for cleansing your system after a period of illness or drug use, radiation treatments, or chemotherapy.

Exercise Steps:
1. Place one hand in the water, palm up, deep enough that the water comes up well above your wrist. Keep the back of your hand *above the bottom of the basin*.
2. Position your other hand above the surface of the water with the palm facing downward

toward the palm of the hand in the water. Your palms are now facing each other, one in the water, one out.

3. Place your attention on both palms, as well as the space between them. Allow the natural exchange of energy between your hands to take place. Simply have your awareness on what is going on between your hands. Give this five minutes.

4. Switch hands. Now the hand that was in the water is above the water's surface, palm down, facing your other hand that is now in the water, palm up—five minutes.

> NOTE: You might find that the space between your hands becoming noticeably *hot*. This is a good sign that your aura is discharging what it wants to get rid of. If this doesn't happen, don't worry, but if it does, just allow it to happen.

5. Now put both hands in the water, palms up—again not touching the bottom of the basin— and allow them to discharge for another five minutes.

6. Pull your hands out of the water and spend a moment visualizing clear light filling your body.

7. Now see clear light filling the water into which you have just released the waste energy from your energy field (in other words, bless it).

8. Empty the water outside in your garden and let nature continue the transformation of the energy you have just released.

These two self-treatments are handy ways to jettison unproductive energy from your system. In the first exercise, you are enhancing your capacity for being like a lightning rod that can conduct energy safely into the ground. In the second self-treatment, you are using the absorbing qualities of water and baking soda to remove subtle debris from your aura. Typically, what these energies need is to get moving again in order to become useful or be transformed.

These exercises are examples of the basic junk-removal level of work with yourself, not unlike cleaning your house so you can live in it comfortably. Let's look now at a deeper level of the twin structures of consciousness. This time, they have to do with hidden attitudes.

### The Trouble with Affirmations

In energy healing, we pay a great deal of attention to the etheric, the layer of energy activity which immediately surrounds and penetrates the physical body This is because it is a bridge between your conscious and non-conscious selves. Whenever you introduce energy-active elements such as sound, color, geometric shape, touch, or rhythm into your practice, they influence your etheric and tend to increase activity at this threshold of your conscious awareness. Meditative practices and work with the energy-active positions in and around your body will stir things up at this vital interface, and one of the consequences is that they can bring you face to face with a lot of twin structures.

Another such element that affects the etheric is language, because it links powerfully to beliefs and feeling. The use of language includes the use of affirmations. When we look at affirmations from the standpoint of what they create in the etheric, they are a very interesting kind of energy practice, and one that can take us well beyond conventional ideas of positive thinking or intention setting.

The etheric is the storehouse of the subconscious, and whenever you hold a charged or emotionally important word or phrase in your thoughts it will activate your etheric, along with the twin structure structures held within it. Our meditations on expression, control, and balance in the last chapter contained numerous examples of using a word to stimulate a response from your etheric. When you introduce a positive affirmation—indeed any time you intentionally move your consciousness toward some specific quality—you might find yourself confronted with its "evil twin." What often comes forward instead of the quality you are affirming is exactly the opposite, especially when you are affirming a quality you're inwardly convinced you don't have. Don't worry, though, it's just an encounter with twin structures, an inherent element of the etheric, and one you can work with.

With this understanding, the practice of affirmations can become a way to lure twin structures out of hiding. They create an opportunity to make elements of your psyche conscious that would otherwise be difficult to get at. The trouble with affirmations and positive visualizations comes when you do them in an attempt to get away from what you think are problems. Wouldn't it be subversive if, instead, you used affirmations in order to do the opposite, to help you to turn toward what is getting in the way? Here is a simple piece of "spiritual judo" to try on yourself for that purpose.

INNER PILGRIMAGE #26: *Affirmation Exercise in Three Persons*
This exercise gives you an opportunity to tease out hidden unconscious twin structures in your etheric—typically, in the form of hidden attitudes and beliefs—that have been getting in the way of new impulses. It helps hidden attitudes to change, not only by giving you insights into what they are, but also by bringing about change in the actual etheric structure of your subconscious. Affirmations tend to contradict the memory stored in your etheric, which is why they can get such a reaction. At the same time, they create an opening for the callings and qualities that want to express through you. This practice helps you to draw out and let go of what keeps a deeper process from taking place.

If you have ever worked through the pages of *The Artist's Way*, by Julia Cameron, you have had plenty of opportunity to see this principle at work. That book is dedicated to connecting you with the creative life within you. Every exercise is a move toward that internal creator. At every turn, the reader is told to note what the author calls the "blurts," the spontaneous objections that boil up when you dare to think anything good about yourself or the artist within you.

The following exercise functions on the same principle as what Hakomi body-centered psychotherapy practitioners call a *probe*. The therapist invites the client to closely monitor what happens when he hears a simple statement like, "I'm glad you are here." The client notes what comes spontaneously, all by itself, whether it is a subtle change in body feeling, a memory, or an internal counterstatement, perhaps something about how "no one could possibly be glad that I am here."

Here is an example of a self-probe, which uses an affirmation stated in three variations. Start with the affirmation in first person as an "I" statement; then in second person, as if you were addressing another person; and finally using third person, as if you were talking about someone else to another person. These three different inflections of the statement each create a distinct set of feelings as you introduce them into your energy system and deeper consciousness. Try this and see what happens.

Exercise Steps:

1. Sitting quietly with your eyes closed, begin this meditative exercise by breathing slowly and deeply. Allow yourself the time to become quiet, centered and relaxed.
2. Internally, make an affirmation:
   - Make it a positive statement about yourself and its meaning for the world in which you live or the people around you.
   - Use your name in the statement.
   - Formulate it in first person, then second person, and then third person.

   Here is a simple example:

   **I**, Jim, like **myself**, and as a result, **I** like other people.
   **You**, Jim, like **yourself**, and as a result, **you** like other people.
   **He**, Jim, likes **himself**, and as a result, **he** likes other people.

3. Internally repeat this triad of positive statements ten or twelve times. Go slowly and feel what the words touch upon in you, as opposed to merely thinking them.
4. Pause and allow whatever comes up to come without judging it.
5. Repeat step three again, then pause again, paying attention to what comes up in you.
6. End the exercise and take note of what took place. With any exercise that activates your psyche, you also have a good opportunity to observe what comes up in your dreams in the days immediately following the practice.

When using this three-person affirmation exercise, or one built on the same pattern, it is possible to encounter deep-seated attitudes, rigid belief systems about yourself or about the "way things are." Consciously encountering these inner structures, stubborn and retrograde as some of them might seem, and simply meeting them with mindful acceptance—neither trying to make anything happen, nor trying to prevent anything from happening—is a step toward change. The affirmation lures the hidden twin into the daylight of your awareness. See if you can let this happen without forcing what emerges to be different than it is.

Here is another example of how to work with twin structures of consciousness, this time in the service of healing your major energy centers.

INNER PILGRIMAGE #27: *Using the Twin structures of Your Major Energy Centers*
In the last chapter, we made use of the fact that words can activate twin structures of consciousness when they link to what has meaning and emotion for you. As a result, they can be important keys to healing when they are used as probes. Here are pairs of words that key in to important emotional and psychological twin structures of your major energy centers:

- *Perineal Center*: Supported/Unsupported.
- *Sacral Center*: Success/Failure; Meaning/Meaninglessness.
- *Hara Center*: Rage/Calm.
- *Solar Plexus Center*: Love/Fear.
- *Heart Center*: Joy/Sorrow.

- *Throat Center*: Expression/Repression.

- *Pineal Center*: Light/Dark; Light/Heavy.

- *Crown Center*: No emotional polarities like the other centers. The Crown will reflect the composite state of the other centers. In other words, as your other centers come more into balance, you will find your Crown Center mirroring that balance.

The pattern of the exercise will be familiar to you from the last chapter:

1. When you have a good contact with one of your energy centers, introduce a word that represents a side of the polarity of that particular center. For example, if you choose to work with your Heart Center, first settle into your contact; choose one of this center's aspects, joy or sorrow, and get a feeling contact with what that word means to you (as opposed to just repeating the word over and over again in your head). In this way, you are placing the *energy* of that word in the energy center so that it can respond.

2. Give this connection of energy center and word a couple of minutes to deepen.

3. Release that contact and settle into a meditation of ten minutes.

4. End the meditation and take note of your experience.

Words used in this way can be like a finger you use to touch something in yourself. They can trigger whole complexes of inner experience. When you use a word in meditation to touch on anything with an emotional polarity, you get both sides of that polarity. Meditating with the word "joy" at your Heart Center, might, for example, bring forward an experience of sorrow in you. Allow that to happen. Conversely, deliberately turning toward sorrow at your Heart Center can reveal emerging joy. Remember that *both* sides of the coin are present when you enter such a practice, and neither is more important than the other. In this case, it is a way of getting to know your Heart Center. So don't be afraid when you encounter the opposite of what you have introduced into your meditation. Twin structures of consciousness are a fact of energetic life, and paying attention to them is the first step in making use of them. The invocation of the *Joyful and Sorrowful Mysteries* has a long history in some Christian contemplative traditions, and it is an example of inviting the twin structures of the Heart Center to become conscious. This process allows these opposites to blend and come into balance, which opens the door your consciousness to move beyond the polarity of joy and sorrow. That is why it is important to work with both sides of the polarities you invoke with such a practice.

Let's move now to an example of twin structures that I encountered in an unlikely place.

*The Twin Structures of Power Places: An Energywork Lesson from a Concentration Camp*
For several years I lived near Dachau, Germany, where one of the largest Nazi concentration camps was located. Even a short tour of the grounds leaves a strong impression. Rows of barracks stretch out in the tidy right-angled enclosure, surrounded by neat, evenly spaced coils of barbed wire atop gray cement walls. Everything is set on a grid in right angles. Men operating under the bizarre trance of the Nazis' "final solution" apparently developed a neurotic worship of the squarish details of their mission in order to keep alive the frame of mind necessary to run a successful concentration camp. According to some accounts, there was always a prisoner whose duty it was to go from barrack to barrack with a carpenter's square and a ball of string to snap

straight chalk-lines on the floors in order to make sure that each bunk was exactly perpendicular to the walls of the room.

The grounds of the Dachau Concentration Camp are well kept. Clean white gravel pathways crunch under the feet of tens of thousands of tourists who come each year. The museum's photo exhibition shows masses of wasted humans. Eyes of prisoners, staring into an unblinking camera lens, reach out to you across generations. Other now-famous photos show piles of their shoes and eyeglasses. Inside one of the crematoria, there is a memorial plaque with the name of Noor Inayat Khan, sister of the late Sufi leader Pir Vilayat Khan.

There is no spreading chestnut tree with a beer garden waiting outside the camp's museum. Germans take their serious youngsters through the Dachau Concentration Camp for a lesson in history. A visit to Dachau at the right time can galvanize a young person's life with attitudes against ever again going through such a national berserk episode. The deep memory of Dachau is intact, scorched into the atmosphere and recorded in the stones underfoot.

Our meditation group visited the convent of Carmelite sisters who live on the grounds at Dachau. Even after a day of tramping around the sterile, depressing concentration camp grounds, I found these sisters unbelievably cheerful. Flying nuns, their light blue hand-washed linens flapped like wind-borne prayers from a clothesline on the convent roof. Behind a screen that marked the boundary to their cloister, we attended vespers and then meditated in their chapel. Dark visions and silent echoes swarmed around us, yet they were accompanied by light every bit as intense. Our group was taken with the strong, palpable feeling of angelic presence.

My meditations and the meditations of those in our group were filled with geometric structures of light. In my own inner vision, blackness covered the concentration camp grounds like an obsidian pyramid, while at the same time a corresponding pyramid of crystalline light extended into the ground underneath. The more I explored the darkness and impressions of the atrocities that had left their mark, the more I saw of the details of that luminous pyramid below us. Here, at this stark reminder of some of history's shadows, I encountered twin structures of terror and darkness paralleled by geometric light structures and great power. Though I was rather baffled by those experiences at the time, I awoke to the strong conviction that we were meditating at a genuine *power place*, albeit one in which the power had enormously cruel manifestations, and that there is an activity of light at the Dachau Concentration Camp equal to the darkness. I now look back at this experience at Dachau as a strong example of an energy-active position on the planet, with its own twin structures.

Many geographic places are influenced by powerful planetary forces, and many of them are sites of healing and restoration, or the opposite. I am fortunate enough to do part of my work at a hot springs retreat center where the healing properties of the land and waters are very palpable. I am accustomed to inviting the energies of the natural environment into my healing sessions. Interestingly, the Native Americans teach that healing lands like this are places where you go for healing, but not places to live full time (in that light, I'm also fortunate to live away from the hot springs). In their wisdom about the forces of the earth, could they have known something about the twin structures that come with such power?

Up to now, our internal spiritual traveler has journeyed to energy-active positions on our bodies. Now, with our knowledge of twin structures in hand, we can take another step by energetically visiting energy-active places on the earth.

INNER PILGRIMAGE #28: *Earth Healing Meditation: Linking to Power Places on Your Body and the Planet*

There is a parallel between the energy-active positions located on our bodies and the power places on the earth. Linking your awareness with sacred sites and power places in meditation is a way to connect with the webwork of energy that moves through the planet and around it. Typically, meditators will link their awareness with places like Macchu Picchu or Stonehenge when doing such a practice, as they are power places where ancient spiritual traditions have had their focus.

But let's take this thinking a step further. In the self-healing energy practices in this book, you have linked your awareness with energy centers, points and streams of energy activity in and around your body—in every way analogous to the energetic grids, vortices, and ley lines of the earth—and moved your awareness among them.[25] In so doing, you have allowed them to interact and harmonize. Remembering that healing often involves bringing together twin structures in harmony, let's try also linking with a power spot associated with negative events, such as Dachau, Auschwitz or one of the other concentration camps, and moving our awareness between it and a power spot that is associated with positive events.

To enter into such a meditation safely, I recommend building up your practice in steps, beginning at the level of your own energetic system. Here is how you can go about it:

> PLEASE NOTE: If you are a person who easily links with energy and find yourself going quickly into other states of consciousness, please use an exercise like this one judiciously. Your greatest safeguard is to do all the steps and observe the time limits for each step. While it is a fact that actually connecting your consciousness with the energies and stored memories of a place can draw you into experiences held in those places, doing this for short, pre-determined periods of time will also teach you how to come back to your normal state of consciousness and integrate such experiences.

## Part 1: Strong Center–Weak Center

One of the simplest ways of bringing balance and healing to your energy system is to connect your awareness with the energy center with which you have the easiest contact, then move to the one that is most difficult for you to contact, and then move slowly and consciously back and forth between them. What you are doing is allowing these two areas of your energy system and psyche to interact with one another. Areas of strength meet with areas of weakness, areas of health with areas of injury, consciousness with unconsciousness. Achieving a balance of activity between such areas is an excellent way to bring overall balance into your system and enhance your self-healing potential. Facilitating this sort of communication between twin structures—in this case, between your essential wholeness and areas that are somehow cut off from that wholeness—is an important piece of the healing puzzle.

If you have been working with your energy centers, you probably have a sense of the ones with which you have easy contact and those less blessed. In other words, you could probably select a relatively strong center and a relatively weak one. If not, begin by connecting your awareness with each of your major centers in turn. Then you'll see which you have the most and the least easy connection. Then you can go on with the exercise.

---

25    Here, you might want to read, or reread, the anecdote "A Visit to Two Scottish Healers" found at the end of Chapter Four.

1. Choose the energy center with which you connect *most easily* and the one that is *least easy* for you to connect with.

2. Bring your awareness into your Heart Center. Take two or three minutes with this initial contact.

3. Move your awareness into your strong center, and give this contact a couple of minutes to deepen.

4. Release that contact and move your awareness into your weak center and give this contact a couple of minutes.

5. Slowly move your awareness from one to the other, pausing with each of these energy centers to let your contact deepen.

6. After moving slowly and consciously between the two centers you have selected, bring your awareness back to your Heart Center, and take some time for a short meditation, about ten minutes, allowing whatever comes forward in you to do so.

7. Take note of your experiences.


Part 2: Healing for Places in Your Known World

Now that you have connected with yourself energetically by moving back and forth between centers that represent areas of strength and areas of need in yourself, let's turn the process toward the world you live in.

1. The first thing to do is to select a place that you know and love for its beauty, peace and power. It could be a favorite spot where you feel the natural power of a mountain or the ocean; it might be a power spot you have discovered in the prairie or along a river. The main thing is that it speaks to you. I think of a giant rock formation at Harbin Hot Springs in north-central California. The energetic emanations from it are massive and peaceful, and even when I can't go there physically, I have no trouble going there in spirit. The energies of the place are that distinct.

2. Now select a place that is known to you where there is damage and need. It could be an area of environmental damage, or a part of your city that is in need, where there is poverty, illness, or where there has been a tragedy. The "place" could be a person in your acquaintance who needs help. The main thing is to select a person or place to which you have a personal link. I think of the people I encountered along the Florida coast right after Hurricane Ivan devastated their homes and towns. I had never seen mass wreckage on that scale before, and I was moved by the way people were pulling together to help each other. To localize this, I might choose the little town of Fort Pierce, Florida, because that is a place I stopped for lunch and talked with local people and heard their stories.

3. Sit comfortably and connect your awareness with your Source. This is a moment in which you raise your awareness to your connection with Spirit or Essence, however you might name that for yourself. Give yourself a couple of minutes in this contact before moving on to the next steps.

4. Connect your awareness with where you are on the planet right now. Feel the location you are in and let this sense of connection extend down into the Earth and outward in all directions immediately around you and your body.

5. Move your awareness into your Heart Center, and let the connection deepen for a couple of minutes.

6. Now move your awareness to the personal power spot you selected in step one. Picture yourself there, firmly rooted in the energies of the place and give this contact a couple of minutes to grow.

7. Let go of the power spot now and move your awareness to the place of need you identified in step two. See yourself there. Feel the place, its spirit and energies. Give this contact a couple of minutes.

8. Now move back to where you are in the present moment and reestablish your awareness in the here and now.

9. When you have centered your awareness where you are, move your awareness back out to your personal power spot, your place of strength and spend a couple of more minutes there.

10. Move again to the same needy person or place you connected with before. Give this contact another couple of minutes.

11. Return to your starting place and reconnect with your Heart Center for a ten minute meditation.

12. End the exercise and take note of your experiences.

It is in the blend and balancing of the energies of each of these places—whether they are "places" within us or external places in the world at large—that this practice has its power. In my work with clients and as a workshop leader, I get to watch the kinds of transformations that come over people when they come, even momentarily, into a state of balance. It seems that when energetic balance is struck within us, we become receptive to fresh impulses that lead us into brand new experiences. The same principle applies to what we are doing in this series of exercises.

Part 3: Energy Healing on the Planet
This time we will intentionally link our awareness with the energies of powerful locations. Some are "positive" power spots, like the Great Pyramid in Egypt or Stonehenge, and some can be seen as "negative" like the Dachau or Auschwitz concentration camps in Europe. We will apply the same procedure of connecting our awareness with such places and intentionally moving it from one to the other.

Exercise Steps:
1. Take a few minutes to *ground and center yourself.*
2. Connect your awareness with your Source. This is a moment in which you connect consciously with Spirit or Essence, however you might name that for yourself. Give yourself a couple of minutes in this contact before moving on to the next steps.
3. Link with your Heart Center and the place where you are. That means to become fully aware of your location on the planet and your connection with the earth on the very spot where you are sitting.
4. Meditate there for five minutes.
5. Move your awareness to a "positive" power spot: for example, the Great Pyramid, Macchu Picchu, or Stonehenge. Picture yourself there. Feel the energies in that

location. Give yourself a couple of minutes there to allow the connection to deepen.

6.  Now release that contact and move your awareness to a "negative" power spot. For example, one of the European concentration camps or the killing fields of Cambodia. See yourself in that location. Feel the place, it's spirit, and energies. Give this contact a couple of minutes.

7.  Release that contact and move your awareness back to where you are in your current location.

8.  Rest your awareness a moment, and then move slowly through this triangle of connections again, from your current location to the same "positive" power spot you chose. Spend a couple of minutes there, then move to the same "negative" power spot your chose. Give this a couple of minutes.

9.  Release that connection and *move back to your current location*. Sit quietly and allow impressions to come forward in you. Take five minutes for this meditation.

10. End the exercise. Write down your impressions.

The earth is a living being whose body conducts energy and consciousness, just like yours does.

The dance with twin structures of consciousness is an essential feature of working on yourself, and you will observe the phenomenon of twin structures at work in those who come to you for help. The factors that keep us from the spiritual heights we long for and from the realization of our callings turn out to be every bit as important as the epiphanies and great breakthroughs, though it is usually harder to appreciate our blockages at the moment we are butting heads with them. Still, the act of turning toward these apparent obstacles means embracing more of the totality of our selves. As acting coach Sanford Meisner put it, "That which hinders your task, becomes your task."

The need for inner work never ends; as you grow and open in compassion, your gifts begin a natural process of turning outward to touch the world around you. Inevitably, you face the challenge of what keeps your spiritual qualities from becoming *expressed* spiritual qualities. In this sense, finding and facing what keeps heaven and earth apart within you is a core piece of your healing work, and may ultimately be one of the most important contributions you can make to this world.

# Chapter Thirteen

## FEAR: A HIDDEN ALLY

*Enlightenment is the essential quality which allows you to express
your spiritual qualities through your body, without fear.*

Bob Moore

Fear is of great interest in energy healing and conscious inner growth. Like our ability to shift into the hyperarousal of a fight-or-flight response, fear is part of our survival, provided by nature to warn us when there is a threat to our well-being. But, as with fight or flight, we were never intended to live permanently in a state of fear. When left unattended, fear gets in the way of communication within your body and psyche; it restricts the expression of who you are. It is a perennial theme in energy healing because it is at the core of so much of what prevents our inner pilgrim from moving along his or her way.

Each of our "negative" emotions has its roots in the soil of fear, and like the quintessential twin structure that it is, fear is typically right there to meet you when you are about to cross an inner threshold into something new. When you pay mindful attention to the sensation of fear, however—neither indulging it, repressing it, nor running away from it—a curious thing happens. It acts like any other internal sensation or obstacle that arises. You find out that fear, too, has its way of shapeshifting and revealing its twin structures of love, openness, and even wisdom. That is when fear becomes an ally.

### Direct and Indirect Pathways

Inner work is a dance back and forth between direct and indirect pathways of action. With a direct pathway, you take action and do some small or large thing that expresses your qualities. In the process, you often have to "jump over your own shadow" by overcoming some resistance or apprehension. Maybe you spend a morning carefully rearranging objects on your shelves, finally go hang gliding, show up on the spur of the moment at the local open mic and sing a torch song by Sarah McLaughlin, or write a letter to an estranged member of your family.

By contrast, an indirect pathway means doing something about the impediments to expressing your gifts. This is like removing the stones and beaver dams that are keeping a stream from flowing. The stream flows just fine all by itself when the obstacles are cleared. You're not trying to determine where the stream is going to flow, but you are attending to the accumulation of debris that was getting in the way. Getting at your fears and facing them is a prime example of such an indirect pathway. Indeed, facing and allowing fear to transform into an ally might be *the* spiritual practice. In a lecture in Kansas City, theologian Matthew Fox once made the point that, in his view, the background reason for such Native American practices as vision quests and sweat lodges is to prepare your heart and help you overcome fear so you are ready for anything. Turning toward your fear as it arises is an indirect pathway into everything we are after in spiritual practice because when you are able to face your fear and allow it to quiet down, love and compassion have a place to work, and your spiritual qualities have a much better chance of flowing all by themselves. Then the processes of enlightenment, according to Bob Moore's definition quoted at the top of this chapter, are able to unfold unimpeded.

### Fear as a Compass

Fear involves closing ourselves off to some degree to life as it presents itself to us, narrowing the channel through which we interact with life. The German word *eng*, meaning "narrow," is close to the linguistic roots of the German word *Angst* (fear), *angina pectoris* (chest pain associated with insufficient blood supply to the heart), and our English word "anxiety," and speaks to the narrowing of our being that occurs when we are in a state of fear. This tightening or contraction is something we all know, and transforming fear when we encounter it means learning to do something that we don't usually do.

Wayne Muller, author of a number of wise books on compassionate living, once said something very interesting about sadness, and it also applies to fear. He said he uses sadness, when it arises in him, as a compass that points him to something worth paying attention to. Instead of turning away from it, as most of us are wont to do, he learned to turn his attention toward the feeling and follow it. In the act of following, a transformation occurs, all by itself. This comes from attending to the sensation mindfully, rather than pushing it away or trying to make it change into something else.

Energywork is full of opportunities to turn your attention toward internal sensations. When you turn your attention toward the sensation of fear within you and relax with it (easier said than done), you have an opportunity to see how mindfulness works. It is like holding an ice cube in your hand. At first, the ice cube is cold and hard. It has sharp edges and stings your skin. But if you hold it a while—no need to do anything else—it will undergo a change of state. It will melt. Water is water, whether you drink it, freeze it into an ice cube, or boil it into vapor and blow it out the window to form clouds that condense and fall down as rain that cools you off and washes the bird droppings off your car. Fear can work the same way when you hold it in your awareness without trying to change it.

*Fear is a question: What are you afraid of, and why? Just as the seed of health is in illness, because illness contains information, your fears are a treasure house of self-knowledge if you explore them.*

Marilyn Ferguson

The sensation of fear can be extremely useful as a compass because it points your attention to what your system deems significant. It will point out where clumps of frozen energy and feeling are lodged. If you let it, fear can become your ally, because facing it the same way we "face" the ice cube when we hold it in our hand will bring about a change in its state, little by little, back into the fluid energy of life.

### Inner Work on Sleepless Nights

Years ago, when I was first learning energy healing, I was employed as an English teacher in Germany. One of my assignments took me weekly into the executive suite of one of the vice presidents of Dornier Aircraft in Munich, the company famous for building the flying boats of World War II. My job was to sharpen the VP's English conversation skills. This job was a distinct pleasure, because my client proved to be an intelligent and engaging man with whom I found I had much in common. My usual classes at Dornier Aircraft were with airplane technicians who explained to me, until I almost understood, how an airplane works. During my one-on-one sessions with this company vice president, however, we explored the inner aerodynamics of how the human spirit takes off and lands.

In the course of our talks, he told me what he did when he couldn't sleep at night. He would get up, sit in a chair and *listen*. Instead of fighting his sleeplessness and struggling to go back to sleep, he assumed that his subconscious mind had something important that it was trying to tell him but had not found an opening during his busy day. Nighttime was its first opportunity, and he saw it as his job to pay attention.

I tried his advice with fascinating results. When I couldn't sleep, I started getting up, finding a place to sit, and listening without trying to make anything happen. I listened into the night and the sounds of the sleeping world around me, from the house as it creaked and settled to my thoughts and the sounds of my own inner world. Early on, the undertaking felt eerie, often tinged with a visceral, low-grade fear, a sense of uneasiness in my body. My turning point came when I decided to turn my attention to the anxious feeling itself and follow what happened when I didn't try to stage-manage what was taking place inside me. Sometimes nothing would happen. More often, though, a whole array of feelings would arise in a chaotic tumble of sensation. The intensity would crescendo and peak all by itself, and carry me into some kind of experience, which often led to a feeling of resolution. Then I would drop into a peaceful state. The whole undertaking taught me to ride the waves of feeling inside me. What started as a feeling of fear and apprehension repeatedly led me through some kind of inner knothole to something that needed my attention or understanding. Then it gave way to a new sense of openness.

After I got the knack of this process, I began to welcome opportunities to get up in the middle of the night in order to see what this other side of myself had in store for me. Invariably, something would fan out before my inner eye. As the aircraft executive had taught me, it was as if something in me was trying to get my attention and had been waiting in the wings until nighttime to come knocking on my inner door. By and by, the practice of getting up in the middle of night and teaching myself to turn, listening and mindful, toward the sensations within me became a personal model for working with the multitude of things that arise in meditation and in my work with others.

There are different grades of fear, some that respond easily to this endeavor, some not. Start small and develop a model that works for you: don't wait until you are in the middle of a full-blown panic attack or some other kind of incapacitating fear to start teaching yourself to turn toward the sensation. If your body and nervous system are flying into defense physiology (fight, immobility, or flight) beyond a certain point, then the only thing on your agenda is survival, which is how it should be!

Just hanging out with the sensation of fear can feel perilous enough when it is a new practice. At first, it makes about as much sense as leaning into a punch. The normal response to such unwelcome feelings is to turn away from them, get rid of them altogether if we can, or at least dull their effect. What this practice asks of you is a paradoxical inner maneuver of turning toward the sensation and approaching it like a doorway or passage into something important. This will probably feel unnatural until you see that what you are actually doing is turning awareness and your ability to feel toward a part of your body and psyche where consciousness has been restricted. It seems paradoxical, but when you actually do it, new things start happening all by themselves. Bear in mind that your attention is made of energy and feeling and that mysterious thing we call consciousness. And you are wielding it in a new way.

If you are prepared to experience yourself in a new way, try this practice with the sensations in your body. Try it with the little threads of anxiety you find there. When you turn your attention to those otherwise neglected or repressed parts of yourself, it's like paying attention to a neglected child. Caring attention is to children what sunshine and water are to a flower: they bloom when they get it. The same thing happens to these neglected corners in yourself, often represented by our aches and pains and what we think of as negative emotions like sadness, anger, and fear.

The fearful little sensations are often your body and energy system's way of saying to you, "Here is something juicy and significant." Certain of those things may even come shrouded in this feeling of fear to ensure that you uncover them when, and only when, you are ready. As your self-knowledge grows, you gain a trust for the internal timing of your processes together with a sense that you truly can choose your battles. You develop a sense of when it is time to "go there," lift the stone that you had previously stepped around, and see what is underneath, knowing that you will be ready when you do.

A colleague recently shared a small example of this process: Sandy told of a recent healing session in which she was a member of a small multihanded healing team of practitioners working together with a woman in the water. One of the woman's complaints was a stiff neck. At one point, the therapist who was working at the woman's head had to leave, so Sandy took over that position. As the session progressed, Sandy began to feel fear rise in her and she became tangled up in trying to figure out "whose fear" it was. Was it her (Sandy's) fear that maybe she would not be competent enough to work with the woman's head and neck properly? Was she feeling fear that was rising up in the woman receiving the treatment? Was Sandy sensing some other deep, dark, un-dealt-with fear emerging from her own psyche?

After a while, Sandy decided to abandon the search for the origin of the fear she was feeling. Instead, she simply turned her attention toward the sensation of fear itself and let it be what it was, regardless of where it came from. By and by, it subsided. She felt herself relaxing, and at the same time, she felt the neck of the woman she was treating letting go as well.

*Five Reasons to Work With Your Fears*
1. Fear can act as a *compass*. By turning your attention toward it, instead of reflexively moving away from the sensation, you can be drawn to a source of insight, renewed strength, and direction.

2. Fear acts like *a negative attractor* in your system. The more submerged and unconscious it is, the more fear will act like a magnet for unwanted energies and events. Working with your fears will reduce the charge around these negative attractors and decrease their influence.

3. Fear tends to *narrow* your attention. While this is an important function in making sure you survive when there is danger, it also creates an excessively limiting filter for the impressions that come to you.

4. Fear is typically at the root of the emotions that leave their residue in your body.

5. Unfaced and unresolved fear is often the reason for energetic *restriction* in the middle of your body and the reason why your upper and lower energy centers don't communicate as they should. In this way, the balancing and healing of your Solar Plexus Center and its etheric storage in the Liver Stream (to be introduced in this chapter) is a major contribution to the meeting of heaven and earth in you.

In the name of finding a new relationship with the hidden ally of fear, let's turn now to a particular movement of etheric energy around your body that will provide a rich field of discovery.

*Introducing the Liver Stream*

The Solar Plexus Center, when unhealed, can be a major bottleneck in our energy systems. Working with the Solar Plexus Center tends to bring background fears into the foreground of your consciousness. Working with your Solar Plexus can't be beat as a way to get at what might be in the way of your personal growth and the expression of your spiritual qualities.

One of the best ways to work on the balance and healing of your Solar Plexus Center is to work with your Liver Stream, one of the etheric streams that run like rivulets within the general flow of etheric energy around your body. The Liver Stream is a band of energy movement that bisects your body, approximately in the middle. Don't miss the significance of this position: the health and openness of your Liver Stream will determine how well your upper and lower worlds—heaven and earth—meet and communicate energetically within you.

I have come to think of the Liver Stream as a doorway to working with the Solar Plexus Center because it contains the *etheric storage* for this important center of consciousness. In turn, the Solar Plexus Center, as it heals, changes from a major source of fear-based blockage to a powerful, open channel of love and consciousness. Once you have made the decision that you want to become skilled in facing the forces that are at work within you, it makes sense to bring this area of your energetic anatomy into your practice.

Before launching into the work with your Liver Stream, first review the basics of making good conscious contact with an energy-active position on your body. You'll find these in chapter four. You might practice on a couple of more familiar energy-active positions—maybe your Heart Center or the energy-active positions at your shoulders or in the middle of your palms— just to remind yourself what this kind of loose, relaxed awareness and letting go into an energy movement feels like. The very same tactics will apply to the Liver Stream. Of course, you'll have to know the physical landmarks in order to have the right starting places—I wouldn't send you in there without a map!—so here is a short subtle anatomy lesson for the region you will be exploring.

### Locating the Liver Stream

Imagine that your Solar Plexus Center is a sun—after all, it's named that way: an indication of the kind of power and energy it can radiate when all's well. The word "solar" also suggests that there might be something orbiting this little sun, and, indeed, there is. Have a look at a human skeleton and find the seventh ribs, which radiate out on both sides from the seventh thoracic vertebra, which is the spinal connection for your Solar Plexus Center. Note how they follow a path that tilts downward slightly, from back to front, passing behind the lower tips of your shoulder blades. Also note that that if you widen that path to include the eighth rib and extend the circle they describe, it would also include the navel. This is the path of the Liver Stream.

Among the stable features of the Liver Stream are four points with which you are going to become familiar. They will act as portals into the Liver Stream and as you learn to contact them consciously, they will provide important access to what affects the health and welfare of the middle of your body and your Solar Plexus Center. Here they are:

- *Spleen Point:* The Spleen Point is like a spark plug in your energy system, a major drawing-in point for the life force as it enters your etheric. It is from the Spleen Point that life force is distributed, in many cases directly, to your major energy centers, which in turn energize their respective endocrine glands. These, in their turn, send their hormonal messages throughout your body via the bloodstream. The Spleen Point is therefore a vital link in the distribution of life force that starts with the sun and what it represents as the Source of Life and flows into each cell and each movement of life in you and through you. Here is how you locate this spark plug:

  *Location:* With your finger, trace the inside margin of your ribs on your left side. Start at your xiphoid process, the bony protuberance at the bottom of your sternum, and follow the lower margin of your rib cage, until you encounter a slight indentation. This will be the place where your eighth rib dovetails with your seventh, approximately eight finger-breadths from your xiphoid process. Here is where you will be able to connect consciously with the energy of the Spleen Point.

- *Liver Point:* This is the counterpart of the Spleen Point on the right side of your body. While the Spleen Point deals in the drawing in of life force, the Liver Point reflects the health and vitality in you, the result of integrating and expressing the life force.

  *Location:* To locate the Liver Point, locate the notch formed by the intersection of your eighth rib with your seventh rib on your right side, approximately eight finger-breadths from your xiphoid process. This is where you can relax your attention into the energy of the Liver Point.

- *Right and Left Shoulder Blade Points:* In energetic terms, the back of your body is home to positions relating to structure and strength, and here we find a pair of *strength points* which make up part of the Liver Stream and lend a certain stability of feeling to this vital movement of energy.

  *Location:* The Shoulder Blade Points are situated behind the lower tips of your shoulder blades. This is just below where your seventh rib passes behind your shoulder blade on both sides.

- *Navel:* I include it here because the Liver Stream, when it expands, covers the navel, an important energy-active position in its own right. We will want to include it as we work with this band of energy movement.

It is interesting to note that the Liver, Spleen, and Shoulder Blade Points are all associated with the seventh rib. It is easy to imagine the right and left seventh rib, joined by the seventh thoracic vertebra, forming an orbit around the Solar Plexus Center.

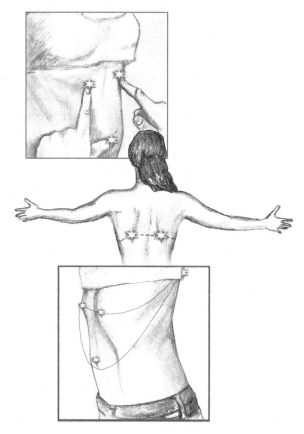

The path of your Liver Stream includes your Liver and Spleen Points, your right and left Shoulder Blade Points and covers your navel, a powerful energy-active position in its own right.

INNER PILGRIMAGE #29: *Pilgrim Enters the Liver Stream*
Our first task is to use the points that have just been introduced in order to activate the Liver Stream and help it both to jettison some of its excess charge and to come into energetic balance. To do this, we are going to move around the stream, visiting each of the points in turn and giving them a chance to become active. Like all etheric streams, the Liver Stream has a dominant direction of movement and, for the purposes of this exercise, we will be moving against that movement. We do this because moving briefly against a stream tends to bring resistance and blockage to the surface, where they can be released.

Preparation:

- Sit comfortably in an upright position and relax your *respiratory diaphragm* so that you can breathe easily.

- Take some time to locate each of the points on the Liver Stream. When they are new to you, it is helpful to briefly touch the positions on your body with your fingertip and, in this way, point them out to yourself. Then remove your fingertip from that position, but remain there with your awareness. Relax your awareness and allow the movement of energy at this position to draw your awareness into itself. As you become more familiar with them, and as they become more active, you will be able to find them internally without using your finger.

The Steps:

1. When you have settled in, move your awareness to your Spleen Point, located at the indentation on the inner left side of your rib cage where your seventh and eighth ribs come together. Let your attention rest there as you breathe into this position. Give this process two minutes before moving on.

2. Release that contact and move your awareness slowly and consciously on your skin surface to your navel. Here, too, spend a couple of minutes, allowing your awareness to gather. Conscious breathing always helps this process.

3. Release that contact and move your awareness on your skin surface to your Liver Point. Like your Spleen Point, it, too, is located at the slight notch where your seventh and eighth ribs meet, this time on the right side of your inner rib cage. Spend two minutes here, allowing your contact to deepen, breathing into this energy-active position.

4. Release that contact. Then, moving your awareness on your skin surface, slowly follow the curve of your body around to your right Shoulder Blade Point, located at the lower tip of your right shoulder blade. Spend two minutes here, and give it a chance to become active.

5. Release this contact and move your awareness to your left Shoulder Blade Point and let it activate—two minutes.

6. From your left Shoulder Blade Point, move your awareness on your skin surface around the curve of your body and down to your Spleen Point and stay with this contact for two minutes.

7. Repeat the circulation. With your awareness, travel once more the path of the Liver Stream, stopping briefly to reconnect with each point and allow the contact to deepen.

8. Now release your contact with these points and sit for about ten minutes with the cumulative effect of this circulation. Allow whatever tries to come up into your conscious awareness to do so.

9. End the exercise and take note of your experiences.

With this initial Liver Stream exercise, we are clearly in the domain of the Solar Plexus Center.

The sensations that arise from that contact might not all be pleasant, but the result of helping this vital stream of energy and consciousness to release its burdens can have far-reaching and very freeing effects.

An Option: Include a Twelve-Breath Cycle

One very effective option here is to move your awareness into each of the points of the Liver Stream and introduce a twelve-breath cycle of energetically balanced breathing into each point. As you'll recall from chapter four, this twelve-breath cycle consists of a series of three breaths in each of these four modes:

- IN through your nose and OUT through your nose
- IN through your nose and OUT through your mouth
- IN through your mouth and OUT through your nose
- IN through your mouth and OUT through your mouth

*Five Reasons for Working with Your Liver Stream*

1. It is an effective way to turn your attention to the residue of fear in your energy system and contribute to its clearance.
2. It opens the middle part of your body energetically and will help open your respiratory diaphragm.
3. It addresses many of the underlying reasons why heaven and earth, yin and yang, masculine and feminine, and your upper and lower energy centers may have trouble communicating with each other in you.
4. It addresses blockages which contribute to mental unclarity.
5. It addresses major impediments—usually relating to fear—to the harmonious, clear function of the Circulations of Expression, Control and Balance.

*The Energy Anatomy of a Panic Attack*

Fear provides much of the mortar that holds dysfunctional patterns together. It inhibits grounding, expression, and the ability to release excess energy from your system. When the charge of fear is reduced in your body and psyche, all kinds of other processes are free to take place.

Many energetic maladies are related to a lack of communication between our upper and lower energy centers. I frequently meet people who are very familiar with themselves from their Heart Center upward. They seem to know a lot about their own mental processes and higher consciousness, and they spend a good deal of time with their upper energy centers. But as soon as they try to drop their awareness into their lower bodies, it is as if they have gone to a foreign country. The threshold is typically the Liver Stream. When this zone is restricted, it is a major source of disruption in the interaction between your upper and lower energy centers.

A clear illustration of the disruptive effects of a distorted or blocked communication between the upper and lower centers can be seen in the extreme example of a panic attack. When we get energetically "all balled up" in the center of our body, due to fear, we are cut off from both heaven and earth, so to speak. We lose our connection to the guidance available from higher dimensions of consciousness, and at the same time we lose our ground, our contact with the earth, which would ordinarily provide us with a supportive foundation and help us draw that guidance to ourselves.

I regularly run into low-grade versions of this basic energetic configuration in my work with others: a disruption of easy, natural communication between my partner's upper and lower energy centers due to some degree of closing down energetically in the middle of their body. We can hold fear in any part of our being, but when it comes to consciously working with that fear, I am often led into my treatment partner's Solar Plexus Center and Liver Stream.

A young woman came for a session, referred by a teaching colleague at a school of massage and bodywork where I teach. Her teacher told me she was having a great deal of trouble focusing and being present in class and, in her estimation, she badly needed help with grounding. The woman showed up right on time and introduced herself as Stardust and told me she was having panic attacks. I asked her to describe what she was feeling. She said it felt to her like all her energy was getting concentrated in her heart and head, so much that they felt like they were going to explode. The sensation was so strong that it set off a fear reaction in her. After her treatment, she felt much better, and after taking it easy the rest of the afternoon, she was able to go back to her class and participate fully the next day.

Please don't read what follows as a "one-size-fits-all" approach to treating panic attacks. I should also point out that Stardust was not, at the time of our session, having an attack. If she were having acute symptoms, such as hyperventilation, abdominal cramping, fear of impending death, and if these had persisted during our whole session, I would have recommended that she seek appropriate medical attention. I present the following informal case history in order to demonstrate my thought processes in an energetically-oriented approach to bodywork that takes into account the overall energetic situation of my treatment partner and the Liver Stream in particular. Here is how I worked with Stardust:

As I scanned her body for anything that felt energetically out of the ordinary, I had no problem locating the charged-up feeling in her upper body and head, which felt like the energetic equivalent of a full balloon about to burst. In contrast, I felt very little vitality in Stardust's lower body and legs. It was easy to see that the static charge of energy around her head and chest wasn't moving into her lower body and, as a result, not grounding. But then came the twin structure question: What's keeping her from being grounded? What's getting in the way of the communication in her body? When two zones are that different, I get curious: Where is the dividing line between these zones, the place where the energy shifts from charged-up to depleted? What's going on there? I compared her upper body with her lower body and watched her breathing patterns. Not surprisingly, the crossover from high to low charge on Stardust was right in the middle of her body, in her respiratory diaphragm and solar plexus region.

I began by engaging her etheric and moving the energy down her body. I massaged her etheric with long strokes on her skin surface from her head out her arms to her fingertips, then down the front of her body, into her legs and feet. As I worked, I made sure I really engaged her legs, both energetically and structurally, making my contact firm enough to feel the bones in her legs.

Then I used some simple structural techniques to bring her feet, legs, hips, and sacrum into alignment. These included some unwinding of her hips and sacroiliac joints and a lumbosacral decompression of the kind used in craniosacral work. When she was structurally in better alignment, I created an energetic connection between her Sacral Center and a number of energy-active positions on her body: both of her Hip Points, her Liver and Spleen Points, both of her adrenal glands and Shoulder Points. I connected each of these positions in turn with her Sacral

169

Center and held the energetic contact for a minute or so to allow the contact to deepen.[26] If you try this, you will notice that these configurations—pairs of energy-active positions connected in turn to her Sacral Center—all form a V. If you connect the paired positions, the figure will be a downward-pointing triangle. I think of this as an arrow, showing my partner's energy which way to go.

Finally, I connected her Heart Center with her Sacral Center. All the while, I was silently, energetically, inviting Stardust to come down into her lower body.

My next move was to do a mini-treatment I call the *Liver Stream Cat's Cradle* to help the middle part of Stardust's body to relax and open. I'll describe that treatment later in this chapter. During that phase of the work, her body quivered and her breathing quickened to a rapid pant as her anxiety peaked and then dropped off into a relaxed state. I followed with some work at her Throat Center and some etheric massage to strengthen and support the movement of etheric energy around her whole body.

After giving Stardust a couple of minutes of "simmering time" to feel everything that was now moving in and around her, and then come back into present time, I asked her to slowly sit up and hang her legs over the sides of the massage table. I scooched my stool close to the table and had her put her feet on my knees, grounding both of us strongly while she got used to being vertical again. Soon, she was out the door and ready to go back to her bodywork class the next day.

I am not telling myself that all of Stardust's fears were taken care of in one session, and certainly she will be working on the underlying issues behind her condition for some time to come. One thing I do know, however, is that our session addressed the energetics of her panic attacks, and that the small breakthrough in her ability to energetically drop down into her lower body would help her ultimately resolve the core fears that have kept this pattern going.

PARTNER TREATMENT #9: *Opening the Liver Stream: Make a Cat's Cradle*[27]
Remember that it was water, the flowing element, that Dorothy in the *Wizard of Oz*[28] threw on the Wicked Witch of the West, who then dissolved into a puddle, no longer able to hold her subjects in fear. Here is where we do what Dorothy did: introduce the element of flow into a place that might be holding fear. Instead of dousing your partner with a bucket of water, however, try this small treatment.

I use this treatment when I detect a palpable energetic division between the upper and lower parts of my partner's body. Breathing patterns can reveal a lot about where energy and consciousness is allowed to go, and not go, in a person's body. One of the surefire indicators for such an upper body–lower body division is when my partner's breathing is restricted to the upper half of their torso. Another tipoff is a palpable difference between the charge and aliveness of the upper and the lower part of my partner's body. This might be the top-heavy, overcharged head and mental aura of a person who is all "in her head" and has difficulty engaging her lower body and energy centers. Remember Stardust with her overcharged head and heart, accompanied by

---

26    I describe these techniques in chapter ten.

27    I gave this exercise the name *Cat's Cradle* because the five energy positions on the Liver Stream and the lines of interconnection between them form a web that reminds me of the familiar string game by the same name.

28    If you have made it this far in this book, you definitely deserve a bonus. To find the Pilgrim Extras, follow the instructions  on the final page of this book. That will lead you to a bonus exercise called *Spiritual Integration According to the Wizard of Oz.*

undercharged legs and feet. Or, going in the other direction, I might run into the feeling of held energy in the lower body of a person who has repressed highly charged emotions ticking away unconsciously in them like a time bomb. Another situation I encounter frequently is in persons who experience a great deal of difficulty in expressing themselves openly. In all of these cases, there is likely to be a charge of fear and blockage in the middle of their body.

The following treatment is an effective way to address your partner's Liver Stream and provide an opportunity for a new flow and blend of activity between its points and energy movements. I will assume that you have, by now, amassed some experience of your own with your Liver Stream. If not, it would be a good idea to spend some time with the basic Liver Stream exercise before working with a partner in this area. As with everything in the world of energy treatments, you are going to be much more effective, not to mention more responsible and authentic, if you first become familiar with your own energy system and learn to appreciate the kind of experiences it can open in you. Here is the treatment:

1. With your partner either standing, sitting or lying on the massage table, activate, two at a time, each of the five points on the Liver Stream. These are her Liver Point, Spleen Point, her right and left Shoulder Blade Points, and her navel. You can do this in any order, using the palms of your hands, which allows the points to interact with the energy centers in your palms. Or you can use your fingertips for a more precise, more penetrating contact. When I choose the latter option, I use the fingertips of my middle and ring fingers.

2. Spend five minutes connecting points on the Liver Stream with each other. With each contact, you will be paying attention to the natural exchange between your hands or fingertips.

3. Give each pair of contacts about a minute to deepen. As you hold these contacts, be aware of the Liver Stream itself as a *circulating band of energy movement* that more or less bisects your partner's body.

4. When you have spent time with each of these combinations of points, place your right palm on your partner's left Hip Point, located at the inside curve of her pelvic crest, and your left palm on her right Shoulder Point, located at the corner of her shoulder. Put your attention on the exchange of energy between your hands. Give this connection a minute.

5. Release that connection and move to the opposite side of your partner's body. Place your right palm on her left Shoulder Point and your left palm on her right Hip Point. Here, too, you will spend a minute with your awareness on the exchange of energy between your hands.

6. End the treatment.

Once you have stimulated your partner's Liver Stream by activating the points on it and then provided the whole area of her solar plexus with the balancing effect of this small polarity treatment using her Shoulder and Hip Points,[29] you can simply release that contact and go on to other things. You will have facilitated the process of change in a number of major areas:

- This treatment creates a way for pent-up energy to move. This way, it helps the fear factor to be reduced in your partner by giving the etheric charge around the middle of

---

29    A full version of this basic polarity protocol can be found in *Energy Healing: A Pathway to Inner Growth*.

her body a means of *discharging excess energy*. This, in turn, makes it possible for many a process to progress that otherwise could not. There will likely be some signs of release, such as a change in breathing patterns and a softening of the tissue in the middle of your partner's body.

- Opening this area makes it possible for your partner's upper and lower energy centers to interact more easily without the distortion created by a sluggish or blocked Liver Stream.

- You have affected energy movement around your partner's head by influencing her Liver Stream—the two zones are energetically related—giving her a better means of releasing build ups of charge around her head, especially at her eyes, teeth and jaws.

> TIP: Next time you undergo some kind of dental procedure—may it be a lightweight one!—place your hands on the middle of your body, along the lower margin of your ribs. Your hands will be covering the area of your Solar Plexus Center, as well as your Liver and Spleen Points, which are major players in your Liver Stream. Bring your awareness into your hands, breath into them, and note what happens there. Place your awareness and stay with it. This process helps to relax your respiratory diaphragm and calms your Liver Stream. Like everything else, it takes practice, but the greater your relaxation in the middle of your body, the more easily and less traumatically you will go through your dental procedure.

- Because of the energetic resonance between the head and the Solar Plexus Center, the balance of activity between the right and left hemispheres of your partner's brain is enhanced by the new energetic balance in the middle of her body. This will indirectly help with your partner's mental clarity.

INNER PILGRIMAGE #30: *Connecting the Circulation of Expression with the Liver Stream*
The idea behind this exercise is to allow your Circulation of Expression and your Liver Stream to interact: they have something to say to each other. When you contact any component of the Liver Stream by contacting one or more of the points on the stream, you are bringing the influence of the entire Liver Stream into the practice. Likewise, when you engage one of the energy centers in the pairings we called the Circulations of Expression, Control and Balance in chapter eleven, you bring the influence of the entire circulation into the practice.

Here is a way to work in a healing way with the Circulation of Expression. This is not only an important healing practice in itself, but it also serves as a model for the kind of inner pilgrimage that brings heaven and earth together in us and addresses the fear that may be keeping that meeting from happening.

Sacral Center
1. Make a good contact with your both your Liver and you Spleen Points at the same time.
2. From this contact with your Liver and Spleen Points, move slowly—either inside your body or on your skin surface—to your Sacral Center in the middle of your sacrum.

Let that contact deepen for a minute.

3. Release that contact and move your awareness up to both your Liver and Spleen Points. Let that contact deepen for a minute.

4. Release that contact and move your awareness back to your sacral center, rest there a minute and then move back to your Liver and Spleen Points and allow that contact to deepen again—one minute.

5. Repeat this movement two or three more times, moving slowly between the points and spending a minute or so in each of these positions. Note that you are creating a letter V as you do this, with the Liver and Spleen Points as the upper points and the Sacral Center at the bottom point. By moving your awareness this way, you are increasing the resonance and communication between your Sacral Center and your Liver Stream.

6. Meditation: Move your awareness into your Sacral Center and let the contact deepen. Relax your attention and, without attempting to analyze or adjust what comes up in you, allow any thought, picture, emotions or impressions that want to come bubbling up within you. Give this meditation five to ten minutes.

7. Open your eyes, stand up, and move around for a couple of minutes before continuing with the next part of the exercise.

## Throat Center

8. Now disconnect your awareness from your Sacral Center and make a good contact with your Liver and Spleen Points once again.

9. This time, after you have established contact with your Liver and Spleen Points, move with your awareness up to your Throat Center. Give this contact a minute to intensify.

10. Now move your awareness down to your Liver and Spleen Points and allow that contact to deepen—one minute.

11. Release your contact with your Liver and Spleen Points and move your awareness back to your Throat Center. Let that contact deepen and then back down to your Liver and Spleen Points, moving on your skin surface. Rest a minute in each of these positions.

12. Repeat this two or three more times. This time, you have inverted the V shape, with your Throat Center as the point at the top.

13. Meditation: When this movement is established, contact your throat center and give yourself a minute to allow that contact to deepen. Release that contact and, again, allow everything to come forward that wants to come forward at this time. Give this five to ten minutes.

14. End the exercise and take note of what happened within you. Though what comes up might not be explicitly about the theme of expression, it is a good idea to see if your experiences are pointing out anything in that aspect of your life.

This same approach can be taken with the Circulation of Control and the Circulation of Balance.

*Conversion of Sensitivity in the Energy Healer*
Your qualities as a healer flourish when you meet another person in the compassionate space we

call healing, which at its best is a joyous, open-hearted, blessing-filled undertaking. Most often, unresolved fear is what keeps this from being a reality. One of the faces of this fear is the anxiety that comes up around connecting energetically with another person. It shows, for example, in the number of times I am asked in classes about how to protect oneself from other people's "stuff" when doing energywork. I'm amazed at how often this question comes from new students of bodywork and energywork who haven't yet even had their hands on all that many people. This fear shows in the elaborate rituals that some of us who work in this field have for keeping other people's energy at bay. This makes energy healers all too easy to caricature, doesn't it?—calling down armies of angels and guides to protect them, visualizing shields of impenetrable light between themselves and the other person, and slinging the other person's energy across the room as if it was a poisonous eel from hell. In my mind, these rituals reveal a good deal of ambivalence and anxiety about touching and truly connecting with other people.

If you find you are afraid of the person you are about to work with, it is better not to work with them. At the same time, it strikes me as absurd to be involved with health care and healing work—which in its most essential terms are about caring and connection—while also being afraid of what contact with the other person might do to you. Don't get me wrong here: there is no denying that our energy fields are entangled—we can't help but influence each other. And I certainly do not mean to belittle the legitimate concerns about hygiene and the phenomenon of unwanted energy transfer in energywork[30]. At the same time, it is also true that many practitioners seem bent on perpetuating their own unexamined fears when they build up in their minds a story of how dangerous other people's energy is.

Not surprisingly, many people who are drawn to energywork already have a highly developed sensorium[31] before they ever get into a class on the subject. By that, I mean that they habitually draw to themselves all kinds of impressions through the medium of their very acute senses. The energies they sense might scare them, or thrill them, or make them curious, but they want to sense more of it. Their ears and noses twitch with activity. Their skin is alive with sensation, and the hairs on their heads and bodies seem to bristle like antennae. Nothing gets by them. Quite often, they are very empathic.

All of this is important. In order to do energy healing in a purposeful way, you have to have some way to make conscious contact with what you are doing, so all that natural sensitivity comes in very handy. It would seem that those who are gifted with such high sensitivity have a great advantage when it comes to learning energy healing, but just as often they are faced with a challenge of another kind.

Many people who have a desire to do energetic healing work were very sensitive, delicate children to begin with. If, in addition to childhood's inevitable bumps and bruises, they may have also been subjected to extraordinary trauma such as abuse, war, and other forms of violence, it is natural for that gift of sensitivity to become organized around the need to feel safe. When such a fear-based core belief about life is carried over into energy healing, it is easy to see how this can color the whole undertaking.

By contrast, if the main intention is to be in an open-hearted connection, devoid of fear, this engenders a matching openness in the person you are treating. Energywork disciplines are

---

30    See the subchapter "Unwanted Energy Transfer and the Myth of "Negative Energy"" in *Energy Healing: A Pathway to Inner Growth.*

31    I use the term "sensorium" to refer to the composite of all our senses when they are working together as one.

full of ways to create a balanced and safe internal environment in which we can meet what comes up in us and in the process kiss the frog of fear. Facing and transforming the fear within is a key ingredient in the conversion of your sensitivity from an early warning system, designed solely for your protection, to a sensory system that is up to the job of helping you to truly meet and engage the person under your hands.

The work with the Liver Stream is useful for addressing many of the underlying issues that keep your inner pilgrim from advancing on his or her path. Every pilgrimage story brings the hero or heroine to a point where fear needs to be mastered. That doesn't mean that fear vanishes; it only means that fear is not dominating your world, and that is a big difference. Some of the greatest accomplishments have been brought by people who were thoroughly scared and yet managed to do what they did. Think of the Freedom Riders in Selma, Alabama. Think of the demonstrators in Tienamen Square in Beijing. Think of all those who have jumped over the shadow of their fear in times of crisis and risen to the occasion in front of them.

Following your calling will present you with all kinds of opportunities to learn to function even when you are in fear. That is why it is so important to learn not to be afraid of fear, but rather to embrace it and let it become your ally. It will teach you about yourself and it may well lead you to a new opening to life, one you never would have suspected.

# CHAPTER FOURTEEN

## RESISTANCE, RELEASE, AND RENEWAL
### THE THREE Rs OF ENERGY HEALING

A thread has been running through the past several chapters. I would sum it up like this: In energetic work, when you bring awareness to sensations arising within you, neither trying to change what is happening nor trying to keep it from changing, you are supporting the process of transformation and renewal. The corollary in subtle bodywork would be: when you connect with your partner and bring mindful awareness to both the structure of his body and the energy that enlivens it and follow the physical and energetic movement without trying to force or hinder change you support the underlying process of renewal in your partner. This seems to hold true in particular with what we tend to view as obstacles, such as fear, pain, resistance, anger, and sadness, not to mention the twin structures that come out of hiding when we take a step toward our innate wholeness. Not only do processes unfold when we finally pay attention to the things we typically try to avoid, they often turn into allies. Facing a fear of failure can lead to finding the strength to succeed. Turning inwardly toward a wistful sadness can lead you to a pool of grief and uncried tears that, when they are finally released, can give your life new depth and soulfulness and lend an unexpected lightness to your spirit. The unlocking of our gifts and qualities often involves embracing apparent obstacles and witnessing their metamorphosis.

Like fear, the triad of resistance, release, and renewal expresses a perennial theme in healing, growth, and development. Taken as a package, they describe a continuum of events, a recurring pattern in processes of change: resistance is often a precursor to the release of excess energy from a person's body or psyche, followed by the potential for a move of consciousness into a new place.

### New Respect for Resistance

There is something about being alive that insists that we grow and change, and the resistance we invariably encounter is likely to occur at the edge of new growth. If it is treated with respect, that resistance often reveals itself as an ally. Using the tools of energywork on yourself and in your work with others will offer you a host of opportunities to witness the dynamics of change. Seldom does a deep change inside a person happen without resistance. In the process, the forces line themselves up: the forces of change over here, and over there, the forces committed to preserving the status quo and regulating the pace of change in our lives. Both sides are undeniable. They converge, yin and yang merge and in the miraculous alchemy of co-creation, something new is born. The whole process begins, however, with resistance.

Resistance, release, and renewal are the daily bread of the energy healer who works at the cusp of the body's structure and the energy that enlivens it. Change is always going on, though typically below the threshold of our awareness. When change is upon a person to such a degree that it creates resistance in their body and psyche and their life's circumstances, that is often the time when they seek help in therapy or some other kind of support in moving through their changes. As an energyworker in whatever field you operate, notice the signs of resistance in those who come to you, because these are often the leading edge of their growth and change. When you skillfully meet that resistance with compassion and mindful awareness, and encourage your partner to do the same, apparent obstacles can turn into *handles* on your partner's whole process.

*The next time someone accuses you of "resisting," tell them, "I'm not resisting; I'm merely regulating the pace of change in my life."*

Let's see what we can learn about the nature of this important triad of events by setting up a situation in which we deliberately run into its leading edge, resistance.

INNER PILGRIMAGE #31: *Dancing with the Demon of Resistance: Deliberately Activating the Twin Structure*

The basic attitude of the pilgrim is a willingness to step into the unknown. Remember that setting out on the three-fold spiritual path has to do with "leaving the world," moving away from your familiar ground, away from your ordinary, habitual state, and moving into something new. There are times, of course, when this just happens: life deals you a wild card; something upsets the applecart, and without having intended it, you are forced into new circumstances. But you don't need to resign yourself to sitting on pins and needles, waiting for the next sneak attack in the dead of night by the forces of transformation. There are more graceful ways to enter the river of change without always having to be thrown in against your will.

Paul Rebillot, in his *Hero's Journey* workshops, used ritual drama to guide participants through the basic archetypal patterns that we all encounter when we enter into processes of transformation. As part of this process, we meet the hero within us, a character not unlike our inner pilgrim, as well as the hero's counterpart, not unlike what we've been calling the twin structure, which Rebillot called the *Demon of Resistance*.

One way to dance with resistance when you encounter it in yourself or in someone you are working with is to *exaggerate* it. This is what Paul taught in his *Hero's Journey* workshops. We are going to do a little update of his idea and braid it together with what we are learning about twin structures and energetic healing. Your encounter with the *Demon of Resistance* begins in your own body. But, as you'll see, this encounter can lead you to areas of resistance that are not physical. Try this:

*Exercise with the Demon of Resistance*
The reason for doing this exercise is to get a distinct, acute sense of your particular resistance patterns—some of them might even be related to the ones that keep your gifts from expressing fully in this world—and, in the process, allow some change to take place.

Exercise Setup:
- Read through all the exercise steps before starting.
- Lie on your back on the floor. Don't use a pillow under your head or knees—this is a deliberately uncomfortable exercise.

Exercise Steps:
1. Begin this exercise by calling to mind your qualities, your own particular gifts which want to be expressed in this world. Take some time and see if you can come into a *feeling contact* with the particular gifts that are yours to express in this world.
2. Now feel into your body. Can you simply be mindful of your body, *without trying to change anything*?
3. Slowly move your awareness along the backside of your body. Take note of the following without trying to change it:
   - How is your weight distributed on the floor?
   - Where is your body touching the floor, and where not?
   - Where is your body holding itself in a particular gesture or position?
   - Where is your body *not* relaxed?
4. Now pick a place on your body that feels like you are holding it in a certain way and slowly, intentionally *exaggerate* the holding pattern. Notice what happens as you do this.

Examples:
- Let's say you find that you're holding your right wrist a bit off the floor and your right hand has a bit of tightness in it. Exaggerate this by bending your wrist even more, and tightening your hand as much as you can. As you do this, become aware of what else changes.
- You might notice that your hips are tilted and that one is slightly higher on your body than the other. Exaggerate this by intentionally pulling the higher hip even further up. Again, pay attention to what else happens when you do this. Do any feelings arise?
- Now, let's say you discover that your chin is sticking up at an odd angle. Increase this odd angle. Make it *really* odd. See what happens in you as you do this.
- You notice that your breathing is a bit shallow and fast. Make it faster. Exaggerate it.
- This would also apply to facial expressions, nervous tics and other small body holdings that you now find going on; if you are smiling, really smile, like a clown; if you are grimacing, go all the way … make it *ugly*!

As if this weren't enough, let's take it a step further:.

5.  By now, you have found several places of physical resistance and exaggerated them, even to the point of discomfort. You might be all twisted up like a pretzel with a gargoyle grin on your face. Hold your body in whatever contortions you have put it in, and then look inside and see what attitudes you can discover.

6.  Exaggerate the attitudes you find. Maybe the thought comes, *I don't want to do this!* Okay, really get into that thought. *I really don't want to do this! I don't like doing this at all!* By now you might be thinking, *What a stupid exercise this is! I'm going to take this book back to the store and get a refund!* Think these thoughts really hard. (But you don't need to take the book back.)

7.  Stay with this Demon of Resistance to which you have given form and even expression. In this way, you are sneaking up on some of your entrenched patterns, giving expression in bodily form to the ways you dig in your heels and resist life. Feel just how rigid and unyielding you can be. Stay with this for some minutes.

8.  Now slowly release this body pattern one piece at a time. With each place on your body, thought, emotion, facial gesture, attitude that you relax, pay attention to what happens. Do this until you are lying, relaxed, on the floor again, your sweet old self again, a demon no longer.

9.  Give yourself some time to lie quietly on the floor, and then end the exercise.

10. Write down what happened.

PARTNER TREATMENT #10: *The Demon of Resistance as a Partner Treatment*

This practice of exaggerating the resistance is something to think of when you are working with someone with a lot of generalized stress on many levels. An example would be if your partner presents with an inability to let go and you sense a high degree of emotional holding behind this inability.

Not everyone will be able to do this, but if your treatment partner is willing to try out something that feels a bit experimental, you can try this paradoxical approach which employs one of the most useful release strategies, that of exaggerating a symptom. It is good to have worked with this by yourself before taking a partner into it. Approach this treatment playfully, and realize that you will need to verbally prompt, even gently coax your partner to move into areas of resistance. Recalling your experiences from the previous personal exercise, try this with your partner:

Steps:
1.  Have your partner lie down on the floor and quietly observe her.

2.  Quietly notice each position on your partner's body that is not touching the floor. For example, her wrist or neck might be slightly off the floor. These are clues as to where there is holding in her body.

3.  Ask your partner to exaggerate any such holding, one at a time. For example, if her wrist is slightly flexed, have her flex it completely; if her head is cocked to the right, have her cock it all the way to the right, as far as she can go.

4.  Similarly, scan her body and, one by one, encourage her to slowly exaggerate every place that is holding. What you are doing is encouraging her to move slowly into an exaggerated version of her resistances.

5. Go slowly, allowing time for each new positional exaggeration to have its effect. This will probably entail some coaxing, and it is best done with humor. This can mean that your partner will briefly be getting into some extreme positions and extreme tension. Encourage this. This extends to small things, such as facial expressions (which, as you know from your own experience, are not small things at all).

6. If you sense an emotion or an attitude in your partner, have her exaggerate it. If she is thinking a particularly nasty—or happy—thought, have her think it really hard.

7. After being in this contorted "demon" state for a couple of minutes, have her let go of the various pieces, one by one, until she is relaxed on the floor. Encourage her to be aware of what is happening inside her each step of the way.

8. Let her rest a bit and then talk a bit about what came up.

The basic idea of this practice, whether you are doing it by yourself or with a partner, is that in consciously, intentionally turning your attention toward resistance instead of away from it, we are allowing something *new* to happen. Often, these resistances have stuck around for as long as they have because our tendency is to sweep them under the carpet where we forget them, and they go further underground. But they are still there as energetic and emotional patterns, and when their charge is strong enough, even the tissues of your body will organize themselves around these hidden patterns. You can help with the processes of change by learning to place your mindful attention on them and briefly exaggerating them.

Here is another dance with resistance that brings this principle into focus.

### The Snow Angel

Now that we have had an opportunity to meet the Demon of Resistance, it's time we met an angel. I originally put this treatment together to address blockage in the upper body, shoulders, arms, and neck in women who have had reconstructive surgery after a mastectomy. It has proven to be useful in other areas as well because of the way it addresses blockage in the Throat Center and the Circulation of Expression.

In the case of the Snow Angel, you will be combining several elements of energy healing:

- The practice of deliberately turning toward stress and resistance and the feelings that come with them

- The etheric streams in your arms, which I will introduce below

- Slow, conscious physical movement, which at first heightens the experience of resistance and then gives way to release

- Your natural ability (when unblocked) to channel energy from the lower part of your body upward into expression and release

As always, your first task is to become familiar with the lay of the land you'll be traveling through, so let's turn first to some of the subtle energetic pathways that conduct energy up your body and out to your arms and hands.

## The Etheric Arm Streams

The etheric acts like a bridge between your physical body and the other dimensions of energy activity that surround your body, and as a result it plays a role in how your body functions and in how your consciousness expresses through your body. In the exercise and treatment to follow, we will use two streams of etheric movement, one positively charged and the other negatively charged, which circulate etheric energy in your arms and hands. Your Arm Streams are part of your energetic means of expressing, since they flow up the center of your body, through your heart and throat areas and then outward. We'll start with a little subtle anatomy lesson to introduce you to the etheric Arm Streams and a number of new energy-active positions.

## Energy-Active Positions on the Negatively Charged Arm Streams

- *Heat Point:* two finger-breadths below your navel (you will recall that the contact position you used for your Hara Center is three finger-breadths below your navel; the Heat Point is one finger-breadth above the Hara contact);

- *Depression Point:* located on the upper part of the indentation just above your xiphoid process, the pointed bony prominence at the base of your sternum (see illustration). It is called the Depression Point because of the accumulation of energy that can occur around this position, especially when you are unable to express yourself and release excess energy. That situation is often accompanied by the feeling of depression and having a weight on your chest.

- *Secondary Depression Point:* located just below the ridge of your manubrium, the bone that joins your sternum with your two collar bones (see illustration): This position, like the Depression Point, is another place where energy stacks up when your expression is blocked.

- *Collarbone Points:* located where your sternocleidomastoid muscles—the large muscles that stand out prominently on either side of your neck when you turn your head all the way to one side—attach to your collarbone. With your head facing forward, trace down the outer lines of your neck to the top of your collarbone. There, you will find the Collarbone Points. As members of a category of energy-active position, these are sometimes referred to as *stress points*, so named because they collect stress.

- *Channeling Points:* These energy-active positions are located on the muscle in the fold at the front of your armpit when your arm is at your side. Think of where the non-mercury end of a thermometer sticks out from your armpit when taking your temperature there. The shaft of the thermometer lies right over your Channeling Point.

- *Hand Centers:* These are located in the center of your palms.

- *The tips of your middle fingers.*

## The Path of the Negative Stream

The negative stream starts at the Heat Point, two finger-breadths below your navel, and moves upward on the midline through the Depression Point to the Secondary Depression Point. From there, it branches out to the right and left along your collar bones to include both Collarbone Points, both Channeling Points, down the inside of your arms, through the energy centers in your palms to the tips of your middle fingers.

181

Energy-Active Positions on the Positively Charged Arm Streams:

- *Waste Energy Position*[32]: so named for its tendency to catch and store energy that moves up your body. It is located between your Heart and Throat Centers on your back, between your shoulder blades, in the area around your second thoracic vertebra. As with the Depression Points on the front of your body, when you have no adequate means of expressing and releasing excess energy from your system, this position acts like an energy trap and can become a site of unproductive, stuck energy when it mounts up.

- *The tips of both middle fingers.*

## The Path of the Positive Stream

The positively charged Arm Streams start at the Waste Energy Position and extend out across both of your shoulder blades and down the outside of your arms to the tip of your middle fingers, where it meets the negative stream on either arm.

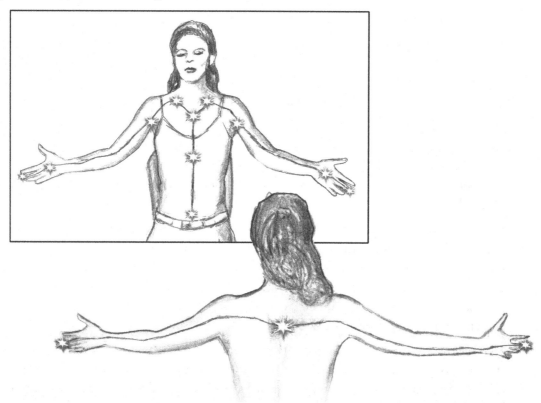

The negative stream starts at the Heat Point, two finger-breadths below your navel, and moves upward on the midline through the Depression Point to the Secondary Depression Point. From there, it branches out to the right and left along your collar bones to include both Collarbone Points, both Channeling Points, down the inside of your arms, through the energy centers in your palms to the tips of your middle fingers.

The positively charged Arm Streams start at the Waste Energy Position and extend out across both of your shoulder blades and down the outside of your arms to the tips of your middle fingers, where it meets the negative stream on either arm.

---

32    I speculate that the Waste Energy Position and the Secondary Depression Point and the space between them are on their way to other functions than being energy traps. As these positions heal and harmonize with the deeper expression of our being, they work together, and may even join into a single energy-active position. The evolution of what some refer to as the *high heart chakra* may be what these positions are ultimately about.

INNER PILGRIMAGE #32: *Navigating the Arm Streams*
Your work with the etheric will bring forward elements of your subconscious world that are in the process of change. In this exercise with your Arm Streams you will enter the pathways of energy movement upward into the area of your Throat Center and then outward, into your arms and hands, which, as you will find, are an important part of your ability to express yourself.

*Preparation:* Locate each of the points on your Arm Streams. Start by reviewing their anatomical landmarks. These are your starting points for connecting with the energy movement at these positions. It can be helpful at first to touch the positions with your finger and, in this way, point them out to yourself. These positions become active as you practice, you will be able to find them internally.

Exercise Steps:
1.  Sitting upright in a comfortable position with your hands apart, begin by bringing your awareness to the tips of all your toes. Give this first contact a couple of minutes to intensify.

2.  Now move your awareness on your skin surface, slowly and consciously, up both your legs to the middle of both your groin muscles. Travel on the *entire skin surface* of your legs. A useful visualization is to imagine that you are rolling a soft stocking up your legs. When moving on your skin surface, the guideline is "never hurry, never stop."

3.  When you have reached your groin on both sides, rest with your awareness in the middle of your groin muscles for about a minute to allow this connection to deepen.

4.  Release your mid-groin contact and slowly bring your awareness into your Heat Point, located two finger-breadths below your navel. Once you have established this contact, stay with it a couple of minutes to let it deepen.

5.  Now move your awareness on your skin surface upward on the midline of your body to your Depression Point, located in the indentation just above your xiphoid process, the bony protrusion at the bottom of your sternum. The energy-active position is in the upper part of this indentation. Allow this contact to deepen for about a minute.

6.  From here, move your awareness slowly up to the Secondary Depression Point, located just below the ridge of your manubrium, the bone that connects your two collarbones, and allow it to rest there for a minute in order to let it deepen.

7.  Now bring your awareness slowly out along both collarbones at the same time and make contact with your right and left Collarbone Points. To find these points, trace the line of the side of your neck down to the collarbone. The Collarbone Points are where the muscle attaches to your collarbone. Give this contact a minute to deepen.

8.  From your Collarbone Points move down to both of your Channeling Points, located on the front part of the fold of your armpits. Give these positions a minute to activate in response to the presence of your attention—one minute.

9.  From your Channeling Points, slowly move your awareness on the skin surface on the inside of both your arms until you reach the energy-active position in the centers of your palms and let that contact deepen. Stay with this contact for a minute.

10. From here, move your awareness on your skin surface to the tips of your middle fingers and allow that contact to get deeper. This is where the negative stream meets the positive stream.

11. Now, slowly move with your awareness over the tips of both your middle fingers, up the back sides of your hands, up the outside of your forearms and your upper arms, across both shoulder blades to your Waste Energy Position. This is located around the second thoracic vertebra in your upper back between your shoulder blades.

12. Spend a couple of minutes with your awareness in your Waste Energy Position.

13. Now you'll start the journey back to where you started the exercise by moving your awareness in the opposite direction along your skin surface. Along the way, stop and briefly visit each of the positions once again and let your contact deepen in them. As always in exercises like this, move your awareness slowly. Here is the return sequence:

   - From your Waste Energy Position, travel across the upper part of your shoulder blades, down the outside of your arms to the tips of both your middle fingers
   - From your Hand Centers up the insides of both your arms to your Channeling Points
   - Collarbone Points
   - Secondary Depression Point
   - Depression Point
   - Heat Point
   - Mid-groin positions
   - Down on the skin surface of both your legs to the tips of all your toes

14. End the exercise and take note of what happened.

INNER PILGRIMAGE #33: *The Snow Angel Exercise*
Now that you have been introduced to your Arm Streams and have had a chance to move your awareness along this important energetic pathway, let's move to a self-healing exercise that can address holding patterns in your upper body and the Circulation of Expression. The key to this practice is slow, conscious physical movement. In deeply relaxing modes of working with yourself, such as Kum Nye exercise,[33] extremely slow movement is used to address deep stress and bring about release. In this self-healing treatment, we will use the same principle.

With the Snow Angel Exercise, you are deliberately placing your body under stress and then performing slow, conscious movement. If there are blockages, this will cause you to encounter them consciously and make it easier for them to move toward release. Here is how it looks when you work with yourself:

---

33    Kum Nye is a Tibetan Buddhist slow movement practice, similar in some ways to yoga or tai chi.

*Exercise Steps:*

1.  Lie down on your back with your arms and hands comfortably at your sides. Make sure there is enough room on both sides for you to extend your arms out away from your body.

    > NOTE: A very effective option is to place a folded towel or massage bolster lengthwise under your spine. When you lie back on it, this will open your chest.

2.  (Assuming your palms are facing down) After you have taken a few moments to settle in, the first thing you will do is turn your palms up toward the ceiling. Do this extremely slowly, so that you feel each and every change of angle in your hands and arms.

3.  Rest a moment with your palms facing the ceiling.

4.  Now bring your arms and hands out away from your body in a slow sweep until they are perpendicular to your body. Again, this is done extremely slowly.

5.  From this perpendicular, or T position, now bring both arms and hands upward, extremely slowly, toward the ceiling. This slow movement will pass through areas of tension which you would miss if you moved at normal speed.

6.  At some point, your palms will be facing each other. Bring your awareness to the *space between your palms* as they slowly come together.

7.  Allow your palms to touch. Rest a moment in that position.

8.  When you are ready, let your hands part and bring both arms slowly and consciously back down to the T position.

9.  Rest there for a few moments.

10. Repeat steps seven through ten two more times.

11. You are now in the T position. Now, slowly move your hands and arms down toward your feet in a slow arc until they are resting once again at your sides.

12. Slowly turn your palms down to the table.

13. End the exercise.

*Here are some tips for getting the most out of this exercise:*

-   Make your movement *slow and conscious.*

-   Don't stop.

-   As for the speed, think of the movement of the minute hand on a clock, very slow, but never stopping.

-   Feel the energy movement up and down your arms.

-   Feel the energy movement between your hands as they approach each other and move away from each other. See if your hands feel like they are being energetically pulled together or pushed apart.

-   Feel the resistance. Practice turning your attention *toward* it.

- If your arms start to tremble or shake as you slowly lift and lower them, *allow this to happen*. See if you can allow the shaking to get as strong as it wants. This shaking is one of the ways your body releases excess energy.

- Similarly, if you feel a heat wave or a quivering deep in your chest or elsewhere in your body as you raise your arms, allow that to happen and continue with your extremely slow movement.

- Keep breathing.

PARTNER TREATMENT #11: *The Snow Angel*

Once you get the hang of this as a self-treatment, it is easy to convert it to a partner treatment. It is good to have done it a number of times with yourself, so that you really know what is meant by "extremely slow" movement, and what it can do. Be aware that this can be an emotional process as you guide your partner through layers of deep resistance. Here is how to go about this with a partner:

Setup*:*

Have your partner lie on her back on the massage table. As you did with yourself, you can place a folded towel or massage bolster lengthwise on the table and have her lie with her spine on the bolster. This is optional, but effective in making the most of this treatment. When she lies back, this opens her chest. Do this only if she can lie on the bolster comfortably.

Treatment with a Partner:

Use your hands or fingertips to briefly activate the energy-active positions on the positive and negative Arm Streams. Consult the illustration for the location of these points. I often use my middle and ring fingers together to activate an energetic point. These are the *fire finger* and *water finger*, and they create a strong, energetically balanced activation. To address your partner's Waste Energy Point, slip a hand under her spine so that you are touching the area around the second thoracic vertebra. This is just below the "knob" at the base of the neck.

The points you will be activating on the Arm Streams are:

Negative Stream
- *The Heat Point*: two finger-breadths below your partner's navel
- *The Depression Point*: located on the upper part of the indentation just above your partner's xiphoid process
- *The Secondary Depression Point*: located just below the ridge of your partner's manubrium, the bone that joins her sternum with her two collar bones
- *Collarbone Points:* located where your partner's sternocleidomastoid muscles attach to her collarbone
- *Channeling Points*: at the front of your partner's armpits
- *Hand Centers:* located in the center of your partner's palms
- *The tips of your partner's middle fingers*

Positive Stream
- *Waste Energy Position*: located around your partner's second thoracic vertebra on her back;

186

- *The tips of her middle fingers:* this is where the positive and negative Arm Streams meet.

<u>Verbal Instruction</u>

Now that your partner's Arm Streams are more active, they are better able to conduct energy. Here is where you start bringing your partner actively into the treatment by walking her through the slow arm movements. I give quite a bit of verbal instruction and active support and encouragement to my partner when I give this treatment. This helps my partner to move extremely slowly through the inevitable areas of resistance the treatment brings up. Here is the gist of what I say to my client:

1.  (If her palms are facing down) "Very slowly turn your palms so they're looking up at the ceiling. Do it as slowly as you can. Pay attention to what happens as you do that."
2.  (When her palms are facing up) "Good, just rest there a moment."
3.  "Now, slowly bring your arms and hands out away from your body. Try to do it really slowly, and when they are straight out from your body, let them rest again."
4.  "Now, slowly bring your arms and hands upward toward the ceiling. See if you can do this really slowly, but without stopping. Very, very slow."

> Tip: While your partner is slowly moving her arms this way, you can enhance the movement of energy in her Arm Streams by massaging these pathways—try it just off the skin surface—with the energetic paintbrushes and brooms of your fingertips and hands.

6.  (As her hands reach the top of the arc) "Okay, see if you can feel what is going on between your palms."
7.  (As her palms touch) "Pay attention to what happens when your palms touch."
8.  "You choose the moment to start the path back down. You're going to bring them back down on the same path they took on the way up. Keep it really slow."
9.  (When her arms reach the horizontal position) "When your arms get all the way back down, just let them rest."

> Encourage your partner to allow whatever trembling or shaking might occur. This is an important part of the process.

10. Repeat these last four steps two more times.

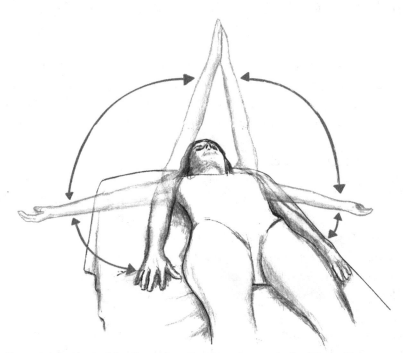

For a detailed look at the *Snow Angel* treatment, come to the Pilgrim Extras on my Web site. (See the instructions for finding the Pilgrim Extras on the last page of this book.)

*Trusting the Dynamic of Release*

In the context of energy healing, we use the term "release" in a specialized way to indicate the discharge of excess energy that is held in our bodies and psyches. In this sense, release can take place in any part of ourselves where we can hold energy. Releases range from barely noticeable finger twitches and knee jerks to sighs and yawns and full-body surges of emotion. Our bodies and psyches use these natural forms of release to regulate and balance the energetic metabolism in our systems, expelling what's old and in the way and drawing to ourselves new impulses and fresh energies that will help us toward our hidden wholeness.

Release that carries a person's experience into new territory underscores the importance of subconscious cooperation between you and your healing partner. One important factor is your acceptance of her process, your capacity to connect and simply be present with her, neither dampening what comes up nor pushing for a release. The energy healer who would facilitate release in a non-forcing way learns the signs and symptoms of impending release and acquires a generous appreciation for the resistance that typically precedes it. Ideally, the healer has also gained enough experience in riding the rapids of her own personal process that she trusts the dynamic of release as it crescendos, peaks and then drops off. She understands that the wave of release, if allowed to do so, can carry her partner onto new shores of peace and insight.

What follows are some of the signs and signals of energetic release that I have learned to pay attention to in my practice of energy-active bodywork. You can find these taking place on the microscopic level as body tissue releases excess charge, partially or fully clears a traumatic pattern and then reorganizes. The same thing happens on a larger scale with full-body emotional releases, often followed by insights and psycho-spiritual renewal.

- *A build-up of resistance* is often a *harbinger of release.* When I am working with another person and there is a conspicuous tightening or drawing together of the tissue under my hands, I become curious about whether a release process might be underway. I find a way to address the area with my hands and my awareness and stay with it, long enough for the release to happen, or long enough for me to catch on that a release is not going to happen this time around.

- *Twitches, sudden flinches, shaking, quivering, trembling,* as energy is discharged from the tissue of the body. Peter Levine, author of *Waking the Tiger,* reported this sort of shaking and trembling in traumatized animals. A related phenomenon in which the body shakes off excess energy is the *therapeutic pulse,* referred to in craniosacral work. Such a pulse can be felt as anything from a tiny "tick-tick-tick" to a bodacious throb, which lasts for a period of time and then diminishes and disappears.

- *Breathing Changes*: It's not uncommon for there to be changes in the depth, rhythm, and speed of your partner's breathing patterns. Spontaneous changes in breathing patterns are one of your body's ways of regulating the energy exchange in your system. This includes the whole range of gasping, panting, sighing, and shallow breathing.

- *Heat* can accompany a release of energy. This can range from localized rises in tissue temperature to radiant whole body hot flashes. Sometimes, energy that has been held for a long time will seem to combust and release outward in a plume of heat, like a solar flare.

- *Fluttering eyelids and rapid eye-movements*: These are outward signals of changes in brain-wave activity, shifts in your partner's autonomic nervous system and entry into hypnagogic states which are like a waking dream, often filled with images, memories, dreams and reflections.

- Emotional release is a common phenomenon. As the word "e-motion" tells us, this is outward-motion of energy. By the same token, if that out-motion is "pressed back" (*re-pressed*) or "pressed down" (*sup-pressed*), the result is a jamming together (*com-pression*) of energies. When your partner's system can relax and come, even for a short time, into a state of greater energetic balance, emotions can be what they were originally intended to be: releases of excessive energy held in your body and psyche.

- *Mental Release*: This refers to the flurries of mental images that can rise up during treatments, which leave little or no impact as memories or information. Cartoon images might cavort past the mind's eye to a soundtrack of internal gibberish that goes in one mental ear and out the other and is gone.

- *"Push-off"*: Sometimes, when working energetically on another person, you will feel as if your hands are being gently pushed away from the area you are working on. It is almost as if, having released energy, the area where you have worked then drinks in fresh energies, and when it is satisfied, it pushes away from the dining table and says, "Thank you very much."

The process of resistance, release, and renewal is not a random process at all. It is a perfect example of the three-fold spiritual path in action. The build up of resistance, which often comes before a release, and the release itself are a vehicle provided by nature for moving our consciousness out of the known world, out of our habitual patterns, into more unfettered contact with what psychologist Robert Johnson calls the "source of our evolving selves," followed by a reentry into our everyday world.

*Release vs. Clearance*

Resistance, release, and renewal, taken as a package, are a perennial theme of energywork and of central importance in energy-oriented healing work. A. T. Still, the father of osteopathy, observed that as organisms we tend toward self-healing when given a chance. I take this to be true on all levels of our being. This self-healing, or self-optimization, invariably involves a shift toward balance, and this seems to always included the releasing old experience—as opposed to merely repressing of it—and the drawing-in of new life force and experience.

It is easy to get the impression that release is a one-time event. In practice, however, that is not always the case. Not infrequently, you can help a partner through a significant release, or go through one yourself, only to find that there is more to do. The need for release will continue as long as the pattern behind the build-up of energy has not cleared. Imagine a stream of water moving along easily and unimpeded. Small sticks and leaves are washed along in the stream, and they, too, move right along with the moving water. Now imagine that, somewhere in the path of the stream, the flow of water encounters a jagged stone. The stone is not so large that the water can't move around it, but because of the stone's particular shape, it has to make a detour. Perhaps some of the water stops moving, and what was once fresh, flowing water begins to pool and stagnate. The sticks and leaves that were moving along with the stream start to hang up on the stone, and in time they accumulate to the point that they impede the free flow of water and maybe even stop it altogether.

We see a similar thing with the movement of life force within us. Energy patterns shaped by the injuries and traumas of your life have their way of impeding the flow of life force through you in the same way the jagged rock collects the sticks and leaves that impede the flow of water in a stream. In your energy system these obstructions can turn into to stagnate pools, and become a collection point for all kinds of energetic debris. You can go into the stream and clean out the accumulation of flotsam and jetsam that hangs up on the rock, but as long as the rock remains in the stream, this accumulation will continue to occur. Likewise, you can periodically release the buildup of energy that collects around trauma patterns, but the permanent release can happen only if there is an actual clearance of the pattern that collects the build-up.

To conclude this chapter, here are some anecdotes from my practice, each illustrating some aspect of the phenomenon of resistance, release, and renewal.

# FOUR ANECDOTES ABOUT RELEASE

## I.
## ENERGY RELEASE WITH
## AN ALL-AMERICAN FOOTBALL PLAYER

I once had a surprise visit in my practice from Albert Strong, an All-American backfield special-ist for the University of Kansas football team. At that time, a lot of the football players at KU went to a very sought-after massage therapist in town named Heidi, one of the kinds of persons you find in the massage community who is physically tiny but finds all kinds of effective ways of elbowing their way into deep tissue. Heidi was out of town, and so a few of her regulars from the football team migrated over to our practice for a session or two. I had rarely worked with football players, and I had forgotten how big they are.

How big? One of Albert's teammates, I'll never forget, had an embarrassing incident that made local headlines. At a local drive-through taco place, he was given one *chimichanga* fewer than he had ordered. When he didn't get what he wanted, he tried to climb out of his car window and through the drive-through window in order to bring down retribution on the offending taco cook. But, alas, he was too large to make it all the way through the drive-through window, and that is where the police found him, unable to get in or out.

Back to the much smarter Albert: he was massive, six-feet-one and 250 pounds with a huge, powerful chest and upper arms bigger around than some people's thighs. He told me he had pain in his right trapezius. It came from repeated shoulder impact while training with the blocking dummy. To me, the picture was clear: blocking practice, repeated impact in the same place on his body, not to mention real blocking, had repeatedly thrown massive amounts of excess energy into the tissue of Albert's shoulder muscles, and it had lodged there.

After a bit of massage, I told him I wanted to shift gears and try something else, and he said that would be fine with him. I pulled up my stool really close and slipped a hand under Albert's right shoulder, spread my other hand out over his right upper chest and settled in. I didn't do much at all beyond getting a good energetic connection with Albert's shoulder, paying attention to the natural exchange of energy between my hands through the area I was holding, and following the micromovements of the tissue. By and by, the highly condensed bundle of energy from all that impact began to make itself felt. It began ticking and pulsing and pretty soon the area was heating up like an electric blanket. We both drifted into a semi-altered state of consciousness for a moment, and everything got quiet. Suddenly, Albert's whole body flinched and jumped a good foot off the table in a massive release of energy. His landing shook the furniture and rattled the windows as if a small bomb had been detonated under the house. We were both utterly shocked with the suddenness and force of it. There we were, stunned, staring at each other with "What the hell happened?" looks on our faces. Actually, I knew what the hell happened, but I had never seen it happen with that much force. Then we started grinning and giggling and couldn't stop for ten minutes. It was quite a release for both of us, and Albert felt much freer in his upper body.

## II.
## AN ENERGY HEALER STEPS IN
## AFTER A CAR WRECK

After a car accident in which the family van rolled over in a ditch, Ruth, a mother of three, came to and was horrified to find that Charlie, her youngest, had been thrown through the window into an open field. Charlie was rushed to intensive care in shock with lacerations all over his four-year-old body. Ruth had been getting treatments from an energy healer, Hanna, whom she called immediately. Hanna spent the next twenty-four hours at the hospital literally pulling the energy of the impact out of Charlie's body. At times, it was as if she was hauling bundles of energy from his body. Other times, it was like she was carefully reaching into a haystack and slowly pulling out long needles, and still other times, she felt like her hand was riding plumes of heat escaping from Charlie like a solar flare. Doctors, who at first feared the boy might die, were amazed at Charlie's quick recovery.

## III.
## ENERGY HEALING AFTER
## AN ACCIDENT WITH A HATCHET

I was visiting the home of my friend Denise Low, some of whose poetry appears in this book. Her husband, Tom, was outside working in the garden and somehow managed to catch the impact of his hatchet on the back of his hand, splitting it open. Tom, with his peculiar sense of irony, sauntered into the kitchen and asked in a casual tone if we thought he maybe ought to do something about this. The gash was awful, and it's a miracle that he didn't chop all the way through his hand! After Tom took a dose of homeopathic arnica, which helps the small blood vessels to heal, I set about attending to the energy of the impact, which was already radiating out from his hand in an angry red-hot wave. For about a half hour, I pulled it our and "unscrewed" the compressed energy in a counterclockwise spiral, guiding it out, giving it an escape route. It also didn't hurt that Tom is a member of the Bear and Turtle Clans of Menominee Indian Nation and had been around energy healing in various forms his whole life, so there was no conceptual barrier to what I was doing. Presently, the heat wave roiling out of the back of Tom's hand began to diminish and cool off, and Denise and I were relieved to watch the tissue of his hand pull together. I think Tom was relieved, too—I sure would be—but he acted as if it was no big deal.[34]

## IV.
## A SMALL OBSERVATION
## FROM THE TREATMENT TABLE

It is a common observation among chiropractors that bones are the "slaves" of the soft tissue.

---

34   If Tom's wound had not responded so quickly and so well, we would have been off to the emergency room. Please use common sense when you are confronted with an emergency. Bear in mind that standard, conventional medical treatment is often the best thing for emergencies and acute, life-threatening conditions. I would like to reiterate the disclaimer I wrote at the beginning of this book: *Please understand that the practices in this book are not intended to be a substitute for care by a qualified health professional.*

That is to say that an adjustment—of a vertebra, for example—is more effective and will last longer if the soft tissue around a bone is compliant. Otherwise, if muscles and other soft tissue are tight and toxic, they will tend to keep the bone where it was, and soon the adjustment will have to be performed all over again.

Similarly, in my experience, the soft tissue has to release its charge of energy and emotion for there to be a change that holds. Susan came into the practice complaining of pressure on one side of her head and tightness in her neck and shoulder blade. As she talked, she was very calm and contained, even when she told me, almost incidentally, that she was about to tell her ten-year-old daughter that she was about to leave her and send her to live with her father. She even speculated that the impending ordeal of leaving her child was in some way behind the bodily sensations she was having. What struck me was her complete lack of emotion about the whole thing as she told about it. On the table it was the same: her body was almost without any of the charge that builds up in a person when they are about to have a release of emotion. The entire session ran counter to my expectations in that way; here was a woman who was about to put herself through what has to be one of the most difficult and wrenching trials imaginable, but it seemed that her emotions were completely on hold. Nothing moved, and although she felt better after the session, I knew that there would be no significant change in her complaints until her emotional process had its day.

## V.
## SYSTEM SHAKERS
### A SPECULATION ABOUT BEING ACCIDENT PRONE

Some time ago I got to thinking about the connection between unreleased concentrations of energy in people's bodies and certain cases of so-called accident proneness. Here, I mean persons who sustain injuries, over and over again, to the same part of their body. My theory is this: when a trauma has "gone underground"—that is to say it is no longer on the surface of our everyday awareness—it operates in our unconscious world. Because of our natural tendency to grow toward our innate wholeness, there inevitably comes a time when that trauma will try to surface and begin drawing attention to itself by whatever means it can find as a means of moving toward release and healing. Knowing that these compressed concentrations of energy create their own force fields with their own kind of magnetism, I believe that if we lifted the lid on chronic, repetitive injury sites, we would often find deeper, more ancient wounds. I speculate that when the ancient wound has healed and resolved—that is when the energetic charge and its magnetic field have cleared—it would be reasonable to expect that the repetitive injuries relating to it would also stop occurring.

Once in a workshop I asked for a volunteer to lie on the table so I could demonstrate an approach to unwinding a partner's head and neck. Gisela hopped up on the table, eager to get a little extra treatment. In addition to volunteering for the demo, she volunteered the information that she was continually clonking her head—she would regularly walk into things and smack her head in the same place every time and knock herself silly. She had no idea why she was mentioning this. It was just this crazy little thing that kept happening to her. I asked if anything had ever happened to her head. She didn't think so ... but yes, come to think of it, she did take a tumble down the stairs once when she was eight years old, but that was a long time ago.

I was seated at the head of the table. Gisela had situated herself too far down the table, so

I asked her to move back toward me. In the process, she sat up and scooted her bottom up the table a bit. At the same moment, I stood up in order to adjust the height on my stool. I leaned forward to do this just as Gisela was lying back in her new position. The crowns of our heads met with such a teeth-rattling, spine-shuddering "clonk!" that we were both stunned. The others in the class reacted sympathetically with "Ooooooh, wow! Are you guys okay?" And then it was over, or was it?

Gisela settled back in, and I began to unwind her head and neck, following the movement of her body and narrating to the group what I was feeling under my hands. This went on for a short time when her body's movements stopped abruptly. Tears started to well up in Gisela's eyes and in a short time her body started to shake uncontrollably. I encouraged her to let this happen, and presently she went into a deep emotional release. As her process emerged, she said that our heads had met at precisely the spot where she was always smashing her head when she would run into things. On the table she vividly relived the experience of being pushed down the stairs by her older brother when she was eight, a time when life at home was difficult for her because her parents were always fighting. The whole emotional context of her fall down the stairs emerged with her release.

Gisela's episode was a prime example a specific kind of synchronicity or outer event which bears a direct or indirect relationship to an emerging process in us. Repetitive injuries at a site where deeper trauma and what are called *energy cysts* are lodged may be something like the "two-by-four approach," a rather blatant form of an unconscious strategy for getting at a deeper pattern. Even though the top of my head was throbbing from our collision, I couldn't help but think, *what a perfect demo!* I talked to Gisela a few times since that workshop and she told me that she had not bumped her head on anything in six months.

There are softer versions of this in which relatively small events act as what I call *system shakers* or openers for larger, deeper processes that may have become stuck in their progress: the camping trip tick bite on a woman's back that gets inflamed and coincides with the opening of an emotional process (interestingly, of all places to bite her, the tick chose a specific acupuncture point on her bladder meridian that relates to release); a man who has a "chance" encounter in coffee shop with a crystal salesman eager to show off his wares who demonstrates the healing qualities of a piece of quartz by stroking the inner edge of his index finger with the tip of the crystal. Interestingly, the man had been living with constipation for quite a while and of all the places to show off his crystal's power, the salesman chose a line on the man's large intestine meridian. Ten minutes after the demonstration, the man had to excuse himself and rush to the restroom.

I run into this sort of phenomenon enough to be especially attentive when clients tell me, maybe only in passing, about seemingly random events that have this kind of system-shaking effect. It seems that when we are in an active process that has not yet crossed over the threshold into full consciousness, or we have repressed something that needs to reach resolution, that we are setting ourselves up subconsciously for a kind of specifically targeted system shaker.

# CHAPTER FIFTEEN

## INTEGRATION

### LIVING ONE LIFE

Your energywork practice delivers a changed person to the world and, in its small way, changes the world. The journey of energy healing has the potential to carry you out of the mass mind and your everyday world, if only for a moment at a time, into encounters with the numinous background of life. There, the pilgrim in your body might find an opening to ecstatic, ineffable states, unfiltered by anything institutional, undefined by psychology or religion or middle class values. At times, new perceptions come cracking through—you sit bolt upright and shout, "Eureka!" and rush out to rearrange the world. Other days, less bombastically, an internal practice might draw you with gentle magnets into deep stillness, after which you calmly reenter your world with renewed clarity and purpose. Similarly, a healing partner might have a profound experience under your hands and come out of a treatment transformed and inspired. Still other times, change happens in imperceptible shifts, below the radar. You go forward on faith and the occasional unnamable tingle and cultivate an eye for the unseen ways that your work in the world of energy and consciousness silently sifts into the world of everyday. Whether quietly or noisily, energywork practice promotes the renewal of the age-old experience of your most essential nature, and this renewal does something to you. Sooner or later, your spiritual growth becomes as undeniable as winter's turn into spring, and with it comes the need to integrate this change into your life.

Much is made in spiritual circles about the best ways to transcend the body, find heaven within, enter bliss or nirvana, but as long as we are in this life, this is only two-thirds of the path. The three-fold spiritual path also involves coming back into the world we inhabit, the ordinary world of washing the dishes, earning a living, visiting Uncle Harold and Aunt Gladys on Sunday, bearing the qualities of our transcendent, ecstatic moments, and the gifts we have cultivated in our soul's work and travels. No longer internally split up into spiritual and worldly domains, the pilgrim's task becomes one of integration. Integration means learning to live one life.

The energy healing practitioner who works at the cusp of the physical structure of her partner's body and the energy that enlivens it is in a unique position to promote the integration of deep inner experiences with the world of everyday. While energy healing works to open the way to transcendent experiences, it also honors the need to come back into the world. Let's look at some practical ways to implement integration in the context of an energy healing treatment.

## *Off the Table and Back in the World*

As an energy healer, it is important to help your partner absorb the changes brought on in your energywork session. We typically underestimate the power of the subconscious, and it is easy to forget that subtle but powerful forces have been activated. As you conclude a session, try to discourage the person you have just worked on from hopping up from the table immediately and rushing out into the traffic of life without first integrating their experience. They may not know it, but they have been in an altered state of consciousness, and they stand to gain something important by making the transition slowly. By intentionally slowing down this reentry phase, you are wordlessly teaching your treatment partner an appreciation for spiritual process by honoring the return phase of the three-fold spiritual path. The nice thing about it is that, in most cases, this integration will happen all by itself when you create the right context for it.

In my practice, my usual *modus operandi* is to complete my hands-on work and invite my partner to stay on the table and simply "simmer," relax and feel what is moving within her. I leave the room for a few minutes, wash my hands, check my schedule, anything to give my partner some space and a bit of time alone. This is part of the session. I frequently come back to find that her process has taken a step in my absence in the form of insights, memories, tears, and reflections. It is often in this short interlude that the arc of the treatment comes full circle.

Another important thing you can do to help this process of integration is to alert your partner to the fact that she will be in a slightly altered state for a while after the treatment, and that this is perfectly normal when energetic techniques have been applied. I often give my partner a bit of homework for the time immediately following an energy treatment as a way for her to integrate her experience and attend to the heightened energetic and psycho-spiritual activity. In my experience, this window is particularly open for about thirty-six hours, a day and a half. Here are some typical hallmarks of the post-treatment integration process, which I call to the attention of the person I am working with in a healing session:

- *Dreams can be very accessible.* Freud called dreams the "royal road to the subconscious," and in the period immediately following an energy healing session they can suddenly be quite active and vivid and instructive about your process. Whether you are aware of them or not, dreams are always part of the interplay between your conscious and non-conscious worlds, and in the aftermath of treatments, it's not uncommon for this important function of dreams to be stepped up. Keeping a dream journal is an excellent way to help this side of your life become more conscious.

- *Similarly, long forgotten memories can come into the foreground.* Energywork affects the etheric storehouse of the subconscious. Energywork that integrates your physical body with your energy field will bring forward held memories. Include a section of your journal for this.

- *Acute and chronic conditions are likely to shift.* For example, a pain might come suddenly and then leave; or a sleep pattern might change.

- *Emotional release* is not uncommon during this period, as excess build-ups of energy discharge from your body and psyche.

- You might suddenly connect some previously unconnected dots in the form of insights and outer events in the form of *synchronicities* that might trigger some significant inner process.

With experience, I believe you will come to see that your involvement with energywork delivers a healthier, more grounded, centered, expanded and spiritually aligned person to the world. Sending your partner out the door in a bit better shape to face her personal challenges contributes positively to her family, society and the world. Likewise, the step taken by the pilgrim in your body raises our collective consciousness and makes you more ready to step more fully into your deepest calling. It is no small thing.

*A Gift of Joy*

Much of this book has spoken to the spiritual traveler within each of us, and to the particular predicament of the healer as she awakens to her calling and consciously steps out on her path. But I hope that it points even inner pilgrims and healers to a more universal path. After all, regardless of what you or I consider our calling to be, there is always more to the picture than any of us are seeing. Ultimately, even the callings we embrace most passionately in this life are partial and transitory and will someday give way to a calling—to paraphrase songwriter Roger McGuinn—to where the rivers of all our visions flow into one another.

If there is a calling that applies to each of us, I believe it is the calling to become universal people. This means progressively embracing more and more of the totality of who we are. Let's assume you have recognized a particular quality in yourself that is asking for special attention, and you set out to cultivate it. That process might take you to schools and experts who supply you with all the techniques and all the state of the art knowledge. It could usher you into the presence of special individuals who initiate you into mystic practices, or drive you up to mountaintops on lonely quests for spiritual visions. By and by, you will have "been there and done that." What then?

At some point your heart opens, and you touch the world you live in with the fruits of your inner work. Think back to the last time you caught someone red-handed in their true calling. When did you last see someone who was truly inspired as they did whatever they did? A musician who enters that magical rapport with his audience, a teacher whose enthusiasm for her subject is so infectious that her students all go away from a class or lecture turned on and changed by what they heard. What's happening when this occurs? At some point, energy fields merge and a connection is made, the kind that happens through the heart when it opens in compassion. That is how a spiritual transmission takes place, no matter what the subject matter or medium. And often, what is transmitted is not information, but joy.

In my experience, one of the glowing examples of the transmission of joy is Richard Feynman, who won the Nobel Prize for Physics in 1966 and served on the blue-ribbon panel of scientists who investigated the explosion of the Challenger Spacecraft. Feynman, acknowledged far and wide as a genius, obviously had great skills and knowledge, but his gift was sparked by his feeling for life and for other people. I know next to nothing about physics, let alone anything of the specific subject matter that made Richard Feynman so famous, and still, he has touched me like few other individuals because of his full-time open-ended inquiry into the mystery of life. His genius lay in the heart and humor he brought to his endeavors, which were wide ranging and whimsical, from unwrapping the secrets of physics to decoding ancient Aztec codices and, once in his spare time, finding a way to get around the security system at Los Alamos; from the mysteries of antimatter to the problem of gaining entry to remote countries in the former Soviet Union by posing as an ethnomusicologist. Even while dying of cancer, Feynman radiated mischievous curiosity about where he was and what was happening to him. In his strange way, he demonstrated the compassion that an open heart makes possible and the way the spiritual qualities of a person can blend with outward activities. Moreover, he showed us the joy that is so often a by-product of finding and living your calling. In his case, that alone was worth a Nobel Prize.

I also find myself thinking about Thomas Merton, who lived in silence for many years, alone in a hermitage, as a Trappist monk, from the beginning of World War II until his death in 1968. After twenty-five years in his monastery, released from his vow of silence, Merton traveled to the Far East. The official reason for the trip was to attend an international conference on religion in Bangkok. Between official events, Merton traveled to various other places in Asia on a more personal pilgrimage that included a number of meetings with the Dalai Lama of Tibet. A short time after his meetings with the Dalai Lama, Merton died of accidental electrocution in Bangkok.

My impressions of Merton started with reading a number of his books, but they grew into a lasting impression when I heard an off-the-record interview with him, recorded just before he embarked on his journey to the Far East, a journey from which he never returned in physical form. It was a time of fierce social and political upheaval in the United States and Europe, when "activism" meant getting out in the street and protesting. When asked if he thought his life as a hermit, dedicated to prayer, meditation, devotion, contemplation, and his writing was truly relevant in a modern world of action, he answered that it was. He said that the monastic calling had to do with attaining the highest possible states of consciousness of the Divine, and then feeding that consciousness back into the world of humanity through prayer.

Hearing Merton speak in this informal interview, I was taken by the palpable lack of neurosis in the man. This came out in his simple presence, grounded and centered. This was not a person who was thrashing around, trying to find himself or his calling—he had found himself and his calling. Nor was he striving to make the world a different place—he was too busy being fascinated by it. His gift was an open-eyed, infectious curiosity about all matters. Like Richard Feynman, his genius came out in his heart-felt joy over his discoveries.

Here, at the close of this book on energy healing and spiritual process, it is my hope that you, too, will find joy in your discoveries.

*Instead of trying to save the world, try savoring it.*

*Nancy Hall*

*A Wish for All Pilgrims*

Pilgrims lose heart when they don't see their path. Sometimes, when things bog down, the simple realization that we are in a process of growth and becoming can be what saves us from believing we are eternally stuck. Each time we take a step, we take what we have absorbed from the past, learning from fellow travelers, both past and present, and move into the strong adventure of the unknown. So encourage that traveler in your heart and in the hearts of those you meet in this life. The final words in the film *Restoration* sum up something of the spirit of this moment for me, and I offer them to you:

> *The stars that once confused me seem now to light a path that is clear—*
> *one that I have, in truth, been traveling for all these days, where I met*
> *what came, and left behind my sorrows and am traveling still.*
>
> Rupert Walters

# APPENDIX

## TWO REFLECTIONS ON
## SPIRITUAL PROCESS AND INITIATION

In spiritual and mystical traditions the world over, the human body is identified as a mystery temple, an alchemical crucible, a place of initiation and transformation. *The point of subtle energy practice is to allow us a means of consciously entering that temple.* By entering into the temple of the body on an energetic level, as a spiritual seeker or as a healer, we enter into a perfect microcosm of the mystery of life and creation. An energywork of spiritual development builds and maintains the bridges between the body and these levels of inner reality.

Spiritual process is the natural process by which we come into the totality of ourselves, and it tends to be brought forward and augmented by energywork practices, which are next of kin to classic disciplines of the inner life like prayer, meditation and contemplation. Traditionally, these classic disciplines were not taught to those who had not dedicated themselves to the spiritual path, since they were recognized as powerful agents of change. The following reflections are part of my personal synthesis of some of the mystic traditions surrounding spiritual initiation. I offer them here for the light they can shine on the psycho-spiritual dimension of energywork practice.

*Reflection 1: Spiritual Initiation vs. Group Membership*
I saw a couple of clients who came one right after the other. It happened to be my birthday. Though they didn't know each other, their sessions bore an uncanny resemblance to one another. They were both going through changes that made them feel they were separating from their former lives and from their circle of friends and family. Big changes. Each felt she was being led away from the life she had known, all the while strangely trustful that the process was a good one and would bring her closer to her truth. Eerily, during their sessions, both of them used the exact same phrase: "I can't see the path I'm on."

I was reminded of old-fashioned initiation rituals in which the initiate is blindfolded and led on a dark path into a secret chamber where, though she does not know it, some deep truth is to be revealed to her. Often the initiate is then guided through acts that give symbolic form to a change in her condition. Initiation rituals of this kind are outer enactments of an inner step that the initiate is in the process of taking. An outer ritual is most effective when it is performed with consciousness and in sync with an inner transformational event; or it might anticipate that internal event, set it up, or seal the transformation into the person's body and awareness.

When I use the term "initiation," I am talking about the turning points in spiritual process, not about being initiated into a group or a belief system. Such things as gang initiations or university fraternity hazings are done mainly to gain acceptance into a particular group or to betoken change of status within a group. They remind me of that long-ago day in Boy Scouts when I had to carry around a sixteen-pound stone all day at Camp Ta-Wa-Ka-Nee, and then at night drink the mysterious "Black Drink," made of bitter-tasting quinine water and charcoal, in order to be initiated into I forget what (maybe it was manhood). Such rituals may even borrow some of the trappings of old serious initiatory practice, but they are typically performed without any pretense of being linked to spiritual process or inner transformation.

In contrast, our spiritual ancestors, the healers and teachers and initiators of the past, were very interested in spiritual process, and evolved their healing practices in harmony with their understanding of cosmic laws and the patterns of the natural world. They saw it as their sacred responsibility to recognize these patterns reflected in those who came to them for guidance and healing so they could perform appropriate rituals in a timely fashion. Of relevance for us here, energy healing, like true initiation, cooperates with natural growth and helps to build a bridge between the microcosm of the initiate's inner world and the macrocosm of the cosmos.

## Reflection 2: Three Octaves of Initiation: Broad Patterns of Spiritual Process

In its broadest terms, something we call an "initiation" marks the completion or end of a cycle and the beginning of another. In spiritual process, it is an alchemical change: something about you is transformed and in the process, the world you live in is also changed. The kernel of a realization that blooms within you and totally changes your outlook might have been planted by something said to you in passing long ago. Sometimes it is the slings and arrows of life that lead you to potent experiences that ultimately require you to change the way you view the world. Or maybe you simply arrive at deep realizations, or awaken spiritually through the process of living your life.

The patterns of spiritual process have traditionally been likened to those found in nature. A seed is planted, rests, out of sight, as it sprouts roots beneath the surface of the earth. Eventually the plant grows and bears fruit. The fruit contains the seed of the next cycle of growth and fruition. Our own alchemical cycles of change partake of the same nature as they pass through their cycles and phases.

In energywork, our challenge is to recognize the cycle even when there's not much happening above the surface. Sufi teacher Samuel Lewis told the story of walking through the gardens in Golden Gate Park in the winter. He ran across the

*Receiving a new world of meaning today would involve complicated experiences far beyond reading a book on acceptable virtues ... The 'body-soul' needs to be changed in order to receive what Joseph Campbell calls "the inexhaustible energies of the cosmos" that pour down toward human beings. Without gratitude to energies much greater than our own, there will be no new meanings. It could be said that we lack the imagination now to imagine any new power to whom we could be grateful. The procedure for young men and women would ask a reintroduction to the dangerous energies of nature, as some Native Americans still ask from their youth. The process is messy, and needs teachers, the out-of-doors, and lots of time.*

Robert Bly

*As the scholar of Renaissance magic and esoterism Frances Yates observes, Hermetic knowledge was not intended for leisurely speculation. On the contrary, it was honored as gnosis, a saving knowledge, an apprehension of mysteries which run deep in nature and in the person, a transforming knowledge which can only be acquired through learning that is far beyond intellect alone.... one can develop a psychological attitude—that is, understand the processes of the soul—only through constant, daily, if not hourly, attention.*

Thomas Moore

gardener, who apologized that most of the vegetation was dormant and not much to look at. Sam assured him that he could see just as much beauty in the dormant plant in winter as when it was in full bloom. Similarly, if we can hone our perception to appreciate this universal pattern of formation, growth, and completion, we will gain what Renaissance scholar Frances Yates called an "apprehension of mysteries which run deep in nature," for they also run in spiritual process. They all partake of the same universal alchemical pattern.

Because we live on many levels, it is useful to think of three magnitudes or "octaves" of initiation: everyday events, life passages that we all go through, and what might be thought of as greater initiations or deeply life-changing transpersonal experiences. Here are some reflections on these three octaves of initiation.

*Everyday Events*

Our first octave of initiation involves all of us in the ebb and flow and small passages of everyday events. This refers to the simple events that begin and end themselves right under our noses, the choices we make, the small and large tasks we undertake, the cycle of each day with its small triumphs and defeats as it begins, takes its course, culminates and segues into the next. The myriad activities of our daily world are often so much a part of business as usual that their slow transformative effect can go unnoticed, so it may, at first, sound strange to call them initiations. But consider the choices you have made since awakening: the choice to see if peanut butter goes well with apples, whether or not to go for a walk before work, the choice to send off a note to an old friend. Small choices, but all together they shape your day, just as your days mingle to shape your life.

The well-known axiom of alchemy, "As above, so below," says that in the microcosm of everyday life, we see the patterns of the macrocosm reflected. Each spiritual tradition has its way of echoing this truth, often joined to the teaching that if we take care of the small things, the big ones will take care of themselves. A good deal of practical alchemy at the level of everyday living starts with this insight, one that humans have cultivated since time immemorial by observing nature, that what is started (initiated) naturally seeks a way to come full circle. This suggests a way to consciously participate in initiatory cycles at the level of everyday life. By attending to the relatively small cycles and passages of your everyday life—getting the kids to school, finally playing a smooth D-minor scale on your oboe, mindfully watching your inner life as you go about your business—you are putting yourself in position to appreciate the bigger initiations when they come.

A decision to do something is enough to start the ball rolling on an alchemical cycle. When you make a firm decision, you set something in motion that will naturally want to complete itself, either by manifesting in this world, perhaps in the form of some action, or by being replaced by another, clearer decision that is allowed to come to fruition.

Some people live with an accumulation of stagnant energy around them from the pattern of barely hatched and then abandoned plans and projects that never resolve themselves in action. Energy loiters in their aura and piles up like unpaid bills. It can be an effective confidence-builder to take this kind of cyclic alchemy by the horns in an everyday sort of way by simply making a decision to do something, however small, and actually following through on it. As an experiment, see how you feel if you deliberately set five tasks that can be carried out in a short time and then actually carry them out.

If you work with clients, it can sometimes be helpful to get an idea of where they are in their cycles of activity. If you sense a good deal of stagnation or lack of vitality around your treatment partner, for example, it can be useful to see how much of their energy is trapped in cycles that have been initiated, but for whatever reason have not come to completion.

I once had a dramatic example of this pattern in my practice. A woman in her fifties came for an energy-active bodywork session. Her chief complaint was fatigue and a kind of burdened feeling. As she relaxed and felt her way into her body, some of that burden began to release emotionally. Midway through the session, her abdomen began to tighten, quiver and release a bit. I maintained my contact, supported and followed her body's movements as this cycle repeated itself several times, building intensity with each cycle. Pretty soon, she was having strong abdominal contractions. I asked her what all this felt like to her and she said it made her think of labor during pregnancy. I asked her if she had children and she said no. I asked if she had ever been pregnant and with that question her emotions broke loose in a torrent of tears. She said she had been pregnant nine times (!), each time terminated, either by abortion or miscarriage. In our session, her body took advantage of the opportunity to release a good deal of held energy by going through the motions of completing a biological process that had long been denied. In a follow-up session, she reported having much more vitality and motivation.

## Life's Passages

The next octave of initiation encompasses the *life passages* we inevitably experience as we grow and mature. In some mystic traditions these passages are called the *lesser mysteries*, denoting the entry into various phases of life, events that are experienced by most of us. These include being conceived and born, entering puberty and reaching the various landmarks of maturity, getting married or finding a mate, having children, embracing a vocation (as opposed to merely getting a job), loss and grief, death. When these points of no return are marked and celebrated by rites of passage, as they are in most cultures, the transition is recognized, solemnized, and aligned with a distinct archetype. Even when they're not celebrated, each of these events has a lasting impact on the individual. It should be said that when a culture tries to deny or downplay the significance of these passages, as is too often the case in our western culture, it runs the risk of denying vital nourishment to the psyche of its members.

## Greater Initiations

Finally, there is the octave of the *greater initiations*, which involve experiences of transpersonal consciousness. They are referred to in various traditions as *Spiritual Initiation*, *Solar Initiation*, entry into the *Greater Mysteries*, or the *Temple Initiations*, to name a few. Not everyday occurrences, these describe spiritual awakenings and conversion experiences, major passages in the greater sweep of the soul's evolution beyond our personal biographies. These awakenings are distinct encounters with transpersonal dimensions of life, conscious steps into a wider spiritual reality. These steps include what might be called *spiritual baptism*—as opposed to baptism as the entry into the congregation of a church or spiritual community—in which we awaken to the fact that we are, first and foremost, spiritual beings. Another such landmark event is what is traditionally called *illumination*, in which the physical body becomes infused with spiritual light, greatly accelerating the processes of spiritual growth. Another such landmark event might be called *self-realization*, in which a person awakens from the illusion of separateness. As with the lesser mysteries, each of these big, life-altering initiations marks the culmination of one cycle of growth and the entry into a new one, and each of these states unfolds and deepens in cycle after cycle in each individual.

The greater initiations happen in varying degrees of intensity. Of course, we have spectacular examples in our religious traditions. Buddha's revelations under the Bodhi Tree, Mohammed's night journey, Jesus' transfiguration on the mountain, and St. Paul's blinding encounter with Christ—so powerful it knocked him from his horse—come immediately to mind. But it is mistaken to assume that these events only occur with saints and monks and founders of religions. Many people have nonordinary experiences that have great power. Some, for lack of a coherent context, file these experiences away and write them off as aberrant quirks of the mind, as a "crazy moment." Others, having no other context than psychopathology, are seen as having psychotic episodes; many of those are forced to tough it out with a psychiatric diagnosis, strong drugs, and even institutionalization.

Of course, not every psychosis is a meaningful spiritual initiation, and certainly not every spiritual experience leads to a psychotic break. But the power of spiritual awakening is often very disruptive to the status quo of a life. It changes everything, and people who already have an active framework of spiritual life tend to roll with these experiences better than those who do not. Thankfully, there are monasteries, ashrams, teachers, and healers connected with traditions that reflect something of the cumulative wisdom that understands these events. These wise teachers can be found both within and outside of established religious and healing institutions, and while it is true that they are not necessarily located on every corner or in the Yellow Pages of your phone directory, they definitely exist. They are in a position to recognize the hallmarks of spiritual initiation as part of a natural process and provide context and guidance to persons who are in the thick of such experiences.

None of this should suggest that you are required to have a crisis or an illuminated teacher in order to experience a profound spiritual awakening. Most of our inner growth is taking place behind the scenes already and comes to us in the process of living life. Wisdom comes less in the form of a spectacular revelation and non-ordinary states of consciousness than in the participation in ordinary salt-of-the-Earth life with its challenges. I remember the last years of my father's life. In the eyes of the world, he lived a long, highly respected but unspectacular life, but there is no doubt in my mind that life was his teacher. As he grew older, living each day as it came to him, it seemed that he shed his burdens and became brighter day by day.

The pilgrim in your body, or in the person who comes to you for help, is often going through one or the other of life's knotholes, and these passages can often be appreciated in terms of one or more of these octaves of initiation. Most of the time we deal in healing work with the aches and pains of daily living and life's inevitable passages. But the more we include practices and treatments which activate the realm of energy and consciousness, the more we enhance and accentuate deeper spiritual processes as well. Typically, spiritual process comes wrapped up in a puzzle package, a multi-layered onion of human complexity. Indeed, getting an eye for spiritual process means becoming a sleuth who detects the clues hidden in what your partner or client presents with when they arrive at your door.

We live in accelerated, post-traditional times in which the setting for initiation is becoming more and more the world of action and everyday life. This world can be a spiritual pressure cooker in its own right. And whether or not you are aware of the fact, the initiate is you and the person before you.

# GLOSSARY OF TERMS

**Arm Streams:** Your Arm Streams are part of the etheric circulation in your hands and arms. They are part of your energetic means of expression, since they flow up the center of your body, through your heart and throat areas and then outward. Points on your Arm Streams are your Heat Point, Depression Point, Secondary Depression Point, Collarbone Points, Channeling Points, Hand Centers, Waste Energy Position and the tips of your middle fingers.

**Centering:** the process of coming into energetic balance or equilibrium; practices that bring you into your center. Practices may be as simple as placing your attention on your breath or a sacred word and then returning there ever so gently whenever you notice your mind wandering. Examples of centering practices are found in Buddhist Vipassana and Christian contemplative traditions.

**Chakra:** Sanskrit for "wheel"; vortices of energy movement located in the etheric. These etheric structures are stable features of the human energy field which play a major energetic role in all aspects of human growth and development. In this book, I have used the more generic term "energy center."

**Circulation of Expression:** the circulation of energy and consciousness between your Sacral and Throat Centers. This circulation relates to all forms of expression as well as the release of excess energy from our systems.

**Circulation of Control:** the circulation of energy and consciousness between your Hara and Pineal Centers. This circulation relates to control, both in the sense of over-control and lack of control and, in energywork, in the specific sense of the kind of control it takes to move your awareness from position to position in energy exercises.

**Circulation of Balance:** the circulation of energy and consciousness between your Solar Plexus and Crown Centers. This circulation relates to how yin and yang balance and blend their activity in us.

**Channeling Points:** a term used by Bob Moore to name the energy-active positions in the front fold of your armpit. To find them, picture where a thermometer would protrude from the front of your armpit if you were taking your temperature there. These points are part of the Arm Streams.

**Collarbone Points:** energy-active positions on the top of your collarbones, located where the outer line of your neck meets your collarbones, at the clavicular attachment of your sternocleidomastoid muscle.

**Craniosacral Therapy, Craniosacral Work:** a gentle manual therapy, derived from the work of Dr. William Sutherland and brought into widespread use, not to mention public awareness, by Dr. John Upledger. Craniosacral work addresses the bones, membranes and cerebrospinal fluid circulation in the head and spine and has a deep effect on the nervous system and the energy field.

**Crown Center:** an energy-active position, a major chakra, that relates to the exchange of energy and consciousness between you as an individual and the cosmos. A good position for connecting consciously with your Crown Center is a bit forward from the crown of your head, and slightly up in your hair. Together with the Solar Plexus Center, the Crown Center forms part of the Circulation of Balance.

**Depression Point:** an energy-active position located in the depression just above the xiphoid process, the bony protrusion at the bottom of your sternum. It is a collection point for energy that, for whatever reason, is unable to be released or expressed. It is so named because of the depression one is likely to feel when expression is blocked and energy mounts up on this position, leading to the sensation of having a "weight" on one's chest.

**Etheric:** the layers of the energy field which immediately surround and penetrate the physical body; also called the "vital aura" or "health aura." The etheric is the storehouse of the subconscious.

**Etheric Circulation:** the movement of the energy of the etheric around the body and the movement of the contents of the etheric, such as memory.

**Etheric Storage:** the content or energetic loading of the etheric, which varies with its location on your body. Each part of your body and each major energy center, for example, has its own etheric storage of energetic charge and memory.

**Etheric Massage:** the use of your hands to influence your partner's etheric, typically either at the skin surface or just off your partner's body. Etheric massage is used to integrate the effects of an energy treatment, calm, activate or "burnish" the energy field.

**Energetic North Pole:** the "North Pole" of the human energy field; associated with an individual's transpersonal aspect or soul; also referred to as the "transpersonal point" and "individuality point." A good position for connecting your awareness with your Energetic North Pole is approximately three feet (one meter) above your Crown Center. See the footnote about this in Chapter Four.

**Energetic South Pole:** the "South Pole" of the human energy field; associated with an individual's grounding and connection with the planet. A good position for connecting your awareness with your Energetic North Pole is approximately three feet (one meter) down in the floor, directly below your Perineal Center. See the footnote about this in Chapter Four.

**Energy-Active Position:** my catch-all term for etheric structures in the human energy field, stable features such as the major and minor charkas, points and streams which play an energetic role in human growth and development.

**Energywork:** the knowledgeable and purposeful use of the energy field that surrounds and penetrates your physical body for healing and personal development.

**Feeling Contact:** This is the first step in connecting your awareness with any of the energy-active positions, such as energy centers and points in the etheric in and around your body. Different from thinking about or visualizing the energy center, a feeling contact involves moving your attention kinesthetically to the position on your body where the energy center is located, then relaxing your attention and allowing the energy movement of the energy center to draw your awareness into itself.

**Foot Center:** an energy-active position, a minor chakra, in the center of the sole of your foot, slightly toward your toes. The Foot Center corresponds to the acupuncture point Kidney-1, or the "Bubbling Spring."

**Grounding:** the process by which we connect energetically with the Earth and with everyday life.

**Hand Center:** an energy-active position, a minor chakra, located in the center of your palm.

**Hara Center:** an energy-active position, a major chakra, located in your lower abdomen. A good position for connecting your awareness with the Hara Center is three finger-breadths below your navel. Together with the Pineal Center, the Hara Center is part of the Circulation of Control.

**Heart Center:** an energy-active position, a major chakra, located in the center of your chest.

**Heat Point:** an energy-active position located two finger-breadths below your navel. The Heat Point is the beginning of the negatively charged Arm Stream.

**High Heart Chakra:** an energy-active position located between the Heart Center and the Throat Center. Some teachers speak of the blooming of the High Heart Chakra as a future development in human evolution. I speculate that the Waste Energy Position and the Secondary Depression Point are part of that evolution. In their unhealed states, these two positions function primarily as collection points for unproductive energy, but as they heal and blend their activity, new possibilities arise and I believe that one of those possibilities is the emergence of the High Heart Chakra.

**Hip Points:** energy-active positions located in the inside curve of your iliac crests.

**Liver Stream:** an etheric stream that runs diagonally around your body, connecting your Right and Left Shoulder Blade Points, your Liver and Spleen Points, and passes over your navel. I have come to think of the Liver Stream as a doorway to working with the Solar Plexus Center because it contains the etheric storage for this important center of consciousness.

**Liver Point:** an energy-active position located at the notch formed by the intersection of your eighth rib with your seventh rib on your right side, approximately eight finger-breadths from your xiphoid process. The Liver Point reflects the health and vitality in you, the result of integrating and expressing the life force.

**Mass Mind:** the largely unexamined unconscious assumptions that underlie the consensus reality of any group of people.

**Mindfulness:** In Buddhist and Vipassana meditation, mindfulness refers to a set of techniques in which you deliberately becomes non-judgmentally aware of your thoughts and actions. In energetic work, I use the term "mindfulness" to describe a state of being connected and present—whether in your contact with another person or in meditative work with yourself—in which you are neither trying to make anything happen, nor are you trying to prevent anything from happening.

**Perineal Center:** an energy-active position, a major chakra, located at your perineum, the position between your anus and genitals. The Perineal Center plays a major role in your grounding function, as it sets up the exchange of energy between you and the Earth.

**Pineal Center:** an energy-active position, a major chakra, located in the center of your head. The Pineal Center is a seat of spiritual sight and insight. Together with the Hara Center, it forms part of the Circulation of Control.

**Pineal Extension Point:** an energy-active position located in the center of your forehead, three finger-breadths above the bridge of your nose, so named because it is an effective position for making a connection with the energy of the Pineal Center.

**Point of Silence:** an energy-active position located at the bridge of your nose, between your eyes. Bob Moore used this term for this position because of its relation to sound and stillness.

**Release:** the discharge of excess energy from your system.

**Spleen Point:** an energy-active position located at the notch formed by the intersection of your eighth rib with your seventh rib on your left side, approximately eight finger-breadths from your xiphoid process. The Spleen Point, part of the Liver Stream, is accorded full chakra status in some systems of energy system nomenclature; it is a major drawing-in point for the life force as it enters your etheric.

**Sacral Center:** an energy-active position, a major chakra, located in the center of your sacrum. Together with the Throat Center, the Sacral Center is part of the Circulation of Expression and plays an important role in your grounding function and in the formation of your psycho-spiritual foundation.

**Secondary Depression Point:** This point is located just below the manubrium, the bone at the top of your sternum where your sternum meets your collarbones. It has a similar function to that of the Depression Point (see the explanation above).

**Solar Plexus Center:** an energy-active center, a major chakra, located in your upper abdomen. A good position for connecting your awareness with the Solar Plexus Center is three finger-breadths above your navel. Together with the Crown Center, the Solar Plexus Center is part of the Circulation of Balance.

**Shoulder Blade Points:** energy-active positions located where your seventh rib passes behind the lower tips of your shoulder blades. The Shoulder Blade Points are part of the Liver Stream.

**Sensorium:** the entire arena of your senses.

**Shoulder Points:** energy-active positions located at the corners of your shoulders, at the outer junction of your collarbones and your shoulder blades.

**Side-Head Points:** energy-active positions located two finger-breadths above the tops of your ears on the sides of your head.

**Spiritual Process:** the processes of psycho-spiritual transformation that take place in a person as he or she awakens, in stages, to the totality of their being. From Chapter One:

"Energywork invites spiritual process, and spiritual process is ultimately about the renewal of an age-old human experience. That experience is often not communicable except in the language of human transformation associated with spiritual traditions, so it is given names like enlightenment, illumination, transcendental experience, self-realization, and others. These are life-changing events when they occur in one's inner life and the processes surrounding these experiences—let's refer to them collectively as spiritual process—are among the perennial themes of energywork."

**Throat Center:** an energy-active center, a major chakra, located in your throat. A good position for connecting your awareness with the Throat Center is at the front of your throat, just below your Adam's apple. Together with the Sacral Center, the Throat Center is part of the Circulation of Expression.

**Three-Fold Spiritual Path:** a universal pattern of psycho-spiritual growth, characterized by three recurring steps: leaving one's familiar world, entering sacred space and then returning to one's former world in a transformed state.

**Twin Structures of Consciousness:** my term for the tendency for any move in consciousness to give rise to an encounter with other phenomena, typically obstacles. Bob Moore referred to this tendency as "double structures of consciousness." In energywork, these terms refer to the way a change in the etheric causes parallel activity. A common example of the twin structure phenomenon is seen in the use of affirmations. Typically, a positive statement, such as "I am a good and loving person," is introduced to one's internal consciousness, whereupon a counter-statement (the twin structure), such as "No you're not! What about the time you snapped at your children?" arises along with it.

**Waste Energy Position:** an energy-active position located between your shoulder blades in the area around your second thoracic vertebra. This position gets its name from the fact that it functions as a collection area for unproductive energy that has not yet found a means of moving into expression or other form of release.

**Zero Balancing:** a form of energy-oriented bodywork developed by Fritz Smith, MD

# BIBLIOGRAPHY

Achtzehn, Jürgen, *Lecture on the Life of Samuel Hahnemann*, Homöopathiewoche, Bad Boll, 1985.

Anthony, Richard, Ecker, Bruce, Wilber, Ken (editors), *Spiritual Choices: The Problem of Recognizing Authentic Paths to Inner Transformation*, Paragon House Publishers, New York, 1987.

Artress, Lauren, *Walking a Spiritual Path: Rediscovering the Labyrinth as a Spiritual Tool*, Riverhead Books, New York, 1995.

Barzini, Luigi, *The Europeans*, Simon and Schuster, New York, 1983.

Birnberger, Anita, *Einsichten*, Selbstverlag, Deggendorf, 1994 (translated by James Gilkeson).

Bruyere, Rosalyn, *Wheels of Light: A Study of the Chakras*, Bon Productions, Arcadia, 1989.

Campbell, Joseph, *The Hero with a Thousand Faces*, Bollingen Foundation, Inc., Princeton University Press, Princeton, 1949.

————, The Power of Myth, Bantam Doubleday, New York, 1988.

Cameron, Julia, *The Artist's Way: A Spiritual Path to Higher Creativity*, Jeremy Tarcher, Inc., Los Angeles, 1992.

Evans, Nicholas, *The Horse Whisperer*, Bantam Dell Publishing Group, New York, 1995.

Feynman, Richard P., *"Surely You're Joking, Mr. Feynman!"*, Bantam Books, New York, 1985.

————, *The Pleasure of Finding Things Out*, Perseus Books, Cambridge, 1999.

Fuller, Jean Overton, *Noor-un-nisa Inayat Khan (Madeleine)*, East-West Publications Fonds N.V., Rotterdam, 1971.

Gilkeson, Jim, *Energy Healing: A Pathway to Inner Growth*, Marlowe & Co., New York, 2000.

Grey, Alex, *The Sacred Mirrors*, Inner Traditions/Bear & Co., Rochester, 1990.

Grof, Stanislav, with Bennett, Hal Z., *The Holotropic Mind: The Three Levels of Human Consciousness and How They Shape Our Lives*, HarperCollins Publishers, New York, 1990.

Hamanaka, Sheila, *In Search of the Spirit: the Living National Treasures of Japan*, Morrow Junior Books, New York, 1999.

Handley, Rima, *A Homeopathic Love Story: The Story of Samuel and Melanie Hahnemann*, North Atlantic Books, Berkeley, 1993.

Hillman, James, *The Soul's Code: In Search of Character and Calling*, Warner Books, Inc., New

York, 1997.

Jackson, Jessica, Lac., Chom., Comments on the life and work of Samuel Hahnemann, personal correspondence.

Johnson, Robert A., *Inner Work,* Harper & Row, New York, 1986.

Kahn, Pir Vilayat, *Introducing Spirituality into Counseling and Therapy,* Omega Press, Santa Fe, 1982.

Kurtz, Ron, *Body-Centered Psychotherapy: The Hakomi Method,* LifeRhythm, Mendocino, 1990.

——, and Greg Johanson, *Grace Unfolding: Psychotherapy in the Spirit of the Tao-te Ching,* Harmony Books, New York,1994.

Leadbeater, C.W., *The Chakras,* The Theosophical Publishing House, Wheaton, IL, First Quest Book Edition, 1972.

Levine, Peter, *Waking the Tiger: Healing Trauma,* North Atlantic Books, Berkeley, 1997.

Levoy, Gregg, *Callings: Finding and Following an Authentic Life,* Three Rivers Press, New York, 1997.

Lovins, Amory B., *Soft Energy Paths: Toward a Durable Peace,* Ballinger publishing Company, Cambridge, 1977.

Low, Denise, *Tulip Elegies: An Alchemy of Writing,* Penthe Publishing, Lawrence, KS, 1993.

——, *Starwater,* Cottonwood Press, Lawrence, 1988.

Mead, Nathaniel, *Wrestling with Demons – Meditation,* (article) Whole Earth Review, Spring, 1994.

Merton, Thomas, *My Argument with the Gestapo,* New Directions, New York, 1975.

——, *The Asian Journal of Thomas Merton,* New Directions, New York, 1975.

Milne, Hugh, *The Heart of Listening: A Visionary Approach to Craniosacral Work,* North Atlantic Books, Berkeley, 1995.

Moore, Bob, *Conversations with Bob Moore,* Anna and Alexander Mauthner (publishers), Kirchdorf, 1992.

Moore, Thomas, *The Planets Within,* Lindesfarne Press, Great Barrington, MA, 1990.

Oschmann, James L., *Energy Medicine: The Scientific Basis,* Harcourt Publishers, Ltd., Edinburgh, 2000.

Palmer, Parker J., *The Courage to Teach: Exploring the Inner Landscape of a Teacher's Life,* Jossey-Bass, San Francisco, 1998.

Pirsig, Robert M., *Zen and the Art of Motorcycle Maintenance,* William Morrow & Co., New York, 1974.

——, *Lila,* Bantam Books, New York, 1991.

Rebillot, Paul and Melissa Kay, *The Call to Adventure: Bringing the Hero's Journey to Daily Life,* HarperCollins, New York, 1993.

Reps, Paul, *Zen Flesh, Zen Bones,* Bantam Doubleday, New York, 1961.

Smith, Fritz, *Inner Bridges: A Guide to Energy Movement and Body Structure,* Humanics New Age, Atlanta., 1986.

——————, *The Vocabulary of Touch*, interview in *Meridians*, published by Traditional Acupuncture Institute, Summer 1995.

Still, A.T., *Philosophy of Osteopathy*, A.T. Still, 1899.

Tartang Tulku, *Skillful Means: Gentle Ways to Successful Work*, Dharma Publishing, Berkeley, 1978.

Tegtmeier, Diane, *Relationships that Heal: Skillful Practice Within Nature's Web*, Infinity Publishing, West Conshohocken, 2009.

Upledger, John E., *Craniosacral Therapy II: Beyond the Dura*, Eastland Press, Seattle, 1987.

——, *SomatoEmotional Release and Beyond,* UI Publishing, Inc., Palm Beach Gardens, 1990.

**Workshops, Lectures and the Energy Healing Newsletter:**
For information on book events, workshops and lectures, contact me via my Web site at http://www.jimgilkeson.com. There, you will also find the archive of my free online *Energy Healing Newsletter.*

**Pilgrim Extras:**
To find the "Pilgrim Extras" page on my Web site (http://www.jimgilkeson.com), go to the page called "Workshops & Retreats," scroll down to the bottom of the page and click on the © symbol in the copyright notice ("© 2008 Jim Gilkeson").

**The Pilgrim Project:**
*A Pilgrim in Your Body* was partially underwritten by a group of donors (see the list of contributors on the page after the Acknowledgments). With their kind support this publishing project has become a reality and this has allowed me to view this book as part of what I call the "Pilgrim Project." As resources become available, the Pilgrim Project will go beyond the publication of these books. I envision a kind of support network and resource for energy healers in the form of teaching materials, educational opportunities, seminar scholarships and inspiration. This goes, of course, way beyond what I as a single individual can do by myself, and this is where it is so gratifying to find other people, like you, for whom this is also important.

For information on how you can contribute to the Pilgrim Project, visit my Web site at http://www.jimgilkeson.com.

**About the Author:**
*Jim Gilkeson* is the author of two books and over fifty articles on energy healing. He was a brother in a semi-monastic order and is now a bodywork therapist, a teacher of meditation and energy-oriented healing and an amateur musician. He lives with his partner, Diane Tegtmeier, in northern California.

**About the Artist:**
*Aimee Eldridge* is an artist and commercial art director/graphic designer who received her Bachelor of Fine Arts from the Milwaukee Institute of Art & Design, WI. She has illustrated multiple publications, books and commercial advertisements. She lives in Wisconsin with her husband, daughter, and several Bengal cats.